Jesus, Mary, and Joseph

Jesus, Mary, and Joseph

Family Trouble in the Infancy Gospels

Christopher A. Frilingos

PENN

UNIVERSITY OF PENNSYLVANIA PRESS

PHILADELPHIA

DIVINATIONS: REREADING LATE ANCIENT RELIGION
Series Editors: Daniel Boyarin, Virginia Burrus, Derek Krueger

A complete list of books in the series is available from the publisher.

Published by
University of Pennsylvania Press
Philadelphia, Pennsylvania 19104-4112
www.upenn.edu/pennpress

Printed in the United States of America on acid-free paper
10 9 8 7 6 5 4 3 2 1

Library of Congress Cataloging-in-Publication Data
Names: Frilingos, Christopher A., author.
Title: Jesus, Mary, and Joseph : family trouble in the Infancy
Gospels / Christopher A. Frilingos.
Other titles: Divinations.
Description: 1st edition. | Philadelphia : University of Pennsylvania
Press, [2017] | Series: Divinations: rereading late ancient religion
Identifiers: LCCN 2017007063 | ISBN 9780812249507
(hardcover)
Subjects: LCSH: Gospel of Thomas (Infancy Gospel)—Criticism,
interpretation, etc. | Protevangelium Jacobi—Criticism,
interpretation, etc. | Apocryphal infancy Gospels. | Jesus
Christ—Family. | Jesus Christ—Childhood. | Mary, Blessed
Virgin, Saint—Biography.
Classification: LCC BS2860.T42 F75 2017 | DDC 229/.8—dc23
LC record available at https://lccn.loc.gov/2017007063

Frontispiece: Max Ernst, "The Virgin Spanking the Christ Child in Front of Three
Witnesses: Breton, Eluard, Ernst." Wallraf-Richartz-Museum—Fondation Corboud.
Photo Credit: Snark/Art Resource, NY. © 2016 Artists Rights Society (ARS),
New York/ADAGP, Paris.

For Amy, Emma, and Joe
We are family

Contents

Preface

Isn't home the place where we truly know others and where, in turn, others know us? No, is the surprising answer in a pair of unusual early Christian gospels. The extracanonical *Infancy Gospel of Thomas* and the *Proto-gospel of James* depict the home life of Jesus, Mary, and Joseph as a scene of misunderstanding and confusion. The *Infancy Gospel of Thomas* recounts the unruly childhood of Jesus. The *Proto-gospel of James* revolves around Mary—her birth and youth, how she met Joseph, and how the pair coped with an unexpected pregnancy.

Since the *Infancy Gospel of Thomas* and the *Proto-gospel of James* are not included in the Christian New Testament, they remain unknown to most modern readers. Even so, readers today may recognize something familiar in stories about the early family life of Jesus, Mary, and Joseph. Consider the frontispiece of the 1926 painting of Max Ernst, "The Virgin Spanking the Christ Child in Front of Three Witnesses."[1] A glance and the floodgates open: Was Jesus ever naughty? Did Mary spank him? What was it like to parent such an extraordinary child? Like the witnesses peering through the window, we want to know more. The same was true for ancient Christians. They asked the same questions and wondered about the same things. The family gospels allow us to peek inside the early Christian imagination.

The second-century authors of the *Infancy Gospel* and the *Proto-gospel of James* pushed into spaces left open by the first-century gospels of the New Testament. While the New Testament does not describe the childhood education of Jesus, the *Infancy Gospel of Thomas* does. In its pages, Joseph tries to find a suitable tutor, only to look on in despair as Jesus humiliates one teacher and harms another. And while the New Testament does not reveal how Mary met Joseph, the *Proto-gospel of James* does. Chosen by lot, an elderly, reluctant Joseph weds (or perhaps does not wed) a twelve-year-old virgin.

As these examples indicate, there is much more to the family gospels than additional stories about Jesus and Mary. When taken as simple expansions of earlier accounts, the *family* aspect of the family gospels is lost. For example, my favorite story in the *Infancy Gospel of Thomas* concerns not only Jesus but also his parents, Mary and Joseph, as they struggle to deal with their precocious offspring. Joseph, determined to educate the boy, hands Jesus over to a teacher. Jesus sasses off, putting in motion a series of events: the teacher strikes Jesus, Jesus curses the teacher, and the teacher falls to the ground, unconscious. Afterward, Joseph takes extreme measures: "And Joseph called his mother and commanded her not to let him out of the house so that those who make him angry may not die."[2] Joseph has had enough, and Mary may feel the same way. Most studies of the *Infancy Gospel of Thomas* have focused on the behavior of the child Jesus. But I think that the angst of the parents is equally important. The *Infancy Gospel of Thomas* is not a one-person play. It, like the *Proto-gospel of James*, is a family drama—an important difference.

Amid a surge of interest in so-called apocryphal gospels, the *Infancy Gospel of Thomas* and the *Proto-gospel of James* remain mere curiosities. Like all apocryphal gospels, biblical writings that never reached full "biblical-hood," they represent paths not taken by the religion. Today, more and more readers are heading down some of these paths. Since at least the 1940s and the discovery of the Nag Hammadi Library, a majority of scholars of early Christianity have come to recognize, even delight in, the vitality and diversity of the religion. For all of this excitement, the *Infancy Gospel of Thomas* and the *Proto-gospel of James* have yet to amass a sizable readership among members of the public. On its own, the failure to thrive does not count for much. In the case of these infancy gospels, however, the lack of interest in the public arena can be explained, at least in part, by the persistent disregard of these accounts in the field of early Christianity. This does not mean that they lack for serious attention among a subfield of dedicated specialists. Rather, it is that this attention has failed to capture the imagination—not only of the public but also of scholars across the discipline. When the history and literature of the New Testament and early Christianity are presented on the scholarly stage, the *Infancy Gospel of Thomas* and the *Proto-gospel of James* are rarely cast in a supporting role.

Jesus, Mary, and Joseph attaches the family gospels to major arteries in the field of early Christianity. The galvanizing work of Peter Brown in *The Body and Society* (1988), Averil Cameron in *Christianity and the Rhetoric of Empire* (1991), Judith Perkins in *The Suffering Self* (1995), and Kate Cooper in *The Virgin and the Bride* (1996) illustrated the importance of images of family life in early Christian storytelling. Some accounts feature apostles preaching sexual renunciation to upper-class families. Others describe the choice of martyrs to reject their biological families, to stand instead with their religious brothers and sisters. The *Infancy Gospel of Thomas* and the *Proto-gospel of James*, like early Christian accounts of apostles and martyrs, are part of a debate over the meaning of family, society, and truth that set fire to the ancient Mediterranean world for centuries. What matters most is what hits close to home.

A Note on Abbreviations

Abbreviations of ancient sources and transliteration of Greek follow *The SBL Handbook of Style for Ancient Near Eastern, Biblical, and Early Christian Studies*, ed. Patrick H. Alexander et al. (Peabody, MA: Hendrickson, 1999). Other abbreviations that appear in this book include the following:

Ga   Recension A, *Infancy Gospel of Thomas* (Burke)
Gs   Recension S, *Infancy Gospel of Thomas* (Burke)
LCL   Loeb Classical Library
PG   Patrologia Graeca
SC   Sources Chrétiennes

Jesus, Mary, and Joseph

Introduction

The *Infancy Gospel of Thomas* and the *Proto-gospel of James* are usually thought of by scholars as early Christian "infancy gospels" or "childhood gospels."[1] This is because these accounts contain stories about Jesus between the ages of five and twelve and stories about Mary, his mother, that likewise cover her infancy and youth. Sometimes they are described as "filling in gaps" in the "missing years" of the gospels of the New Testament.

The *Infancy Gospel of Thomas* is a short account of seventeen chapters—references are included below in parentheses—that describes events in the life of Jesus between the ages of five and twelve. The gospel lacks a strong narrative arc and can seem to readers little more than a loose collection of childhood episodes.[2] It begins with a series of episodes about the five-year-old Jesus: he turns toy birds into actual birds (2); curses one boy, leaving him disabled (3); curses another child to death (4); fights with his father and afflicts neighbors with blindness (5); and, during his first lesson in a classroom, humiliates a teacher (6–7).

Jesus suddenly reverses course in the next chapter, restoring to health all those he had previously cursed (8). In Chapter 9, Jesus is accused of pushing another boy, Zeno, from the roof of a house. With Zeno lying dead on the ground, his parents pointing the finger at Jesus, Jesus raises Zeno from the dead, who in turn testifies to the innocence of Jesus. At the age of seven, Jesus performs miracles for his mother, fetching her water, and for his father, helping him with planting (10–11). Jesus, now eight years old, continues to help his father, this time supernaturally extending the length of wood planks for making ploughs and yokes (12). Two classroom scenes follow: in one, Jesus curses the teacher, who falls down dead (13); in the other, Jesus speaks to a crowd while the teacher looks on with approval (14). Jesus performs a couple more miracles, healing a boy from a snakebite and raising from the dead a man who had died from an errant stroke of an axe while chopping wood (15–16). The *Infancy Gospel* concludes with a version of the only childhood story found in the New Testament, the story of the twelve-year-old Jesus in the temple of Jerusalem (17; cf. Luke 2:41–52).

The *Proto-gospel of James*, which focuses on Mary, likewise includes childhood episodes. But it is a more sophisticated account than the *Infancy Gospel*, building to a climax in a story of the birth of Jesus in a cave outside of Bethlehem. Early chapters relate the story of Mary's parents, Anna and Joachim, who are childless and upset because of it (1–3). After seeking divine aid, Anna miraculously conceives a child, whom she dedicates to a lifetime of service in the temple (4). The child is born—a girl, whom Anna names Mary—and spends the next three years at home with her parents (5–6). At the age of three, Mary is escorted by her parents to the temple, where she lives until the age of twelve (7–8). The priests in the temple worry that she will soon begin to menstruate and defile the holy site. The priests seek divine counsel and are instructed to choose a husband for Mary by lot: an elderly widower is selected—Joseph, who already has sons of his own (9). Joseph, perplexed and troubled by the situation, refuses to have sex with Mary and leaves her in his house while he goes off to work on a construction project.

The next several chapters follow an unfolding crisis, one that includes details familiar to readers of the gospels of the New Testament as well as some unfamiliar elements: an angel appears to Mary, and she conceives a child without having had intercourse with Joseph (11). She promptly forgets what the angel has told her (12) and thus cannot explain her pregnancy to Joseph when he finally returns home (13). Distressed, Joseph considers divorcing Mary, but an angel reassures him (14). But this reassurance is short-lived: Joseph and Mary are hauled before the high priest to explain Mary's condition (15–16). Neither one is able to do so, so the high priest orders an ordeal to reveal whether they have had sex. They pass the test, confirming the miraculous origins of Mary's pregnancy (17).

The remaining chapters continue to weave together details from earlier gospels with new information. Joseph and Mary travel to Bethlehem to comply with the census of Augustus (17), but Joseph decides instead to stop in a cave outside of Bethlehem (18). From a distance, Joseph witnesses the miraculous birth in the cave (19). After the child is born, skepticism about the source of Mary's pregnancy continues, and a midwife, Salome, attempts to examine Mary's postpartum genitals (20). She is stopped short, however, when her hand catches fire and begins to disintegrate. The child Jesus heals her (21). The family is soon threatened by King Herod. He consults Magi, who have arrived looking for the child (21), and orders the killing of every infant in his domain (22). Mary hides her child from the soldiers in a manger (22). But Zacharias, high priest and father to the newborn John, is unable to escape the soldiers, and they kill him in the temple (23). The narrative comes to an end when the priests gather to choose a new high priest (24). It is Simeon, who, according to the Gospel of Luke, will hail Jesus as Messiah when Mary and Joseph bring the infant to Jerusalem shortly after his circumcision (Luke 2:21–35).

*　　*　　*

The *Infancy Gospel of Thomas* and the *Proto-gospel of James* are the strange gospels at the heart of this book. They include stories about the childhoods of Jesus and Mary. But are they "infancy gospels"? Tales about a wonder-working child could be told to testify to the power of the individual. They could be used to reveal something important about the figure's character and forecast future greatness. And all of this could be accomplished without telling readers anything about the family life of the child. It is my contention that the *Infancy Gospel of Thomas* and the *Proto-gospel of James* are underread when taken as narrow chronicles of holy figures. So long as they are approached as odd character sketches of Jesus and Mary, the family gospels and research into them will, I fear, languish on the borders of the field. *Jesus, Mary, and Joseph* makes a case for a different perspective, one that sees the stories as something more than profiles of Jesus and Mary.

In the past, scholars often dismissed these gospels as tabloid accounts meant to satisfy a craving for tidbits about the celebrities of the faith.[3] Recent treatments, however, have exchanged scorn for empathy. Tony Burke argues that the portrayal of the child Jesus in the *Infancy Gospel of Thomas* reflects the "idealized child" of antiquity.[4] Stephen Davis asks whether the stories of the *Infancy Gospel of Thomas* reflect cultural memories of childhood in antiquity.[5] And Reidar Aasgaard argues that the *Infancy Gospel* represents an early example of Christian childhood literature.[6] As for the *Proto-gospel of James*, Jennifer

Glancy and Lily Vuong wonder whether the unusual womb of Mary reflects or resists ancient assumptions about the female body.[7] These studies have illuminated important aspects of both gospels and have sharpened my thinking on the accounts. I want *Jesus, Mary, and Joseph* to add to the momentum of this new wave of interest. I think it does so by focusing attention on why these stories make a difference to the study of early Christianity.

My use of the term "family gospels" reflects the chief argument of this book. Both family gospels depict a *family* in crisis. If we look at the stories as family dramas, new questions emerge: How well did Mary and Joseph know each other? How much did they understand about the strange events that they witnessed? What did Mary and Joseph see in their son? What did they fail to see? What did they know that others did not? And what did they not know at all? *Jesus, Mary, and Joseph* is about these new questions. It is the depiction of the give-and-take of familial relationships that makes the *Infancy Gospel of Thomas* and the *Proto-gospel of James* important to the study of early Christianity. Before I describe in more detail my approach, I first outline my assumptions about where to plot the *Infancy Gospel of Thomas* and the *Proto-gospel of James* on the timeline of early Christian literature.

Where Did the Family Gospels Come From?

The family gospels are not unique. After they had been written and began to circulate, ancient Christians continued to tell stories about the family life of Jesus, Mary, and Joseph. Many of the written sources that document this storytelling combine details from the Gospels of Matthew and Luke with new elements and perspectives. Some sources include the *Gospel of Pseudo-Matthew*, a Latin text that includes most of what we know today as the *Proto-gospel of James*. Something similar happened among eastern Christians, as the family gospels were taken up into the Syriac *Life of the Blessed Virgin Mary*, later translated as the *Arabic Infancy Gospel*. Other sources focus on the "wise men" from Matthew: the *Revelation of the Magi* and *On the Star*.[8] In the Afterword, we will encounter a different account, the *History of Joseph the Carpenter*, which describes the death of Joseph and the grief of Mary and Jesus.

Even so, the family life of Jesus, Mary, and Joseph did not fascinate at first. The birth of Jesus did not matter to the author of the oldest gospel. Neither the narrator of the Gospel of Mark nor the characters in the story refer to the birth of Jesus. Jesus enters the picture as a lone adult. He goes to the Jordan River, where John baptizes him (Mark 1:9). The first chapter does not mention Mary and Joseph, nor does it imply that Jesus has left behind his natal household Instead, it refers to kinship of the supernatural variety: "And a voice came from heaven, 'You are my Son, the Beloved; with you I am well pleased'" (Mark 1:11). The rest of the gospel is a fast-paced narrative about an itinerant holy man, culminating in his arrest, trial, and crucifixion in Jerusalem. The tone is established early: before Chapter 1 reaches the halfway point, Jesus has taken up public ministry. He travels to Galilee, "proclaiming the good news" (Mark 1:14). Mark 1:1 locates the "beginning" of the gospel of Jesus in the activity of adulthood, not in his nativity.

From the standpoint of modern biography, the absence of a birth story in Mark is merely the first in a series of omissions. After all, Mark ignores many crucial milestones: the first words of Jesus, his adolescent years, the moment he departs from home and sets out on his own. Mark's lack of a birth story stands out because the two later Synoptic gospels, Matthew and Luke, added infancy narratives. Without Matthew and Luke, the present book would likely not exist. It does so because of the decision of this pair of evangelists to begin the story of Jesus with a family drama instead of with the sudden appearance of a fully formed, independent adult. The Synoptic accounts set the parameters for the contents of the *Infancy Gospel of Thomas* and the *Protogospel of James*. In their telling, the story begins with an infant, not an adult Jesus, who belongs first to and with Mary and Joseph. The relationships of this small household, hinted at in the infancy narratives of Matthew and Luke, are what proved attractive to the writers and readers of the family gospels.

How was the additional storytelling of the family gospels received by ancient Christians? Answering this question depends on how one thinks about the authority of the gospels of the New Testament at a time *before* there was a New Testament. An influential list of the twenty-seven books of the New Testament dates to the late fourth century, in the thirty-ninth festal letter of Athanasius of 367 CE. Most of the writings of the New Testament were written by 100 CE. What happened in the nearly three centuries between this date and the canon of Athanasius?[9] One view is that the process of forming the New Testament followed a linear path. It was a rather neat, multistaged process, led by charismatic figures such as Irenaeus, bishop of Lyons in the second century. Christians gradually reached decisions about which books to include and how many. Consider this recent summary: "Patristic evidence shows that in the final quarter of the second century a kind of *communis opinio* had already been reached about the exclusive authority of Matthew, Mark, Luke, and John. For Irenaeus (around 180 CE), it was an established fact that these four were the only gospels with general authority."[10] According to this model, by the end of the second century, Christian leaders and followers had reached a decision about which gospels to read and which to reject.

Irenaeus's *Against Heresies* is often regarded as a crucial hinge in canonical development, establishing once and for all the four-gospel canon. Yet, as Annette Yoshiko Reed shows, in many places, it is unclear what Irenaeus has in mind.[11] For Irenaeus, "gospel" can refer to "divine knowledge," something much bigger than, strictly speaking, written gospel narratives.[12] Consulting the "correct" books did not in and of itself protect against error; faithful interpretation required the right blend of tradition and gospel.[13] So too the explosion of early Christian literature in the second and third centuries undercuts the claim that Irenaeus reflects a second-century consensus. Many, it seems, favored the expansion of the Christian library, adding apocalypses, acts, letters, and, gospels. How does one make sense, as Harry Gamble puts it, of the "ongoing production . . . throughout the second and well into the third century" of "additional literature in similar genres—gospels, letters, acts, and apocalypses"?[14] Among these books are of course the family gospels and many others: the *Gospel of Peter*, which describes the exit of Jesus from the tomb; a *Third Letter to the Corinthians*, attributed to Paul; and the *Apocalypse of Peter*, a prototype of Dante's *Divine Comedy*. The list also includes the Gospel of Thomas, a sayings gospel not to be confused with the *Infancy Gospel of Thomas*.[15] Christians would not have written such "copycat" books unless there was an audience waiting to receive and read them. If so, a widespread consensus did not yet exist about which books should and which should not be read. From the perspective of second- and third-century Christians, a closed canon lay on the other side of a distant horizon.

Making sense of the flourishing of early Christian writing in the second and third centuries means moving away from an evolutionary model, as a recent essay by David Brakke suggests.[16] He outlines three different modes of scriptural practice in the early Christian era. The proposal allows for a broader and more flexible assessment of early Christian literature and separates the question of "scripture" from that of "canon."[17] One mode of scriptural practice involves "Study and Contemplation" and features the editing of texts and spotting corruptions. A second mode is "Revelation and Continued Inspiration," which covers the writing of "new texts that mimic the genres of existing scriptures." The third and final mode involves "Communal Worship and Edification," which focuses on "careful consideration of what should and should not be read at gatherings for worship."[18] Of these modes, only the third, "Communal Worship and Edification," would lead eventually to the closed canon of Athanasius.[19] The other two modes were quite different. "Study and Contemplation" required the perspicacious gaze of the scholar, who could distinguish truth from corruption in a text or set of texts and restore them to pristine condition.[20] Those who accepted "Revelation and Continued Inspiration" welcomed new volumes into an expanding religious library.[21]

I suggest that we think of the *Infancy Gospel of Thomas* and the *Proto-gospel of James* as products of "Continued Inspiration." The family gospels present themselves as supplements to the authoritative storytelling of the Synoptic gospels—extending, expanding, and rewriting.[22] Now they do not call themselves "gospels."[23] The titles I use were assigned secondarily, but I retain them because this is how they are best known, and I persist in the use of "gospel" because of their generic affinity to earlier gospels.[24] Moreover, we do not know who wrote the family gospels.[25] The *Infancy Gospel of Thomas* first circulated anonymously. And while the *Proto-gospel of James*, or *Protevangelium Jacobi*, includes an epilogue stating that the account comes from the hand of James, it is a dubious claim.[26] So too we cannot be sure of where or when the family gospels were written.[27] *Jesus, Mary, and Joseph* assumes that both were composed in Greek and first circulated by Christians in the eastern part of the Roman Empire in the second and third centuries, after the Synoptic accounts had acquired authority in some Christian circles but before Christian leaders of the fourth century began to insist on an exclusive club of New Testament writings.[28]

The writers of the family gospels were deeply familiar with earlier storytelling about the figures of Joseph, Mary, and Jesus.[29] What they received, especially from the earlier Synoptic birth narratives, is an image of Jesus, Mary, and Joseph as a family. By expanding into "gaps" or open spaces, they mimic, perhaps unwittingly, the interpretive practice of Matthew and Luke. These two Synoptic gospels famously add on to the Gospel of Mark the birth accounts of Jesus. Why did they do so? Did Matthew and Luke hope to replace Mark with their own, better accounts?[30] Did they want to complement Mark's version with another one? In any case, it is the methodology that matters: the family gospels share with Matthew and Luke the use of an earlier source or sources as a narrative framework.

The family gospels tell us something about how early Christians read and interpreted the Synoptic tradition. The authors of the infancy gospels saw in the Synoptic infancy narratives an invitation to add more stories. Seeing the family gospels as extensions of the Synoptic tradition may help readers to appreciate their sincerity, for lack of a better term. For some, it will not be enough to overcome what is, on any measure, provocative storytelling. But perhaps a shift in perspective will begin to put to rest the idea that these stories are *simply* "gap-filling" measures. Scholars would not accept as a sufficient explanation that all that Matthew and Luke do is "fill in gaps" in Mark. When the Gospels of Matthew and Luke add infancy narratives to the front of Mark, they do so to draw the eye to divine affairs and human intimacy. The same is true for the storytelling in the family gospels.

Family Dramas of Knowledge

Jesus, Mary, and Joseph, guided by elements in the family gospels, investigates themes of Roman-era culture. We explore a range of ancient literary sources, especially from the second and third centuries CE, looking for images of empire, family life, spectacle, and education. These images, I contend, illuminate aspects of the family gospels. In this, my book is an example of what is sometimes called "cultural poetics." Daniel Boyarin glosses the term as "a practice that respects the literariness of literary texts (that is, as texts that are marked by rhetorical complexity and for which that surface formal feature is significant for their interpretation), while attempting at the same time to understand how they function within a larger socio-cultural system of practices."[31] To relate this gloss to *Jesus, Mary, and Joseph*, the chapters that follow investigate the ways that the family gospels appropriate themes of Roman culture ("a larger socio-cultural system of practices") as well as how they resist them. I want to understand how the family gospels belong to the world in which they were written. So too I want to understand how they interpret that world.

Cultural poetics is a powerful method for connecting text and context. Even so, it has limitations, or at least it does in the way that it is practiced in this book. For one thing, *Jesus, Mary, and Joseph* does not offer a social history of the ancient family. Rather, it dwells mostly on representations of family life. The same is true for themes such as empire, education, and spectacle. What did these practices mean to the authors of the family gospels and their readers? How is this meaning captured in the storytelling of the *Infancy Gospel* and the *Proto-gospel of James*? Most important, how do questions about domestic life and knowledge posed by the family gospels echo the questions that come to the surface in a diverse set of ancient sources? Written by ancient Roman pagans, ancient Jews, and ancient Christians, the primary sources that surround the family gospels in *Jesus, Mary, and Joseph* indicate that knowledge—where it can be found, how it is acquired, how it should be interpreted—was a topic on people's minds.

But what about the "literariness of literary texts" that appears in Boyarin's gloss of "cultural poetics"? While all of the chapters concern themselves with this question, Chapters 4 and 5 focus to a greater degree on the "literariness" of the family gospels. Much of my thinking has been shaped by Meir Sternberg's poetics of narrative in the Tanakh, especially his view that a parallel drama of knowledge between *intratextual* characters and *extratextual* audience operates in biblical stories.[32] Sternberg argues that the organizing principle of biblical narrative is the difference between the omniscience of God and the limited understanding of human beings.[33] In perhaps his most compelling case study of a palace and household drama, the account of David, Bathsheba, and Uriah in 2 Samuel 11–12, Sternberg points up the kinds of questions that the story raises and refuses to answer.[34] How widespread is news of the affair in David's Jerusalem? Does Uriah know about the affair? Does David suspect that Uriah knows? Definitive answers are hard to maintain; more than one hypothesis can be argued. These kinds of questions both expose the fallible perception of characters in the narrative and remind readers of the limits of their own understanding. Readers may accept that 2 Samuel 11–12 offers a truthful telling of the events and, at the same time, concede that the full story or the "whole truth" extends beyond their grasp. The narrative remains complex and unsettled—a lesson learned time and again through engaging with the laconic reporting of biblical stories. Human beings only ever know in part, if it can be said that they know anything at all.

Biblical writers assume the omniscience of God. I think the authors of family gospels share the same view of things.[35] But I do not think that readers must adopt or share their theological presuppositions to appreciate their accounts or the way they pose the dilemma of human ignorance. In the family gospels, characters must make decisions in the face of uncertainty.[36] As a comparison, consider a different account, the book of Tobit. Of the ancient family dramas in narrative form, the one that comes closest in spirit to that of the Christian family gospels is a Jewish book. The book of Tobit was addressed to a Jewish audience, although it is not included in the Tanakh.[37] Like the family gospels, it is "parabiblical" in the sense that it reflects the language and pacing, not to mention many of the theological assumptions, of biblical narrative.[38] And while its composition was likely not affected by the rise of the Roman Empire—it belongs first to the Jewish Diaspora of the Hellenistic period— Tobit shares with the family gospels an interest in the intimacy of family life. One scholar observes that the "whole book [of Tobit] is generally unusual for its detailed portrait of family life."[39] What should fathers teach their sons? What should sons inherit from their fathers? What is the value of marriage? So too, like the family gospels, the book of Tobit unfolds at the intersection of divine and human affairs, and this gives a particular resonance to its exploration of what human beings know and do not know under such circumstances.

"What God has joined together, let no one separate" (Matt 19:6; cf. Mark 10:9). Demons ignore such injunctions. One of the plot lines of Tobit features a woman, Sarah, who has been married seven times. Each wedding was followed by demonic savagery: as soon as the groom enters the bridal chamber, a demon appears and kills him, leaving Sarah a widow. Her story intersects with the story of Tobias, the son of Tobit, who travels to where Sarah lives to collect his family's riches and return them to his father. He learns all about Sarah's misfortune and the danger that awaits any man who enters the bridal chamber. Tobias nevertheless intends to marry her. As it turns out, Tobias has a friend in heaven: the angel Raphael, who disguises himself as Tobias's traveling companion. He gives the benighted Tobias instructions for defeating the demon in Sarah's room: "When you enter the bridal chamber, take some of the fish's liver and heart, and put them on the embers of the incense. An odor will be given off: the demon will smell it and flee" (Tob 6:17–18). When Tobias enters the bridal chamber, the family of Sarah waits. Tobias follows the instructions of his friend, and the demon is expelled. This good news is verified for family members when a maid enters the bridal chamber and finds "them sound asleep together" (Tob 8:13). After so much suffering, the sight of Tobias and Sarah at rest brings relief for all parties.

The book of Tobit builds suspense for an audience that trusts that God's purposes will not be thwarted. Readers know who Raphael is, and they know that Raphael will defeat the demon. At the same time, they are aware of the limits of Tobias's knowledge—that he does not know Raphael's identity, nor does he know whether the smell of fish liver will prove efficacious. So too with Sarah, who shows courage in trying to marry again despite the lessons of her tragic history. This combination of suspense and "anti-suspense factors" eventually yields to a satisfying resolution. Not only are Tobias and Sarah married, but Raphael also reveals his true identity (Tob 12:11–15), a moment that leads to the prophesying of Tobit about the restoration of Israel. As Ryan Schellenberg puts it, "Tobit's narrative world has no loose ends."[40]

Are there loose ends in the family gospels? *Jesus, Mary, and Joseph* argues that this is so. Uncertainty persists in the household of Jesus, Mary, and Joseph. Yet, they share with the book of Tobit an important focus. Ignore for the moment Raphael's "big reveal" at the end of the story, which is the instant that he takes off his disguise and declares his true identity. Prior to this, Tobit is a story about human beings making a choice to act. They have been given some but not all of the relevant information. Tobias's crossing of the threshold into the bridal chamber, while Sarah braces herself for yet another demonic attack and crushing loss, is a scene about courage in the face of the unknown. Readers may guess that all will be well. Tobias and Sarah must trust that it will be so.

Like Tobias and Sarah in this suspenseful interlude, the members of the holy household of the family gospels must choose over and again to remain a family. The chapters of this book frame and interpret the family gospels as dramas of knowledge, as stories about what is known and what remains unknown in a small household. I do not think that these accounts give us access to what really happened, but I do not always couch my claims in ways that call attention to the fictional character of the stories. I want my readers to focus on the storytelling and to recognize in it a rich depiction of familial conflict and misunderstanding.

Chapter 1 explores the historical context of the family gospels, especially the widespread rhetoric of familial concord in the Roman era. Christian writers responded, sometimes arguing for a rather conservative vision of patriarchal household authority. At other times, they told stories about the breaking up of marriages, replacing this with a celibate household learning at the feet of an apostle. If the prevailing image of the household was as a place of teaching, learning, and knowledge, then scenes of domestic confusion, like those in the family gospels, pose a stark contrast.

The first chapter then turns to the earlier gospels of the New Testament, especially the infancy narratives of the Gospels of Matthew and Luke. What did Mary and Joseph understand about the events in which they were swept up? How much did they know (and not know) about their extraordinary child? How much did Jesus disclose about himself to Mary and Joseph? Several early Christian authors offered explanations. The second-century heresiologist Irenaeus, for example, notes the belief of a rival Christian group, the "Marcosians," that the twelve-year-old Jesus taught his parents secret knowledge. In the fourth century, John Chrysostom rejected the idea that Jesus had performed childhood wonders. Both Irenaeus and John Chrysostom seek to overcome ambiguity. The family gospels accept it as a feature of human relationships.

Chapters 2 and 3 explore aspects of Roman-era culture and images of family life in the family gospels. The grim Roman-era fascination with public spectacles forms the backdrop to Chapter 2. I argue that the family gospels include *narrative* spectacles of their own. When a midwife tries to examine Mary's genitals in the *Proto-gospel of James*, her hand begins to burn and disintegrate. In the *Infancy Gospel of Thomas*, Jesus' indiscriminate use of supernatural power—he curses and heals, kills and brings back to life—leaves neighbors and parents in a state of fearful uncertainty in the *Infancy Gospel of Thomas*. Hard to ignore, these spectacles are also difficult to decipher. Like other stories from the era, the family gospels use narrative spectacles to expose the limits of human understanding, as both characters in the text and the audience outside of it struggle to make sense of them. And when the smoke clears, the intimate drama of family life comes into view.

The difference between human perception and divine omniscience is central to Chapter 3. Joseph in the *Infancy Gospel of Thomas* wants Jesus to be educated, while Anna, the mother of Mary in the *Proto-gospel of James*, wants her daughter to train in the temple. This chapter contends that broader conversations about the value of classical Greek education and culture may help to illuminate this conflict. Lucian of Samosata, a Greek-speaking satirist from the Roman period, describes his own youthful dilemma over whether to pursue education and its rewards or the skilled labor of masonry and sculpture. In it, Lucian offers a young person's perspective on a disagreement with parents about the future.

The family gospels, by contrast, emphasize the perspective of parents who "want what's best" for their children. But the dreams of Joseph, on one hand, and those of Anna, on the other, go unrealized: the child Jesus is not a good student, and Mary is forced out of the temple when the priests fear that the onset of her menstrual cycle will defile the house of God. Do the parents err in wanting a future for their children that is at odds with the plans of heaven?

Chapters 4 and 5 change somewhat in approach. Rather than use examples from both gospels to explore a common theme, each of the chapters focuses on a specific family gospel. Chapter 4 shows that the *Proto-gospel of James* gives a twist on an ancient biblical idiom—that is, the use of the term "know" as a euphemism for sexual intercourse. The Mary and Joseph of the *Proto-gospel* do not "know" each other in the biblical sense (i.e., sexually) or in any other sense. They meet by accident, and once Joseph installs Mary at his house, he departs for a months-long work project.

It will of course not shock anyone to learn that an early Christian account denies Mary and Joseph a robust sex life. But why present the holy couple as strangers to one another? In the *Proto-gospel of James*, the nature of the relationship between Mary and Joseph remains vague, and it is only the crisis of Mary's unexpected pregnancy that throws the man and woman together. Yet, together they brave doubt, scandal, and a potentially lethal ordeal. Their bond is forged in a crucible of miracle and courage, and their fidelity to one another scrapes away at expectations about what constitutes conjugal intimacy. They bond over "unknowing." And this shared ignorance disrupts assumptions about what counts as a "husband" and what counts as a "wife."

The willingness of the family gospels to put domestic strife on display is just as striking in the case of the *Infancy Gospel of Thomas*. Chapter 5 begins with Gospel of Luke's story about a twelve-year-old Jesus debating with religious experts in the Jerusalem temple. It is sometimes referred to as the "Finding of Jesus" because, for a span of three days, Mary and Joseph lose track of their son. When they finally discover him in the temple, Mary reproaches her son: "Why have you treated us like this?" (Luke 2:48).

A version of this story forms the conclusion to the *Infancy Gospel*. It is perhaps the episode that inspired the entire family gospel. Rather than smoothing over the dysfunction of the holy family, the *Infancy Gospel* piles on more examples of parent-child strain. Jesus kills playmates and sasses off to adults. When Joseph reprimands the boy, Jesus warns his father not to upset him. Against this background, Mary's question to her twelve-year-old son takes on new urgency. Because the child Jesus uses his astonishing powers for good and evil, the audience, like the characters in the story, cannot predict how the child will react. Through episodes of suspense and surprise, the *Infancy Gospel* instills in readers the same loss of comprehension that bedevils Mary and Joseph. By so doing, it also gives readers a new perspective on the blowup in the temple. The parents have a choice to make, and so does Jesus. Will they remain a family?

In the Afterword, I look at one sixth-century source, the *History of Joseph the Carpenter*, that offers another scene of family drama. In it, Joseph, lying on his death bed, begs the forgiveness of his son, and the son, in turn, weeps for his father.

Note on Texts and Translations of the Family Gospels

One of the long-standing obstacles to scholarship on the *Infancy Gospel of Thomas* has been the lack of a critical edition of the Greek text. The obstacle has been overcome with the publication of Tony Burke, *De infantia Iesu*. It includes a critical edition of the Greek text based on the "S Recension" (Gs) of the text. This is the text and translation that I follow, including Burke's chapter and verse divisions and subdivisions. On occasion, I point out variants in the other influential "A Recension" (Ga). When I do so, I indicate this in the notes and use Gs and Ga to distinguish between the different texts. While Burke makes a convincing argument for Gs as the earliest representation of the Greek text, scholars continue to find value in comparing readings from Ga.[41]

For the *Proto-gospel of James*, or *Protevangelium Jacobi*, the edition of the Greek text and English translation that I use comes from Bart D. Ehrman and Zlatko Pleše, *Apocryphal Gospels*, including chapter and verse divisions. It is based on the critical edition in Émile De Strycker, *La Forme la plus ancienne*, 63–191. I occasionally modify the translation, indicating where I do so in the notes.

I have kept most quotations of the Greek text of the family gospels and other ancient sources in the endnotes. Where I think it is essential to include a Greek term in the main text, I use a transliteration.

Chapter 1

Family Matters

Ancient Christians wrestled with the meaning of family life. The letters of Paul and the sayings of Jesus raise fundamental questions about the worth of the household. Paul urges his unmarried followers in Corinth "to remain unmarried as I am" (1 Cor 7:8). Marriage is a distraction: "those who marry will experience distress in this life" because "the appointed time has grown short" (1 Cor 7:28–29). Paul could see the beginning of the end in his own day: "The present form of the world is passing away" (1 Cor 7:31). Society would soon vanish, along with institutions such as marriage. Would the basic social unit, the family, survive? No, said Jesus. In the Gospel of Luke, he tells his disciples, "Do you think that I have come to bring peace to the earth? No, I tell you, but rather division!" (Luke 12:51; cf. Matt 10:34). "From now on," Jesus continues, "five in one household will be divided, three against two and two against three; they will be divided: father against son, and son against father, mother against daughter and daughter against mother, mother-in-law against her daughter-in-law and daughter-in-law against mother-in-law" (Luke 12:52–53; cf. Matt 10:35–36).[1] In these passages, the axe is laid at the root. They predict that the apocalypse will begin at home.[2]

To move forward in time to the second and third centuries of the Common Era is to find a range of Christian positions on "family values."[3] For some early Christian authors, faith and family life went hand in glove. The Pastoral Epistles of the New Testament envision the patriarchal household as the ideal. Men should be in charge; women should remain silent and focus on childbearing (1 Tim 2:8–3:7). Their emphasis on harmony and order in the household follows the drumbeat of the Roman era. On the opposite end were

Christians who rejected sex, marriage, and procreation. They told stories about charismatic and miracle-working apostles—some of them female—proclaiming a gospel of lifelong chastity. A new relationship, an ascetic "family," comes to replace the conjugal bond. Young lovers turn away from each other and gaze instead on the face of an apostle.

For some time now, historians have documented the ways that early Christians used various notions of the family to define their religion. But the *Infancy Gospel of Thomas* and the *Proto-gospel of James* have been left out of the conversation. This book offers a new perspective. It claims that the *Infancy Gospel of Thomas* and the *Proto-gospel of James* turn the family life of Jesus, Mary, and Joseph into a laboratory for testing ideas about human understanding. What can human beings comprehend of divine affairs? What can human beings know about each other? The stories, in other words, are about relationships. How are they created? How are they maintained? How much and how little understanding travels along the lines that connect the members of a family to each other and to the deity they worship? These are the questions that readers will encounter in these stories about Jesus, Mary, and Joseph. What emerges from the accounts is a family that is both strange and familiar, unusual and ordinary.

Why did *family* matter to ancient Christians? And how do the *Infancy Gospel of Thomas* and the *Proto-gospel of James*, with their focus on the religion's founding family, fit into the picture? These are the guiding questions of the first chapter. To answer these questions, we explore overlapping contexts. The first section turns to the historical context. Should Christians marry? Should Christians try to have children? Ancient Christians debated the meaning and value of family life at a moment when the household became a symbol for order in the Roman Empire. Family life, in other words, was deeply relevant to the broad society to which ancient Christians belonged. The stress on family life in the historical context can help to explain why the authors of the family gospels expanded storytelling about Jesus into the domestic sphere. It may also help us to understand why these stories gained traction with early Christian audiences. No less than their pagan and Jewish neighbors, ancient Christians talked and wrote about what mattered in their world.

The second section describes the literary context. If the historical context suggests the reason why stories about the holy family gained traction with early Christian readers, then the literary one can begin to tell us why the family gospels take the shape they do. A study of the *Infancy Gospel* and the *Proto-gospel of James* must consider their relation to the earliest narrative references to the family of Jesus, scattered among the first four gospels of Matthew, Mark, Luke, and John. What information do these accounts contain? As we shall see, when it comes to the household of Jesus, Mary, and Joseph, the four gospels of the New Testament leave much to the imagination. What happened behind closed doors? How much did Mary and Joseph understand of the events in which they were swept up? Did the parents of Jesus know who he was? Did they understand his significance? Gaps in the earliest literary portrayals put the imagination of Christian storytellers in motion.

But it was not only what is missing that attracted the authors of the family gospels. They also wondered, I think, about what is present, especially the strain and confusion that is evident in the single childhood story found in the earliest gospels: Luke's story of the twelve-year-old Jesus and his parents in the temple of Jerusalem (Luke 2:41–52). This story plays a leading role in third section on the interpretive context. We look at three different interpretations of this story. Themes of familial intimacy and the limits of human understanding come to the surface, themes that likewise run through the family gospels. The *Infancy Gospel* and *Proto-gospel of James* report surprising, even shocking, details about the household of the first Christian family. But the questions they raise pop up in a number of Christian sources, from the earliest gospels to the writings of Irenaeus in the second century and those of John Chrysostom in the fourth century.

Family Squabbles (Historical Context)

Christians, according to some ancient observers, were the enemies of "family values." Around 177 CE, one critic described a day in the life of Christians. The report is unkind.[4] It comes from the hand of Celsus, a Greek-speaking pagan, perhaps of Alexandria, who issued a rebuttal of Christian claims in his work, *The True Doctrine*. As part of his takedown of Christians, Celsus includes a vignette of suspicious activity:

In private houses also we see wool-workers, cobblers, laundry-
workers, and the most illiterate and bucolic yokels, who would not
dare to say anything at all in front of their elders and more intelli-
gent masters. But whenever they get hold of children in private and
some stupid women with them, they let out some astounding state-
ments such as, they must not pay attention to their father and
school-teachers, but must obey them; they say that these figures talk
nonsense and have no understanding. . . . And if just as they are
speaking they see one of the school-teachers coming, or some intel-
ligent person, or even the father himself, the more cautious of them
flee in all directions; but the more reckless urge the children to
rebel.[5]

Christians, according to Celsus, are too dense to realize what is good for them.
Plus, they are dangerous. They try to brainwash youngsters and "urge children
to rebel."

Christianity threatened the foundation of civilized society, according to
Celsus. He points to unrest in the household: fathers are being wronged by
early Christian "yokels," and thus the strength of "private houses" is being
weakened from within. On display, then, is the corrosive effect of Christianity. It rejected the rightful place of fathers in teaching the young how to take
up their proper roles in adult society. Of what value, then, was this new-
fangled religion? Very little, as could be inferred from the company that
Christians kept. They wallow in the muck with "the foolish, dishonourable,
and stupid" and prey on "slaves, women, and little children."[6] If their own
tactics doomed Christians to irrelevance, why did they cause Celsus so much
dismay? Because, as Celsus and his audience believed, if households were
being infiltrated by this menace, Roman society at large was put at risk. The
social web of the public Roman world was held in place by "private houses."[7]

How seriously should historians take the claims of Celsus? It is unlikely
that Christians urged their children to rebellion. At the same time, Celsus put
his finger on a reliable aspect of the early history of the religion: it began in
households. Long before Celsus, Paul's first-century letters afford a view of a
network of communities in the houses of followers of Christ. Decades before
the use of the term "Christian," a new kind of belonging was taking shape in

the collection of Gentile house churches. Spend any time reading Paul's letters, and one learns a good deal about the ancient household: the role of
slaves, the importance attached to questions of inheritance and adoption,[8]
and the top-down "command structure" of the patriarchal household. Paul's
letters indicate that early Christian communities, while meeting in households, were nevertheless challenging assumptions about familial and societal
order.[9]

The household gave Paul an important metaphor for describing the followers of Christ. Christians of every household are supposed to be united in
the family of Christ. Paul describes himself as mother and father (1 Thess 2:7,
11–12). Even so, as Paul's letters make clear, strife was often present. People of
different statuses, who would have never mingled together in the outside
world, were suddenly thrust together. It led to conflicts that Paul tried to resolve. For example, in his letter to Philemon, Paul takes on Philemon, the
head of his household, over his treatment of a slave, Onesimus (Phlm 8–14).
While Philemon is the first addressee, the letter is also for the "church in your
house" (Phlm 2). Over this Christian "family" Paul holds a claim to authority, and he uses it to challenge Philemon's position. Convinced of the nearness of the end, Paul used metaphor and manipulation to chip away at—but
not do away altogether with—assumptions about order and hierarchy within
households.[10]

Paul's appropriation of familial terms hints at an alternative to the traditional household. Full-blown opposition is found later in some Christian
writings of the second and third centuries. Agents of Christ are homewreckers
in the so-called Apocryphal Acts, a set of five narratives modeled on the canonical book of Acts. One of them features none other than Paul: he recruits
an adolescent girl, Thecla, away from a life of aristocratic matrimony. As she
sits at her window, she hears a beatitude from the mouth of Paul, one that
cannot be found in canonical beatitudes attributed to Jesus: "Blessed are those
who have kept the flesh chaste, for they will become a temple of God."[11] Salvation in the Apocryphal Acts depends upon the renunciation of sexuality.
For Thecla, the rejection of marriage and procreation is empowering in a very
specific sense: no longer bound to her fiancé, she is free to take up the mantle
of apostle. In the final chapter, Thecla returns home to call her mother to salvation: "For if you desire riches, the Lord will give them to you through me;

if you desire your child, see, here I am!"[12] Marriage lies in ruins, but family ties endure. Thecla yet hopes to persuade her mother, speaking to her as only a daughter can.[13]

Apostles fan out across the Mediterranean basin in the Apocryphal Acts, from Rome to India, carrying a message of celibacy: sex and marriage are evils, so too are offspring. In the *Acts of Thomas*, Christ himself appears as the apostle Judas Thomas ("the twin") in the bridal chamber for a pair of royal newlyweds. He begins at once to enumerate the virtues of chastity: "Remember, my children, what my brother said to you, and to whom he commended you; Know that if you refrain from this filthy intercourse, you will become temples holy and pure, being released from afflictions and troubles, known and unknown, and you will not be involved in the cares of life and of children, whose end is destruction."[14] Warming to his theme, Christ in the *Acts of Thomas* spells out for the couple what they have to look forward to, should they decide instead to bring children into the world: "But if you get many children, for their sakes you become grasping and avaricious . . . and by doing this you subject yourselves to grievous punishments. For most children become unprofitable, being possessed by demons, some openly and some secretly. For they become either lunatics or half-withered or crippled or deaf or dumb or paralytics or fools. And though they be healthy, they will be again good-for-nothings, doing unprofitable and abominable works."[15]

Accounts like the *Acts of Thomas* or rumors of such accounts would have set off alarm bells for Roman-era elites such as Celsus. The *Acts of Thomas*, like the other Apocryphal Acts, specifically features the breakup of aristocratic betrothals.[16] Legal marriage was by and large a concern of the upper crust: as an institution, it protected the transfer of wealth between families and from one generation to the next. If well-heeled young people chose to "refrain from filthy intercourse," elite society would face a crisis. What would happen if there was not a next generation to inherit the wealth and good taste of the current one?

The erotic literary twin of the Apocryphal Acts is the popular Greek romances of the Roman era, also, canonically speaking, five in number. They celebrate the marriage of young aristocrats. Their stories were popular among those who had the most at stake in the maintenance and passing down of elite Greek culture: the wealthy Greek-speaking audiences of Asia Minor who lived in the shadow of Rome. Tales of separation and reunion shored up the notion of public Greek identity in this context by expressing and maintaining a connection to an idealized, Hellenistic past. Wealthy lovers—"to the manor born"—are separated by shipwrecks, bandits, kidnapping, and war. But dislocation ultimately comes to an end: the pair reunite and pledge their love to one another. The Greek romance sets the "happy ending" in a suitably Hellenized city.[17] The union guarantees the stability of well-to-do society.

The Apocryphal Acts, with their tales of apostles breaking up aristocratic betrothals, have been read as targeting an upper-class anxiety of "social reproduction." But they may also be attacking a set of ethics based on conjugality, like the one found in the happy endings of the Greek romances.[18] The upper-class argument for a conjugal morality is precisely what is denied in the Apocryphal Acts, which depict conventional marriage as a cesspool of iniquity. "Men and women giving up *sex* may tell the story of asceticism and subversion," Andrew Jacobs argues, "but men and women giving up *marriage* tell a story about families and Christian ethical resistance along social status lines."[19]

What apostles offer instead is a spiritualized relationship, an "apostolic love triangle."[20] Christ in the *Acts of Thomas* urges the couple to eschew one form of married life and replace it with another kind of commitment: "But if you obey and preserve your souls pure to God, there will be born to you living children, untouched by these hurtful things, and you will be without care, spending and untroubled life, free from grief and care, looking forward to receive that incorruptible and true marriage, and you will enter as groomsmen into that bridal chamber full of immortality and light."[21] Lovers turn away from each other and look for guidance from another figure: the apostle and, in the case of the *Acts of Thomas*, Christ, the twin brother of Thomas. The story continues: "And when the young people heard this, they believed the Lord and gave themselves over to him and refrained from filthy lust, and remained thus spending the night in the place."[22] The message of salvation comes to the bedroom, breaking up the carnal union. In its place is a pledge of lifelong continence. Following the example of the apostle, the converts follow the path of salvation to a place where everything is illuminated. A chaste bedroom leads to perfect knowledge.

The Apocryphal Acts contrast their vision of spiritual marriage and heavenly knowledge to the "filthy intercourse" of conventional marriage. But

Christians were not the only ones to try to raise marriage to a higher plane. Pagan authors of the Roman era also cast marriage in elevated terms. Plutarch, the Greek moral essayist of the Roman era, portrays the institution as nothing less than a philosophical school. He creates an image of the bedroom as a schoolhouse of discipline in *Advice to a Bride and Groom*.[23] The husband's role is to teach his wife and to create order and harmony in the household.[24] This includes behavior in the bedroom: the husband should train his wife in the arts of pleasure (without giving into excessive desires or wantonness). But there is also the education of the mind to consider. By teaching his wife mathematics, the husband guarantees that she will be rightfully ashamed to dance and make a spectacle of herself in public. By teaching his wife the science of astronomy, the husband ensures that she will recognize the tricks of astrologers. Instruction leads to wisdom and the possibility of overcoming the inherent weaknesses of her sex.

Plutarch and the Apocryphal Acts are unlikely bedfellows! Their appraisals of the value of marriage could not be farther apart. Nevertheless, they hold something in common: the notion that the household—traditionally conceived or transformed into a spiritual version—can be a setting for increasing and perfecting knowledge.

This is not the only point of contact between Christian and pagan sources. In the decades following the death of Paul, some of his interpreters took it upon themselves to develop a vision of family life and household order.[25] Perhaps the best known of these passages are shared by Ephesians and Colossians (and 1 Peter): "Wives, be subject to your husbands, as is fitting in the Lord. Husbands, love your wives and never treat them harshly. Children obey your parents in everything for this is your acceptable duty in the Lord. Fathers, do not provoke your children, or they may lose heart. Slaves, obey your earthly masters in everything. . . . Masters, treat your slaves justly and fairly, for you know that you also have a Master in heaven" (Col 3:18–4:1; cf. Eph 5:21–6:9; 1 Pet 3:1–7). The stratified Household Codes project a vision of domestic order.[26]

A similar Christian voice speaks in the three Pastoral Epistles of the New Testament, also attributed to Paul. Hierarchy of gender is essential: "Let a woman learn in silence with full submission. I permit no woman to teach or to have authority over a man; she is to keep silent" (1 Tim 2:11–12). Some scholars have argued that the assertion of patriarchal authority in these letters is meant to undermine the female heroes of accounts such as the *Acts of Paul and Thecla*.[27] By the time the Pastoral letters were composed, Christian communities were no longer on the lookout for the end of days. What was needed instead was leadership. In an early "job description" for the office of bishop, the pseudonymous author of 1 Timothy contends that a bishop "must manage his own household well, keeping his children submissive and respectful in every way—for if someone does not know how to manage his own household (*tou idiou oikou*), how can he take care of God's church?" (1 Tim 3:4–5). A successful bishop fosters harmony at home and in "God's church."[28]

The link between household and wider society, in this case "God's church," runs parallel to the public imagery and rhetoric of the Roman Empire.[29] The Roman Empire was a well-managed household, overlapping with the "sentimental ideal" of the Roman family that projected concord in marriage, dutiful children, and slaves. The first Roman emperor, Augustus, championed this comparison: he presented the empire as a harmonious family.[30] He accepted the title *pater patriae* or "father of the country."[31] In imagery and coins, the Augustan household was advertised across the empire.[32] Subjects were encouraged to see Augustus as their benevolent head of household. Practical measures of tax relief for aristocratic, childbearing families were passed during his reign.[33] Romans included images of the genius of Augustus on home altars. In the provinces, such as the Greek-speaking area of Asia Minor, Augustus was proclaimed the "father of the human race." A century later, it reached an apogee, as Peter Brown observes: "The second century witnessed a striking convergence around the image of familial unity as a reflection of the harmony of the Roman Empire."[34]

Under the watchful eye of Roman emperors, a new religion grew up in homes throughout the empire. Much of the language that Christians use to this day reflects the early appropriation of familial imagery and metaphor. Even so, the household soon became a source of controversy. By the second and third centuries, Christians were preoccupied with debating different models of family life. Some of these models corresponded to broader imperial notions of family as a symbol of harmony. Others rejected altogether marriage and childbearing. What binds all of these Christian attitudes together is the assumption that the closeness of the household, when properly understood, offers a natural setting for mutual understanding. When Christians authors wanted to evoke intimacy, they turned to family: " 'For this reason a man will leave his father and mother and be joined to his wife, and the two will become one flesh.' This is a great mystery, and I am applying it to Christ and the church" (Eph 5:31).[35] Members of a family are supposed to know one another. And this is why accounts of confusion and misunderstanding between Jesus and his parents warrant our attention.

The Family of Jesus in the Gospels (Literary Context)

Much of what readers know about the family of Jesus comes from a handful of chapters—five in all—at the beginning of the Gospels of Matthew and Luke. Take out these few chapters about the birth of Jesus, and what is left are only tantalizing glimpses. The father of Jesus is mentioned only once—and not by name—when Jesus travels to his hometown of Nazareth (Matt 13:54–58; cf. Mark 6:1–6; Luke 4:22). Jesus begins to speak, and his former neighbors are taken aback. He seems haughty; they know better: "Is not this the carpenter's son? Is not his mother called Mary? And are not his brothers James and Joseph and Simon and Judas?" (Matt 13:55). Two thousand years later, one can still feel the disdain in their questions. There are also poignant moments. One of the best-known passages involves the death of Jesus. The Gospel of John reports that Jesus, as he was being crucified, made provision for his mother: "When Jesus saw his mother and the disciple whom he loved standing beside her, he said to his mother, 'Woman, here is your son.' Then he said to the disciple, 'Here is your mother'" (John 19:26–27). Michelangelo's *Pieta*, the sculpture that depicts Mary cradling the dead body of her son, lacks an explicit reference in Christian scripture. But the familial sentiment of the *Pieta* may perhaps be echoed in the story about Jesus' final act of filial devotion, in which he asks a friend to take care of his mother and his mother to take care of his friend.

In death there is affection, but in life there is strain.[36] The cold welcome that Jesus receives from erstwhile neighbors is not unlike the chilly relationship he has with members of his family. Jesus spends far more time with his disciples than with his mother. When he does speak with Mary, at a wedding in Cana in the Gospel of John, the exchange does not bespeak filial devotion (John 2:1–11). Mary says to Jesus, "They have no wine." Jesus, sensing what his mother wants, replies curtly, "Woman, what concern is that to you and to me? My hour has not yet come" (John 2:3–4). But Jesus relents and turns water into wine—"the first of his signs" (John 2:11). Mary, at least, believes that Jesus is capable of great things, which is more than can be said for other members of his family. Elsewhere the Gospel of John reports, "not even his brothers believed in him" (7:5).

A pair of moments in Chapter 3 of the Gospel of Mark raises more questions about the relationship of the adult Jesus and his family. At this point in Mark, Jesus has already made a name for himself as an exorcist, attracting a "great multitude from Galilee" (Mark 3:7). Jesus and his disciples go to his home for supper. The mob follows, creating so much chaos that Jesus and his disciples "could not even eat bread" (Mark 3:20). Somehow a report of the event reaches the family or "relatives" of Jesus, and "they went out to restrain him, for people were saying, 'He has gone out of his mind'" (Mark 3:21). Why does the family act to stop Jesus? Their motive remains unstated. Do they act from a protective instinct, worried that the crowd might turn on Jesus? Have they grown accustomed to the noise around Jesus? Is this why, when the news comes, they do not hesitate but immediately strike out for the scene?

Amid the uproar inside the home, scribes begin to question the source of Jesus' supernatural powers. They accuse Jesus of demon possession. Jesus rebukes the charge with a rhetorical question: "How can Satan cast out Satan?" (Mark 3:23). And then, in terms that may gesture to wider societal divisions, Jesus remarks, "If a kingdom is divided against itself, that kingdom cannot stand" (Mark 3:24–25). At this point, the "mother and brothers" of Jesus arrive at the house. Because of the crowd, they must "stand outside" (Mark 3:31). They send word inside, asking to see him. The crowd relays the message: "Look, your mother and brothers are outside seeking you" (Mark 3:32). "Who are my mother and brothers?" Jesus responds (Mark 3:33). Then, looking around the room at the people encircling him—both to gesture to those listening and, perhaps, to take the temperature of the room, so to speak—he continues, "Look, [you] are my mother and brothers. For whoever does the will of God, this one is my brother and sister and mother" (Mark 3:34–35). The family of Jesus is unable to penetrate the barrier of the crowd. In a gospel that returns frequently to the image of those on the outside and those on the inside (Mark 4:10–12), the scene is telling: the family of Jesus is on the outside.

If this collection of passages is jarring, it is a credit to the stories of the birth of Jesus. In them, Mary, Joseph, and the baby Jesus seem bound tightly together by a secret, known only to them. The infancy narratives of Matthew and Luke put the story of one family at the center of large-scale events.[37] Otherwise, the two versions of the Christmas story are quite different.[38] In the Gospel of Matthew, Joseph and Mary are forced to flee Bethlehem after the client-king Herod of Judea orders the slaughter of all babies under the age of two: "Then was fulfilled what had been spoken through the prophet Jeremiah: 'A voice was heard in Ramah, wailing and loud lamentation, Rachel weeping for her children; she refused to be consoled, because they are no more'" (Matt 2:18). The "Massacre of the Innocents" is not part of the Gospel of Luke. Instead of regional bloodletting, geopolitics is the backdrop to the Lukan account of the birth of Jesus. Joseph travels with Mary to Bethlehem (from Nazareth) because the Roman ruler Augustus has called for a census: "In those days a decree went out from Emperor Augustus that all the world should be registered" (Luke 2:1).

The story of the new family begins amid turbulent circumstances. It takes place against the backdrop of the pious curiosity of shepherds and Magi as well as the implacable quest of ruling powers to acquire information.[39] In the Gospel of Matthew, a mad client-king seeks to wipe out an entire generation of children. In the Gospel of Luke, the Roman emperor wants to consolidate power by gathering census details on each and every family within the realm; Rome is an empire of data in Luke's telling. Together, the two accounts suggest a dark parallel: the birth of Jesus happens under rulers who seek to control the production of knowledge and, grimly, the production of offspring.

If we want to understand the later *Infancy Gospel of Thomas* and the *Protogospel of James*, the stories of the birth of Jesus in Matthew and Luke are a good place to start.[40] They supply the characters that people the family gospels. Mary and Joseph, the parents of Jesus, are the most important figures, although we do not learn from Matthew and Luke any specific details about how old they are or how they met. Neither account digs too deeply into the emotional life of their relationship. The reticence to do so is more conspicuous in one gospel than the other. Luke offers a moving portrayal of a couple, but it is not of Mary and Joseph. The first chapter relates a "prequel" to the birth of Jesus. It features Mary's elderly cousin, Elizabeth, who, after living for years without children of her own, finally conceives a child with her husband, Zechariah. In a span of three verses (Luke 1:5–7), the reader learns crucial information, including the family backgrounds of Zechariah and Elizabeth, the upright character of each, their lack of children, and their advanced age: "But they had no children, because Elizabeth was barren, and both were getting on in years" (Luke 1:7). It is a slender but powerful combination of facts that gives an emotional depth to the relationship. They are running out of time to have a child.

By contrast, since we are told so little about it, the relationship of Mary and Joseph does not possess the depth of Elizabeth and Zechariah's. This flatness is striking because the first two chapters of Luke spill over with emotion. Mary is moved to sing a song about the events that have overtaken her (Luke 1:46–55). Indeed, readers are afforded more than one glimpse into the heart and mind of Mary. The earliest example comes when Mary learns that, like Elizabeth, she is about to become unexpectedly pregnant. This set of circumstances is even more shocking in her case than in her cousin's, and Mary voices her confusion: "How will this happen? I have not known any man" (Luke 1:34).[41] As the story develops, Mary's own emotions about the pregnancy bubble to the surface time and again. Meanwhile, the only reference to Joseph in all of Chapter 1 comes in the verses cited above (Luke 1:26–27), as the stage is being set for the visitation. Joseph does not utter a word of direct discourse in the gospel, and Luke's profile of Joseph is restricted to his lineage. We are not told of his reaction to Mary's pregnancy, nor are we given enough information to infer what it might have been. We learn how Mary feels about her child and her God, but her feelings toward Joseph and his toward her remain invisible.

The central feature of the accounts is the miraculous conception of Jesus by Mary. In Matthew, Mary is already engaged and pregnant, while in Luke, Mary is already engaged and then becomes pregnant. Mary and Joseph are bound together in a liminal state, on the threshold of parenthood. This bit of information is repeated by Luke later, in the same unadorned way, when the couple travels to Bethlehem: "Joseph also went from the town of Nazareth in

Galilee to Judea, to the city of David called Bethlehem, because he was descended from the house and family of David. He went to be registered with Mary, to whom he was engaged and who was expecting a child" (Luke 2:4–5). The evangelists carefully circumscribe the when of the supernatural conception of Jesus: it was after this (engagement) and before that (sex).

While the Gospel of Luke includes a long prologue in the story of Elizabeth and Zechariah, the Gospel of Matthew dives into the problem of the relationship between the two. Joseph intends at first to "dismiss her quietly," hoping to save Mary from public humiliation. He wants to protect Mary from public ridicule, but he is also worried about his own reputation. He decides to seek a "quiet" divorce. But then an angel appears to Joseph in a dream and offers reassurance: "Joseph, son of David, do not be afraid to take Mary as your wife, for the child she conceived in her is from the Holy Spirit" (Matt 1:20). Joseph sets asides his worries, and "he did as the angel of the Lord commanded him; he took her as his wife" (Matt 1:24). Matthew then implies, perhaps, that the couple eventually had sex, after the birth of Jesus (Matt 1:25).

Joseph's moment of hesitation is so brief that it can be quickly passed over. But it should not be overlooked since it is one of two instances of uncertainty in the early family life of Jesus, Mary, and Joseph in the Synoptic tradition. The other belongs to the Gospel of Luke (2:41–52). Although the episode rests in close proximity to the stories of birth and infancy, it belongs to a later period in the life of Jesus. At the age of twelve, Jesus wanders off on his own, distressing his parents. When Mary and Joseph find Jesus in the temple of Jerusalem, they reproach him. Jesus responds in kind: "And his mother said to him, 'Child, why have you treated us like this? Look, your father and I have been searching for you in great anxiety.' He said to them, 'Did you not know that I must be concern myself with the things of my father?' But they did not understand what he said to them" (Luke 2:48–49).[42] It seems that mother and son "talk past one another" here. The awkward exchange between Mary and Jesus in the Lukan "Finding of Jesus" may seem unusual, even alien to the spirit of the rest of the earliest gospels. But perhaps it is better understood as one in a range of images of family life that stretches across various canonical and extracanonical accounts. On one end are stories of conflict and confusion, such as when Jesus refuses to speak with his mother and brothers. On the other are moments that evoke a sense of profound intimacy, such as when Jesus, dying on the cross, asks a friend to take care of his mother, something that he will no longer be able to do.

The Nativity and All That (Interpretive Context)

If the history of Christian debates over family life can tell us why early Christians expanded storytelling into the family of Jesus, then the moments of uncertainty in the earliest gospels can tell us why the storytelling takes the shape it does. The Lukan story of Jesus and his parents in the temple acts as a dividing line between different kinds of Christians of the second century. The clash shows how different Christians used the family of Jesus to explore the relationship between human and divine beings, as well as the limits of human understanding in the face of divine activity. In the examples that follow, we look at two different moments, one in the second and the other in the fourth century. One of the through lines of these examples is the story of the twelve-year-old Jesus. The other is the rejection of the kinds of stories that are part of the family gospels.

Irenaeus of Lyons, a figure who would later be accorded "orthodox" status, reports on the interpretation of a rival group of Christians. In the late second-century *Adversus haereses*, or *Against Heresies*, Irenaeus describes the "Marcosians," followers of a Christian teacher named Marcus.[43] Irenaeus attacks them, first, for their use of apocryphal stories.[44] Irenaeus accuses his followers, the Marcosians, of creating a number of "apocryphal and spurious writings" to mislead others.[45] Irenaeus gives an example: "When the Lord was a child and was learning the alphabet, his teacher said to him—as is customary—'Pronounce alpha.' He answered: 'Alpha.' Again the teacher ordered him to pronounce 'Beta.' Then the Lord answered: 'You tell me first what alpha is, and then I shall tell you what beta is.' This they explain in the sense that he alone understood the Unknowable, whom he revealed in alpha as in a type."[46] This story about Jesus and the letter alpha closely resembles an episode in the *Infancy Gospel*, one of at least three "schoolhouse" scenes that belong to the childhood tradition.[47]

Irenaeus ramps up his ridicule of the Marcosians when he takes up their use of a different source. Unlike the "apocryphal and spurious" story of Jesus in the classroom, this episode comes from a gospel that Irenaeus revered: the Gospel of Luke. Irenaeus reports: "For example, the answer he gave to his Mother when he was twelve years old: *Did you not know that I must be about my Father's business?* [Luke 2:49] They assert that he announced to them, the Father, whom they did not know."[48] As the Marcosians understand it, the story depicts a divine child who enlightens his ignorant parents. The scorn of Irenaeus for this interpretation comes through in the biting sarcasm at the chapter's end. The Marcosians posit an unknowable God and "still they announce him!"[49] If God is unknowable, Irenaeus scoffs, on what basis can the Marcosians claim to discuss the deity?

The interpretation of the Marcosians, however loathsome and illogical to Irenaeus, made sense to at least some ancient Christians. It did so, I suspect, because it addresses a problem that is difficult to resolve: the surprising parental ignorance of Mary and Joseph. Why did the parents of Jesus not understand his words in the temple? The Marcosian rendering of the twelve-year-old's question both acknowledges the puzzle and attempts to solve it. The parents did not understand because the truth of the "Unknowable One" is beyond their grasp, or so goes the thinking of the Marcosians. They are lost in the darkness of a malformed world. Ignorance remains a film over the eyes of Mary and Joseph. The twelve-year-old Jesus peels it away through his teaching.

Two centuries later, the commentary of John Chrysostom, reflected in his *Homilies on John*, takes on the problem of Mary and Joseph's failure to understand their twelve-year-old son. It also explores more broadly the question of intimacy and understanding between Mary and her son, touching on themes that belong not only to the *Infancy Gospel of Thomas* but also to the *Protogospel of James*. To understand his perspective on the story, we must first grasp his position on childhood miracles attributed to Jesus. John Chrysostom— alternately bishop and exile of fourth-century Constantinople—affords a glimpse inside the head of an early Christian familiar with the family gospels or of an account that resembles them. Like Irenaeus, he rejects such stories.[50] He ascribes preeminence to the canonical gospels; they are the benchmark against which all other traditions are measured. In them, according to John Chrysostom, the miracles of Jesus begin in adulthood. His specific objection to childhood tales about Jesus rests largely on a claim in the Gospel of John, which records the water-to-wine miracle in the wedding at Cana as the "first of his signs" (John 2:11).[51] John Chrysostom insists that accounts of "childhood deeds," such as the *Infancy Gospel of Thomas*, attributed to Jesus are "false, and merely products of the imagination of those who bring them to our attention." This is because reports of childhood deeds contradict the letter and spirit of John 2:11: "If he [Jesus] had worked miracles beginning from his early youth, neither would John have been ignorant of him, nor would the rest of the crowd have needed a teacher to reveal him."[52] In addition to John 2:11, John Chrysostom has in mind the Baptist's own words: "I myself did not know him" (John 1:31).

Some studies of the *Infancy Gospel of Thomas* view John's judgment as a historical rather than a theological one. John, contends Reidar Aasgaard, rejects the *Infancy Gospel* for being "historically untruthful," not for being "heretical."[53] But the problem is neither history nor heresy. The problem is knowledge. The notion of childhood miracles violates John Chrysostom's sense of coherence or what we may be tempted to call "plausible deniability." If Jesus had performed wonders as a child, the masses would have heard about Jesus long before his dunking in the Jordan. Miracles speak for themselves, creating their own publicity. To follow the logic of John Chrysostom a bit further: John the Baptist, a relative of Jesus according to the Gospel of Luke, would certainly have learned about the childhood wonders of Jesus, had the boy performed any. It would turn implausible the "plausible deniability" of the Baptist in John 1:31. To side with the approach of John Chrysostom for a moment, readers of the gospels of the New Testament may have noticed that not one of the neighbors in Nazareth recollects anything special about the childhood of Jesus. On the contrary, they ask, "Is not this the carpenter's son?" (Matt 13:55; cf. Mark 6:3; Luke 4:22).[54] They remember an unremarkable childhood.

In a later homily, John Chrysostom again appeals to plausible deniability: "If, I repeat, he who within a short time, because of the number of his miracles, became so famous that his name was quite plain to all, had worked wonders from the first, with much more reason he would not have remained hidden in this longer period."[55] The sheer quantity of miracles let loose a flood of reports about the adult Jesus. The same would have happened, argues John Chrysostom, if he had performed wonders as a boy.

His next step is to address the lone childhood story of the earliest gospels, the Lukan episode of Jesus and his parents in the temple. His stresses the

limited scope of the incident. "For as a child he did nothing (*ouden*) except
that one thing of which Luke bore witness, that, he sat, when he was twelve
years old, hearing the teachers, and, through his questions, he appeared to
them to be amazing." Does this qualify as a miracle in John's mind? Perhaps.
But its effect is limited. A single event, no matter how amazing, need not have
raised the profile of Jesus.

But John Chrysostom's case for the absence of childhood miracles threatens to come apart in the next section, as he begins to explore more broadly the
character of the relationship between son and mother. Here we take note of a
rhetorical question that John poses: if Jesus' childhood was not extraordinary,
"then how did his mother become aware of the greatness of her son?" John's
response outlines a progressive scheme of awareness. First, John points out,
Mary was given access to an unmatched, if inchoate, mode of knowing, one
uniquely hers as mother: "The conception itself, and all the events connected
with the nativity, implanted in her the suspicion of her child's greatness."[56]
Now Mary kept this "suspicion" entirely to herself throughout Jesus' early
years. Bearing in mind the Gospel of John's account of the "first sign," John
Chrysostom insists that Mary did not have the "confidence" to ask her son for
a miracle during the latent period of Jesus' childhood. "Before this," he goes
on to say, "he lived as one of many": there was thus no way for Mary to know
that the young Jesus, ordinary in all respects, had it in him. Whatever insight
Mary had, it was partial and submerged, "implanted" at the same time as
conception. Mary waited to act on this instinct until "she had heard that John
had come for his sake . . . and that he had disciples." Only then, at Cana, did
she dare to nudge Jesus into performing a miracle.

The relationship between Mary and Jesus tests the limits of plausible
deniability—a problem that still bedevils commentary.[57] John Chrysostom
tried to confront head-on the puzzle within the framework of miracles and
knowledge. Even if the young Jesus did not perform any miracles in front of
her, Mary must have sensed something, if only because of the unusual nature
of her pregnancy—"the Nativity and all that," to paraphrase. Here, John
Chrysostom's thinking overlaps with questions in the *Proto-gospel of James*:
How much did Mary understand about her own pregnancy? Did she know
how she became pregnant and why? The challenge pushes John Chrysostom
to specify two ideas somewhat in tension with each other: one, that Mary had

an inkling of Jesus' greatness—call it "mother's intuition"—and, two, that she refrained from acting on her hunch because, having taken the full measure of her son's modest abilities, she could not quite believe it herself. In so doing, John Chrysostom separates Mary's interior life from observable behavior. He restricts Mary's perception of the growing Jesus to a gut feeling, rough and unsure. In support, John Chrysostom quotes from the evangelist: "But Mary treasured all these words and pondered them in her heart" (Luke 2:51).

At the same time, John Chrysostom does not blame Mary, and his view of the correspondence of miracles and knowledge offers a way out. In this section, he dabbles in counterfactual storytelling, suggesting that childhood miracles would have attracted the wrong kind of publicity and sent the young Jesus too soon to the cross. Everything in its appointed season: the miracles of the mature Jesus led to celebrity, and celebrity led to the cross. Thus, it comes as no surprise that Mary regarded Jesus as an ordinary boy, "one of many": the less others knew about Jesus, the more control Jesus exerted over his own fate.

In a different collection, *Homilies on Matthew*, John Chrysostom describes a messianic smokescreen: "For while at twelve years old he showed himself, he was quickly overshadowed again."[58] In the temple, Jesus revealed himself: he taught "things which the Jews had never seen nor heard." It was a flash of light that a moment later dimmed, as the twelve-year old shrank back into an ordinary life.[59] John Chrysostom's correlation of miracles and knowledge remains intact, as does his view of Mary. Of course, John Chrysostom might have said, Mary wanted to know the truth about her son, to see him for all that he was and all that he would become. And had she seen her son perform miracles as a child, she would have been able to perceive his brilliance. But she did not and so could not, and that is the way Jesus wanted it.

*   *   *

Why did *family* matter to ancient Christians? We have seen that Christianity began in households and that familial language pervades early Christian writings. Soon Christians, like others in the Roman Empire, were engaged in a debate over the meaning and shape of the ideal family. Images of family life pervaded culture and society. In the Roman era, they could be found in the monuments to imperial households and in the moral essays of Plutarch. Some ancient Christians embraced images of familial harmony and order. Others waged an assault on this vision. They nevertheless exchanged one ideal for another. The Apocryphal Acts describe a "love triangle" between chaste couples and a charismatic apostle, an ascetic family already experiencing the glory of the God, together sharing perfect knowledge and heavenly insight. In this sense, it was not all that different from the domestic unity envisioned in the Pastoral Epistles.

Within and against these projections, the *Infancy Gospel of Thomas* and the *Proto-gospel of James* offer something different and messier. The family gospels gather together strands of storytelling in earlier gospels to create a profile of family life, one that at once alludes to the source material and goes beyond it. Much is ambiguous in what the earliest gospels report the relations between Jesus and his family, including the Lukan story of the twelve-year-old Jesus and his parents in the temple. Like Irenaeus, the Marcosians, and John Chrysostom, the authors of the family gospels saw this ambiguity and used it as a basis for exploring the limits of human understanding. And like these interpreters, the family gospels call attention to the problem of what the parents know about the child and, more important, what they do not and cannot know about him.

One could say that the family gospels owe something to the "antifamilial" strain of early Christianity. Mary and Joseph do not have sex in the *Proto-gospel of James*. So too both family gospels portray the domestic life of Jesus, Mary, and Joseph as a scene of distress and ignorance. Confusion travels along horizontal as well as vertical lines, for Mary and Joseph fail to understand one another just as they fail to understand Jesus. Still, against this strictly "antifamilial" view is the worth given to familial relationships in the *Infancy Gospel of Thomas* and the *Proto-gospel of James*. While their stories expose the limits of human understanding, they also affirm the capacity of human beings, in the face of uncertainty, to choose to stick it out together. In so doing, the family gospels give to Jesus, Mary, and Joseph a dysfunctional and weirdly plausible domestic life.

Family mattered in antiquity, and this is why the family gospels matter. Their stories are about more than just filling in gaps of earlier sources. In the *Infancy Gospel of Thomas* and the *Proto-gospel of James*, family life is the setting for examining the reach of human knowing and the problem of ignorance.

What happens when human beings are caught up in the plans of God? Under such circumstances, what are human beings able to know, and what remains beyond their comprehension? In the chapters that follow, we explore how these questions shape the storytelling of the family gospels. Chapter 2 looks first at the way that the supernatural spectacles recounted in the family gospels bring into relief the push and pull of human relationships.

Chapter 2

Made You Look

How did *this* happen?

In the *Proto-gospel of James*, lots of people want to know how Mary got pregnant. Even after the birth of Jesus, questions persist. A woman named Salome confronts Mary while she holds and nurses Jesus. The new mother is told to prepare for a full examination. Then, in what is arguably the most jaw-dropping moment in all of early Christian literature, Salome extends her hand to probe Mary's genitals (*physis*).[1] A moment later, Salome recoils in horror, crying out, "Woe to me for my sin and faithlessness! For I have put the living God to the test, and see, my hand is burning, falling away from me."[2] As her hand turns to ashes, Salome kneels and begs the help of the "God of my fathers."[3] Mary looks on or looks away—the text does not say—holding her child.

People want answers. A different story, found in the *Infancy Gospel of Thomas*, makes a similar point. It describes divine punishment and the longing to understand the why of it. It begins with the five-year-old Jesus walking down the road. Another boy runs into Jesus, hitting him in the shoulder. "You will go no further on your way," Jesus declares, and the unnamed child falls dead to the ground.[4] The parents of the dead boy blame Joseph for what has happened.[5] Although the detail is not stated outright, we can perhaps picture the parents gathering the lifeless body of their child in their arms and presenting it to Joseph. Look at what *your* son did to *our* son.

How do these two stories compare to one another? If there is something prurient about Salome's attempted examination of Mary's private parts and her ensuing suffering, then horror and sorrow is what the sudden death of a clumsy child evokes. What does this supernatural pain and suffering mean? It stands for and points to divine mysteries that exceed the grasp of human beings. But this does not stop anyone from trying to find out answers. The family gospels show characters trying to understand a baffling turn of events and doing so amid the tangle of domestic life and familial relationships. Salome bursts in upon a mother, child at her breast, while the parents confront Joseph, the father of their son's killer.

This chapter is about unlikely events and the way they attract attention, the way they make people look and wonder. Why did this happen? How did it happen? What does it mean? What goes for characters in the stories holds true for readers, who look on as Salome and the parents of the dead boy struggle to make sense of what they witness. In other words, readers play a role that mirrors that of *intratextual* characters. They are *extratextual* observers who want to find purpose and meaning in these accounts.[6] So too readers become watchers of the watchers, taking in the reactions of characters. They lean forward to find out what Salome discovers and to see how Joseph will respond to the mother and father of the dead child. One task of this chapter is to show that this way of captivating readers owes something to the broad culture of public viewing under the Roman Empire. Within this framing, we can better appreciate the visual dimension of family gospels. Their narrative spectacles of violence do not take place on the battlefield or in the amphitheater but in the unexpected settings of small village life—in the common play of children and the quiet moments of postpartum bonding.

If we want to learn how the family gospels captivated an early Christian audience, then their episodes of sudden death and dismemberment are a good place to begin. A flash of otherworldly violence will turn heads, and so too will a miracle that reverses the harm.[7] But the family gospels offer something else in these moments: close-up scenes of loss and love. It is the back and forth of human relationships, illuminated by sparks of supernatural power, that remain the most salient feature of the storytelling.[8] For all of their strangeness, the family gospels draw the eye to something that is quite ordinary but no less meaningful for being so—the intimate drama of family life.

Body Language in the *Infancy Gospel of Thomas*

Does the supernatural violence of the boy Jesus teach a lesson to those who suffer and those who witness it? Yes and no, depending on one's point of view. The family gospels were written under the Roman Empire, at a time when public spectacles of pain and death were designed not only for entertainment but also for communicating messages of authority and order. Romans were used to looking for meaning in dead and maimed bodies on the battlefield and in arenas. At the same time, their stories seem to trump the one-way shows of the Roman amphitheater. As abruptly as Jesus kills a clumsy boy, he turns around and brings him back to life. In the same way, Salome's hand reappears as soon as she reaches out to touch Mary's baby. What is the meaning of these acts of restoration? What is the message? What is the point of this violence if it can be so quickly reversed?

There is also the matter of location to consider. The family gospels describe spectacles of violence taking place where they are not supposed to—not in the amphitheater or in a war zone but in the small comings and goings of village life. The play of children turns lethal in the *Infancy Gospel of Thomas*. In the *Proto-gospel of James*, the cry of Salome shatters the quiet calm of a mother bonding with her newborn. The "everydayness" on display in these scenes amplifies the unexpected and confusing nature of the suffering.

This section relates the spectacles of death and dismemberment in the *Infancy Gospel of Thomas* to the culture of viewing under Rome. It then turns to an analysis of the strange episode of Zeno, a boy who falls off a rooftop and dies. The parents of the dead boy accuse Jesus of the deed. This results in a stunning reversal: Jesus resuscitates Zeno, who in turn testifies to the innocence of Jesus.

Spectacles of Death

Jesus does not get along with others in the *Infancy Gospel of Thomas*. When something or somebody vexes Jesus, he vents his frustration through curses. And whatever he desires to happen in that moment instantly comes to pass. The account begins, for example, with a beguiling story about Jesus playing with and hiding his toys from adults and ends in supernatural wrath and pain. The five-year-old boy sits at a stream, playing on the Sabbath day. He molds toys by hand out of the spongy clay, twelve sparrows, and all is well. But an onlooker, "a certain Jew," is offended and reports what he sees to Joseph, the father of Jesus, "saying that, on the Sabbath he has made clay, which is not lawful, and formed twelve sparrows!"[9] When Joseph arrives at the stream, he begins to speak sharply to his Jesus, trying to correct him. Jesus claps his hands together, and the toys turn into real birds and fly away. Soon another onlooker joins the action at the stream: a child, who is identified as "the son of Annas."[10] With a "willow twig" in hand, he scatters the water that Jesus had gathered.[11] He drains the pools from which Jesus had taken mud to create the toy birds. Now Jesus is mad, and he curses the son of Annas: "Your fruit shall be without root and your shoot dried up like a branch scorched by a strong wind."[12] The son of Annas "withers" (*exēranthē*) on the spot.[13]

While the *Infancy Gospel* is full of miracles, some of them beneficial, these scenes of cursing and harm stand out because of their contrast to miracles in earlier gospels—or so it is often maintained. Not so fast, say some scholars, pointing to biblical accounts of cursing prophets and apostles.[14] The prophet Elisha curses a group of boys for making fun of his baldness, and a pair of "she-bears" come onto the scene to kill scores of the children (2 Kings 2:23–24). In the Synoptic gospels, Jesus teaches his disciples to curse villages that do not welcome them (Matt 10:13–14; cf. Mark 6:11; Luke 10:10–12). Jesus himself curses his opponents in the Gospel of Matthew: "Woe to you scribes and Pharisees, hypocrites!" (Matt 23:1–36). He curses the villages of Chorazin, Bethsaida, and Capernaum for unbelief (Matt 11:23; cf. Mark 6:11; Luke 10:13–15). And in a strange interlude, Jesus curses a fig tree for not bearing fruit, even though it was not the season for figs (Mark 11:12–14, 20).[15]

So, yes, the adult Jesus of the canonical gospels sometimes lashes out in word and deed. Are such bursts of anger equivalent to the supernatural harm meted out by the boy Jesus? I do not think so. When Jesus makes a whip of cords to drive out the moneychangers from the temple, it is not a display of superhuman strength (John 2:15). His victims flee because the adult Jesus brandishes a whip. Had the cursing of scribes and Pharisees been accompanied by a description of their immediate death and dismemberment, then this would be comparable to the violence of the *Infancy Gospel*. By and large, the canonical Jesus does not inflict physical pain on enemies or friends. Indeed, his miracles mostly point in the opposite direction. Consider the story of the demoniac in the synagogue in Capernaum. In Luke's version of the exorcism, which he takes over and modifies from Mark, Jesus casts out a demon that exits the victim "without having done him any harm" (Luke 4:35).[16] When a miracle could potentially cause physical suffering, the adult Jesus preserves the demoniac from any side effects.

If the adult Jesus, like a physician, first does no harm, the boy Jesus seems to do nothing but. Jesus creates more trouble in the next scene of the *Infancy Gospel*. The withering curse has been described as a "response in kind": as the son of Annas intentionally dries up the pools, so Jesus dries up the son of Annas.[17] Symmetry is missing from the next curse, in which an anonymous boy, running along, bangs into Jesus' shoulder.[18] Jesus retaliates by cursing the child to death. Stories of suffering can sometimes suggest a moral or imply a didactic interpretation; biblical accounts of punishment very often do. But looking for a "teachable moment" in the killing of a clumsy boy seems perverse. Children run into one another all the time. What is the lesson—that kids should avoid running into one another or, at the very least, avoid running into Jesus?

A recent study suggests that the story reflects the rough-and-tumble of ancient childhood education.[19] Stephen Davis contends that the location of the collision—the boy "tore into his shoulder"—gives away the agonistic setting.[20] It is a move in a wrestling match, a picture of Roman-era "gym class" that an ancient audience would have recognized. Davis goes on to suggest that the anonymous boy poses a threat to the villagers because of his violence and that Jesus, heroically, puts a stop to it.[21] But the scene does not mention a gymnasium, and no one expresses gratitude to Jesus for his curses.

Moreover, if these clues were apparent to some readers, they were not at all to others. Ancient and medieval scribes were flummoxed by the story. Some variants in the manuscripts try to justify the actions of Jesus. In the Ethiopic translation, the collision is not a glancing blow to the shoulder but a direct hit to the chest of Jesus. In the Irish version, the boy annoys Jesus.[22] The rewrites are meant to show that the anonymous boy deserves harsh, measure-for-measure treatment.

What kind of savior kills children? As the bodies pile up, the *Infancy*

Gospel describes the mounting pressure on the parents of Jesus. Onlookers gather around the dead body of the clumsy boy, asking, "Where was this child born that his word becomes a deed?"[23] Their astonishment is followed by a confrontation between the dead boy's parents and the father of Jesus: "From wherever you have such a child," they tell Joseph, "you cannot live with us in the village. If you wish to be here, teach him to bless and not to curse; for we have been deprived of our child."[24] The grief of a single family comes through in their outrage and recriminations. But the death of their son is also an assault on the corporate body of the village. Their words link the harm done to the bodies of children and the safety of the community in which these children had—until crossing Jesus' path—run and played. They speak for the village, and the village must protect itself. Exile is a punishment and a safeguard. When he takes Jesus aside to scold him for cursing, Joseph connects the dots for his son: "Why do you say such things? They suffer and hate us."[25] Joseph's reprimand underscores an important point—the words of Jesus, his curses, inflict physical harm; they are like weapons or fists. For this reason, other manuscripts render Joseph's question as "Why do you do such things?"[26] His father's plea does not gain traction. Jesus does not show remorse. He rebukes his father for his ignorance and turns on his accusers, blinding them.[27]

The child Jesus has everyone's attention. As he calls down pain on the bodies of other children, Jesus makes a spectacle of himself. The *Infancy Gospel* is more than a record of marvels from the childhood of Jesus. It is also a story about how observers in the narrative, the intratextual audience, react to what they see from the child Jesus. In this, the *Infancy Gospel* reflects the times. If public life under the Roman Empire was about anything, it was about watching. The second and third centuries, for example, witnessed regular performances of "showing and telling" about the greatness of the *pax Romana*. Declamation was a hallmark of Greek civilization; it was transformed under the Roman Empire. What the empire of Rome needed was "public affirmation" of its rule—or what we might call "branding"—rather than the give-and-take of debate in the public square of classical Athens.[28] Orators enumerated the benefits of Roman rule before crowds that gathered to watch and listen. Perhaps the *Infancy Gospel* picks up on this aspect of Roman-era life, or perhaps it is an example of second-order borrowing, for the earliest gospels, as we shall see, also bear the imprint of a wider "spectator culture."[29]

Not all watching in the Roman Empire involved public speaking and the like; sometimes the display was a spectacle of death. Ancient Rome is remembered for vicious public spectacles—the combat of gladiators and prisoners fed to wild animals. Less well known is that emperors and other patrons sought to present displays of violence as an art form. They financed a combination of brutality and stagecraft that has been described as the "theatricalization of death," a phenomenon that would strike most today as a callous and shocking disregard for human dignity.[30] In the choreography of gladiatorial combat, staged animal hunts, and public executions, brutality was staged. Orchestrated violence became a form of communication, not unlike public speaking. Spectators learned how to "read" the bodies of victims for messages about the Roman order of things. A prisoner, dressed in the costume of Daedalus, was led up to a tower and then pushed off so that he plummeted to his death on the floor of the Colosseum of Rome.[31] Roman emperors and other patrons thus grimly brought myth to life. Killing became play in elaborate performances of "fatal charades."[32]

Other artists took note, writers in particular, who peppered their stories with episodes of violent spectacle. Scenes of bodily harm can be found across the library of pagan, Christian, and Jewish writings of the Roman Empire. Subjects of the Roman Empire were taught in text and in life to look for meaning in "teachable moments" of violence. Jesus' youthful killing spree and Salome's burning hand may have appealed to an audience that was used to searching for meaning in the display of disfigurement and death, whether put on in an amphitheater or described in narrative. Many ancient Christians, after all, found profound meaning in accounts of the passion of Jesus. When the Johannine Jesus speaks of his universal appeal, he does so in "viewing" terms: "And I, when I am lifted up from the earth, will draw all people to myself" (John 12:32). The gospels of the New Testament culminate in the crucifixion, a Roman spectacle of violence and the "lifting up" to which the Johannine Jesus knowingly and ironically alludes.[33]

Like the canonical gospels, the *Infancy Gospel* put all eyes on Jesus. The difference between them, of course, has to do with what takes place before these eyes: the adult Jesus suffers while the boy Jesus causes others to suffer. As

he scatters injured and dead bodies about the village, the *Infancy Gospel* turns
the suffering of earlier gospels on its head, carving out a far different role. Instead of the victim, the child Jesus is the producer of the show.

Speaking with Corpses

When the *Infancy Gospel of Thomas* and the *Proto-gospel of James* describe harm
done to human bodies or the threat of such harm, they may imply a kind of
body language or, more accurately, a language of "talking" with bodies that
came out of the "spectacle" milieu of the Roman Empire. When armed conflict took place, Roman generals and their opponents exported the "theatricalization of death" from the stage into true theaters of war. In the second-century
account of the "First Jewish War" (66–73 CE) by the Jewish historian Josephus, the manipulation of dying and dead bodies announces the intentions of
the agent and, as Maud Gleason observes, illustrates "the disquieting ease with
which a human subject can become an object."[34] Josephus, an eyewitness to
the events he describes, records the actions of the Roman general Titus, who
crucified captives before the walls of Jerusalem. Titus arranged the victims in
humiliating poses as a form of negotiation with the besieged Jewish rebels.
Josephus decoded the message of Titus in the following way: "But his (i.e.,
Titus's) main reason . . . was the hope that the spectacle might perhaps induce
the Jews to surrender, for fear that continued resistance would involve them in
a similar fate."[35] *Read these bodies and weep.* "When people use the bodies of
others to send a message," Gleason concludes, "the body's appeal as a semiotic
instrument seems to lie in its promise of a universal language."[36] In the service
of imperial police actions, body language was designed to slice through cloudy
films of difference in language and culture. The pose of a dead body would, it
was hoped, reduce or remove altogether the ambiguity of spoken and written
discourse. It would also testify to the authority of the figure, in this case Titus,
who had the power to arrange the bodies of victims just so in order to communicate with the enemy.

Does the child Jesus of the *Infancy Gospel* likewise send a message through
dead and dying bodies? If so, it is no wonder that such bodily messages are
hard to "read" in the setting of quiet village life. When violence was used to
communicate on the battlefield, in the arena, or on crosses, the message was

designed to be intelligible, a point that Josephus drives home for his audience. Body language could be "read," acknowledged, and disputed. But translate it to the domestic setting of the play of children, as the *Infancy Gospel* does, and the "language" suddenly becomes incoherent.

Can one find meaning in the suffering and death of children? This question had as much meaning in the ancient world as it does for the modern one. Plutarch, the second-century biographer and philosopher, composed *A Consolation to His Wife* on the death of their infant child, urging stoicism. Meanwhile, Fronto, a contemporary of Plutarch, concludes that philosophical ideas cannot overcome parental sadness at the loss of children.[37] The author of the *Infancy Gospel* is aware of the pain that comes with the loss of children, and this is why the narrative spectators that matter the most are the parents who have lost the most. It is not that they are confounded by the parables of Jesus or his metaphors. Nor do they doubt the supernatural power of the strange boy. In this moment, they do not care to learn how Jesus does what he does, and they do not spot a lesson in the violence. Instead, the parents ask Joseph to make it stop: "Teach him to bless and not to curse; for we have been deprived of our child."[38]

When Jesus harms children, he also hurts the parents. The web of family life comes into view—not just the victim's but also Jesus'. Joseph is just as shocked as the parents of the dead boy, as his question to Jesus indicates: "Why do you say such things?"[39] It is the speech of Jesus that poses the greatest danger since the curses he utters instantly come to pass. Beyond instilling fear and loathing in the community, the message in the violence of Jesus, if there is one, remains unintelligible to intratextual onlookers. The same holds true for the extratextual audience. Appealing to biblical prototypes or explaining Jesus' killing as grappling in the schoolyard may satisfy some. But what if the point of these spectacles is to frustrate attempts to explain? By taking spectacles of death out of the arena and dropping them, incongruously, into the play of children, the *Infancy Gospel* creates a set of jarring images that defies expectation and compels the audience to take a closer look.

Zeno's Testimony

Then the *Infancy Gospel* does it all over again. At the midpoint of the narrative, Jesus, going against type, laughs and saves those he has cursed.[40] While it may feel as if a great distance has been traveled, only two brief chapters separate the death of the clumsy boy from the charming tale about the toy sparrows come to life. And only one story about Jesus in the classroom separates Jesus' curses from the grand gesture of healing. The reason that Jesus gives for the reversal is mysterious. Jesus declares, "Now let the barren bear fruit and the blind see, and you, the foolish in heart find wisdom, because I am here from on high so that I may deliver those below and call them to the heights just as the one who sent me to you commanded me."[41] A mass healing follows: "And at once those who had fallen under his curse were saved."[42] Do his words and deeds clarify or further muddy the waters? Jesus takes credit for the spectacles of death. He creates the pain that he heals, a supernatural version of the Roman "fatal charades" that turned cruelty into a transcendent work of art. Or is it parody? Is Jesus playing with human bodies just as earlier he played with toy sparrows? Not surprisingly, the villagers decide to keep their distance from this unpredictable child: "And no one dared to make him angry from that time on."[43]

The lifting of the curse is not the last of the abrupt reversals. The most astounding feat involves Jesus and his playmates. Readers are given a glimpse of the secret life of children, as some time later, Jesus plays with other children on the roof of a house. Fun suddenly turns into tragedy: "One of the children fell and died."[44] When the parents arrive, they accuse Jesus of knocking the child off the roof. Jesus denies the charge: "I did not knock him down."[45] The parents do not accept Jesus' word and continue to accuse him. Finally, Jesus calls out to the dead boy, "Zeno, Zeno—for this was his name—rise and say if I knocked you down." Zeno stands up and replies, "No, Lord." The parents praise God and worship Jesus.[46]

The guilt or innocence of Jesus in this episode is less significant than the question itself. To be sure, the hero of the *Infancy Gospel* now brings salvation instead of suffering. Yet, for a moment that lasts at least the length of the interval between the accusation of the parents and the raising of their dead child, there is suspense, a turning of the screw.[47] If readers are not thrown by the accusation of murder, it is because we remember all too well the curses of the child Jesus. What we do not know is whether Zeno fell by accident or was pushed (as the parents suggest). There are suspicious details: Why, for example, do the other children flee the scene? Whom are they running from—the adults or Jesus? The scene manipulates the expectations created by Jesus' earlier random acts of violence. The gospel gives the audience—an early Christian audience that might otherwise quickly dismiss the accusation of Zeno's parents—reason to suspect the boy Jesus. Readers do not know what happened. Even if most would think the parents are wrong in their accusation, it is at least understandable why some would think Jesus capable of such a thing. His reputation precedes him.

Does the testimony of the resurrected Zeno put to rest all doubts? "Talking corpses," like the "theatricalization of death" more broadly, are a regular feature of second- and third-century narratives. Maud Gleason sees in these stories a reflection of this "ritual dramatization of the state's coercive power" in the miraculous "talking corpses" that appear in a range of literature under the Roman Empire.[48] Shot through with reversal, the narratives share three elements. First, there is a "truth contest" to resolve a conflict between parties. Second, dead bodies serve as witnesses, miraculously testifying for or against a character under scrutiny. Third, the ordeal unfolds before a "lay" intratextual audience, not a tribunal or magistrate, which is prepared to accept the testimony of erstwhile corpses.[49] The "Tale of Thelyphron" in the *Metamorphoses* of Apuleius features a revived murder victim who not only identifies his killer but also exposes a malevolent act of sorcery against another man.[50] The *Acts of Peter* describes a showdown between Peter and Simon. Both men seem to bring the dead back to life, but it is Peter's more impressive ability to make a restored corpse talk that wins over the crowd.[51] Stories like these, as Gleason has shown, allude to and parody the actual forensic brutality of the Roman era and, especially, the customary torture of witnesses.[52] Like a reflection in a funhouse mirror, the flip-flopping bodies of fictional truth contests mimicked and mocked the judicial torture.[53] The *Infancy Gospel* likewise stages a provocative "truth contest" in the story of Zeno: Jesus defends his innocence to a skeptical audience, a resurrected boy confirms the claim, and the parental spectators convert from witnesses for the prosecution to worshipful followers.

But parody always risks eating itself. By turning Zeno's testimony into a rather morbid performance, a "talking corpse," the *Infancy Gospel* raises more questions about cause and effect than it answers. To explore further, let us compare the story of Zeno to another pair of resurrections. Aside from the accounts of Jesus' resurrection, the New Testament includes several stories of the dead being brought back to life. All of them are of course noteworthy, but not all share the same degree of performance. Consider, for example, the story of Eutychus in the canonical book of Acts. It takes place late at night in the city of Troas. As Paul and his companions talk, a "youth," Eutychus, sits on a window ledge, three floors above the discussion. Then Eutychus falls off the ledge: "overcome by sleep, he fell to the floor below and was picked up dead" (Acts 20:7). Paul takes Eutychus into his arms and restores him to life. There is little ambiguity about the death of Eutychus. Nothing is to blame but fatigue (and perhaps the garrulousness of Paul). Nor is the miracle that Paul performs especially dramatic. It lacks buildup and emotion, as if Eutychus tripped and fell down, and Paul offered him a hand up.

Contrast this story with a better known one, the raising of Lazarus in the Gospel of John. When he hears news of Lazarus's illness, Jesus does not go immediately to his aid. He hangs back with his disciples until he becomes aware, preternaturally, that Lazarus has died. Jesus relates the news to his disciples, but they do not understand what he means. Jesus says, "Lazarus is dead. For your sake I am glad I was not there, so that you may believe" (John 11:14–15). When he finally does come to the tomb of Lazarus in Bethany, the two sisters of Lazarus, Mary and Martha, both say to Jesus, "Lord, if you had been here, my brother would not have died" (John 11:21, 32). They wonder why Jesus did not rush to save Lazarus, as do others who remark that Jesus, who had given sight to the blind, "could have kept this man from dying" (John 11:37).

The raising of Lazarus is a *performance* of supernatural power, more so than the relatively unspectacular raising of Eutychus. Jesus himself announces his plan for the event to his disciples. Questions about his tardiness propel the drama, leading to the realization that his lateness in coming was, it turns out, part of a larger plan. And if the calculations involved in the story may at first strike readers as cold, the story includes other details that soften the edges. The emotional life of the family of Lazarus is described: Mary weeps for her dead brother at the feet of Jesus (John 11:33). So too Jesus weeps, either in sympathy with the sister or from the pain that he feels at the death of his friend.

Like the story of Lazarus (and in contrast to the story of Eutychus), Zeno's story in the *Infancy Gospel* amplifies the spectacular nature of the resurrection. Unlike the story of Lazarus, it leaves out details that could tie the episode to a larger purpose, allowing readers to fill in the gaps. Note that the setting is childhood amusement: "Jesus was playing with other children." Jesus' defense against the accusation of Zeno's parents is grimly playful in its own way. As with the toy sparrows that he brought to life, Jesus brings what is dead (or inanimate) to life in order to escape punishment. Moreover, if Jesus has the power to raise Zeno, he, like a child with a doll, must also possess the power to make Zeno say whatever is convenient. The revivified Zeno calls attention to the staging of its own miracle—a staged performance with a lifelike prop. There may be a larger plan in the Zeno story to inspire belief as in the raising of Lazarus. But the possibility is disturbing. Does Jesus allow Zeno to fall off the roof so that he could then raise the boy from the dead? The story raises a series of questions about cause and effect and the specter of uncertainty about the motives of the child Jesus. With the culprit, if there was one, left unnamed, the testimony of the revivified Zeno betrays a degree of desperation. It is as though the storyteller recognizes that the reader, aware of past injuries caused by Jesus, may be hesitant to accept Jesus' denial. The whole truth of what happened on the rooftop lies beyond our grasp. All we see is the strange spectacle that follows.

Is the story of Zeno's death and resuscitation the key to understanding the *Infancy Gospel of Thomas*? Does it illuminate the other spectacles of death that Jesus performs before and after? Since the *Infancy Gospel* is disjointed as a narrative or at least lacks the transitional scaffolding of a more sophisticated account, it is hard to make the case that any single scene is the hermeneutical key. Who is to say whether the resurrection of Zeno or the earlier report of Jesus' sweeping reversal of earlier harms is the more important moment? Still, the Zeno story is crucial in at least two ways. First, it shows that Christians could tell stories in which it was possible for a sympathetic audience to *not* take Jesus' word for it—to wonder, even for a moment, if he is telling the truth. This is only possible because of the surrounding stories of mayhem, which pull readers in, turning them into observers and interpreters.

Second, it is important in the way that it depicts the intimacy of family life. In the raising of Lazarus, Jesus weeps. Not so the child Jesus. Affective bonds are reserved for the family of Zeno. They are participant-observers, passing through stages of grief over a tragedy and rejoicing at their son's sudden recovery. The parents of Zeno first accuse Jesus and then worship him. The parents of Jesus, meanwhile, are conspicuously absent from the scene. What would Joseph and Mary have said? Would they have defended their child against the accusations? Celebrated in his vindication? How would they have reacted?

Truth Tests in the *Proto-gospel of James*

In the Gospel of Matthew, Mary's unexpected pregnancy is the first sign of drama. Joseph and Mary are engaged when he discovers Mary's condition. He realizes that he is not the father of the child. Joseph wants to spare Mary humiliation and "dismiss her quietly," out of the public eye. But an angel pays a visit to Joseph and delivers a message of reassurance (Matt 1:20–21). The crisis passes, never to be mentioned again. In the *Proto-gospel of James*, by contrast, Mary's ill-timed pregnancy becomes public knowledge, prolonging the crisis.

The *Proto-gospel of James* begins with the backstory of Mary's parents, Joachim and Anna, and then shifts to Mary herself: her birth, her childhood, and her dedication in the temple. The bulk of the story deals with her. Moreover, scholars have detected rhetorical features that favor a Maria-centric approach—specifically, the resemblance between the family gospel and *encomia*, ancient declarations of praise.[54] In line with the conventions of *encomia*, the *Proto-gospel of James* highlights Mary's virtue, especially her self-control. Why develop a saintly profile of Mary in the second century? The most popular explanation for its origins is the "apology" theory. Whatever else ancient Christians did when they told stories about Mary, the basic objective, it is surmised, was to mount a defense. The theory proposes that the *Proto-gospel of James* was written as an apology of Mary against attacks from outsiders. Traces of these attacks can be found in Celsus's polemic against Christianity and in the legends of the *Toledot Yeshu* (*Generations of Jesus*).[55] Ancient Christians responded by expanding storytelling around Mary. For example, against those who questioned the truth of Mary's virginity, the *Proto-gospel of James* shows that the same kind of skepticism was present in Mary's own day. She was subjected to scrutiny.[56] And Mary passed all of the tests. Other related accusations—that Jesus was the offspring of an illicit encounter or, as some critics said, that Mary herself grew up on the wrong side of the tracks and was thus morally questionable—are likewise countered by the storytelling of the family gospel, according to the theory of apology.

Mary is unquestionably the star of the *Proto-gospel of James*.[57] But what is the point of subjecting Mary to testing, of making a spectacle out of her body?[58] Recent scholarship has examined the family gospel's fascination with the strange body of Mary. This is what Jennifer Glancy has in mind when she calls the *Proto-gospel of James* "Mary's book."[59] Glancy and Lily Vuong describe the ways in which Mary's body changes and does not change, as well as the ways in which it conforms to and alters definitions of purity found in biblical texts and elsewhere.[60] At first most characters in the story, Joseph included, suspect that she has conceived a child the old-fashioned way. Her ill-timed pregnancy attracts attention, something readers know she has nothing to do with. Mary herself is uncertain about the pregnancy because she forgets the "mysteries" that the angel tells her. When Joseph asks how she got pregnant, Mary says, "I don't know how it got inside me."[61] She becomes the object of intense curiosity—first in private, then in public, and finally in a setting that falls somewhere in between the two, in a cave outside of Bethlehem.

People want to know the truth about Mary, and they are willing to go to great lengths to find it. What is at stake in these stories, I propose, is not just the truth of Mary's body but that of the relationships among the members of the holy household. Since Joseph's interrogation of Mary belongs to the private sphere, it is not examined here, but we will return to it in Chapter 4. Instead, we investigate the public and quasi-public examinations that Mary undergoes.[62] The first is a spectacle of danger, the ritual trial of Mary and Joseph in a "drink test." Their lives are left up to the supernatural testing of the ordeal, and they face it together. The second is Salome's digital inspection, which goes up in flames. It will also serve as the setting for a supernatural healing, the first miracle of the baby Jesus.

Passing the Test Together

When Joseph's neighbor, scandalized by what he takes to be evidence of illicit sexual intercourse between the pair, reports Mary's pregnancy to the high priest, the high priest steps in to investigate.[63] He first interrogates Mary, who claims not to know how she became pregnant. Then he turns to Joseph, who insists that he is not the father. Mary's unexplained pregnancy and Joseph's denial of paternity upset the community, and now the high priest must get to the bottom of the situation.

The high priest orders the couple to take the "Lord's water of refutation."[64] The story alludes to a procedure in the book of Numbers (5:11–31); this test is altered from its biblical form. In Numbers, only the woman drinks, while in the *Proto-gospel of James*, both Mary and Joseph submit. They are ordered to drink the "water of refutation" and wander, separately, into the wilderness. One after the other they return, unharmed. The crowds look on in wonder, perhaps not entirely convinced: "All the people were amazed that their sin was not revealed." The high priest declares, "If the Lord God has not revealed your sin, neither do I judge you."[65] In this different narrative setting, the priest's remarks seem circumspect, withholding judgment rather than affirming the innocence of Mary and Joseph, as if to say, I cannot really believe it myself, but the test results say so.

Virginity was a hot topic for writers of second- and third-century fiction. Jews, Christians, and pagans all wrote stories about sex and abstinence.[66] One example, the Greek romance, *Leucippe and Clitophon*, includes a test of virginity that resembles the ordeal of the *Proto-gospel of James*. The stars of Achilles' novel are Leucippe, the daughter of an affluent general of Byzantium, and Clitophon, the scion of a wealthy family of Tyre. They meet and instantly fall in love, but before they are able to consummate their relationship, fate forces them to follow separate paths. Leucippe maintains her virginity against assaults, while Clitophon gives into temptation, seduced by an older, married woman, Melite. At the end of the romance, the women, Leucippe and Melite, face a pair of public ordeals to test claims of virginity and fidelity. The women enter sacred areas, a cave and a spring; in them, false claims result in death. Both survive: Leucippe because she has maintained her virginity and Melite because she has worded her claim of fidelity in such a way that her "slip" with Clitophon does not count as adultery.[67]

Things are not always what they seem. Tests can be "gamed." Like other examples of the genre, characters in *Leucippe and Clitophon* masquerade as and are mistaken for others. Sometimes they fake their own death; at other times, what appears to be a murder turns out to be only theater.[68] Part of the delight for the reader comes in already knowing the truth of events. Readers often know more than do characters in the story. While the *Proto-gospel of James* is not as playful as *Leucippe and Clitophon*—it does not go as far in exploiting the theme that appearances can be deceiving—it nevertheless creates an asymmetry of knowledge between readers and characters. Readers know what the high priest and the crowds do not know—that Mary and Joseph are telling the truth, that neither of them had anything to do with the pregnancy. In this moment, the perspective of the extratextual readers is at odds with that of the intratextual spectators to the ordeal. The early Christian audience shares a bond with Mary and Joseph in the very same moment that the relationship between the couple is put to the test.

Baby's First Miracle

The second episode of testing happens after Mary has delivered Jesus. Joseph takes Mary to a cave outside of Bethlehem for the birth of the child. He leaves her there and meets a midwife who travels with him back to the cave. Joseph and the midwife return in time to witness not a typical birth but a strange series of events: first cloud cover, then a bright light, and finally and suddenly an infant at the breast of Mary.[69] Thunderstruck, the midwife says, "My soul has been magnified today, for my eyes have seen a miraculous sign: salvation has been born to Israel." She enters the cave and finds Mary nursing her newborn.[70] When the midwife encounters Salome, she tells her that she has seen "a new wonder": "A virgin has given birth, contrary to her natural condition." Salome's response sets up the test: "Unless I insert my finger and examine her," announces Salome, "I will never believe that a virgin has given birth."[71] When Salome arrives, she says to Mary, "there is no small controversy concerning you." She advises Mary: "Brace yourself."[72]

Is Salome's test a public or private investigation? It is both. The cave where Joseph brings Mary is by now crowded with people—family members and strangers crammed into the airless space. Mary's pregnancy continues to attract widespread curiosity and, as Salome tells it, generate "controversy." At the same time, the cave is the setting for intimate physical contact. On one hand is the image of the child nursing at Mary's breast, and on the other is Salome's impending pelvic examination.[73] But Salome, we will recall, is blocked from performing the test: "Then Salome inserted her finger in order to examine her condition, and she cried out, 'Woe to me for my sin and faithlessness. For I have put the living God to the test, and see, my hand is burning, falling away from me.' "[74]

The *Proto-gospel of James* forces an adjustment in the perspective of readers. In the earlier test, the water ordeal, the extratextual audience has a privileged point of view. Readers have access to more information than do the intratextual crowds. So too readers know more than does the high priest. In the cave, however, readers must depend entirely on Salome's testimony. They only see what Salome describes. The view of the extratextual audience is suddenly and radically limited. Readers watch Salome watching her hand, seeing it all happen through her eyes.[75]

What is the meaning of it? It should be noted that Salome's testimony is not dispassionate: she condemns herself for doubt. Hence, readers learn what happens to Salome's hand through Salome's own didactic interpretation of the event. Is Salome's the final word? Some scholars suggest as a parallel the story of "doubting Thomas" in the Gospel of John.[76] After being told by other disciples that Jesus has been raised from the dead, Thomas refuses to accept the claim. "Unless I see the mark of the nails in his hands," he says, "and put my finger in the mark of the nails and my hand in his side, I will not believe" (John 20:25). When Jesus appears a week later, he holds out his hands to Thomas. Unbelief is overcome, and Thomas calls out to Jesus, "My Lord and my God!" (John 20:28). Salome is to Mary as Thomas is to Jesus. Yet, for all of the ways that the stories resemble one another, their differences are equally compelling. Why, for example, does Thomas remain unharmed, while Salome watches her own hand fall away? To reduce the episode to a cautionary tale, I suggest, does little more than reproduce Salome's cry of regret.

Moreover, the image of Mary—a new mother nursing her child, preparing to be searched by a stranger—artfully combines frailty and strength. At the same moment that Mary is exposed, her body becomes a channel of holy power. She is a sacred vessel, and this makes her dangerous.[77] A divine fire continues to burn inside Mary after the baby has exited. Salome's hand thus gathers information even as it is being consumed by fire. It is crucial that at this moment, Salome declares her ancestral heritage. She cries out, "O God of my fathers, remember that I am a descendent of Abraham, Isaac, and Jacob."[78] Salome, a Jew, becomes a surrogate for a Christian audience. Her brazen probing of Mary's genitals creates knowledge of Mary's sacred, postpartum virginity for a Christian audience.[79] And her disintegrating hand, Jewish "flesh," is evidence of the presence of God. Early Christian readers of the *Proto-gospel of James* could watch all of this happen from a safe distance.[80]

But Mary's fiery womb is not the only source of supernatural power in the cave. There is also her newborn child. Salome, like Zeno in the *Infancy Gospel*, enjoys an abrupt and otherworldly reversal of harm. When Salome prays "before the Master" for aid, an angel appears. The angel instructs Salome: "Salome, the Master of all has heard your prayer. Bring your hand to the child and lift him up; and you will find salvation and joy."[81] As Salome does so, she is healed. She worships the child, "for he has been born a great king to Israel." Once again, Salome's Jewishness gives and takes away. Positively, Salome belongs to the biblical past—she refers to the glory of the royal house of David—from which ancient Christians acquired in part a sense of self. But the value of an ancestral connection to this past is diminished. The patriarchs that Salome summons up in her suffering recede as the worship of the baby Christ comes into the foreground.

The newborn Jesus is vulnerable. Salome can hold him in her arms and lift him up in the air. At the same time, he is endowed with supernatural ability: like mother, like son. Spectacles of violence in the *Proto-gospel of James*, like those of the *Infancy Gospel*, turn the gaze of readers toward familial ties. The water ordeal that Mary and Joseph endure does not have much to do with proving their innocence to readers. The audience already knows the truth. The point instead is to show Mary and Joseph as a couple, suffering together and vindicated together. In the same way Salome's inspection illuminates a tableau of family life. Mary's body is not the only body on display in the cave. Nor is Salome's fiery hand, which cools and heals as suddenly as it burst into flames, the only image that lingers. There is also the picture of a newborn baby at Mary's breast. Readers are thus given the poignant sketch of a mother nursing her child: both of them helpless, both of them powerful.[82]

*   *   *

Ancient readers knew about spectacles of violence. Some had seen one in person; others had heard stories. They lived in a world in which the display of suffering could be presented as a work of art, where spectacles of violence could be "teachable moments" about wealth, authority, and the Roman order of things. Traces of what was staged before live audiences remain in the literature of the era: Josephus records the "messaging" of Roman generals, who turned the bodies of captives into a kind of universal alphabet for broadcasting their intentions. As we have seen, other sources, while exploiting the attraction of theatrical scenes of violence, ramp up skepticism and irony. The apparent deaths of Greek romance show authors using spectacle to fool their readers: things are not always what they seem. The same could be said for passion narratives: the crucifixion of Jesus, in the eyes of the Christian faithful, was not a sign of humiliation but just the opposite.

The common denominator of the examples in this chapter is the power of spectacle. It was a reliable narrative device for captivating an audience, or so I have argued. It made readers look. And when they looked, they asked questions. The family gospels push this exercise to its limits. Jesus' curses and Salome's hand are hard to ignore and difficult to decipher. Spectacular violence, common to the arena and battlefield where it can be "read" and understood, is rendered unintelligible when set amid the intimate moments of everyday life. And if these moments startle the intratextual audience, then they must have been designed to do the same to the extratextual audience. Yet, as gripping as they are, the violent spectacles of the *Infancy Gospel* and the *Protogospel of James* are temporary and reversed.

The violence of Jesus in the *Infancy Gospel* is fleeting. But the questions raised by the incidents remain. The parents of dead children do not understand why Jesus is hurting their offspring. And when the parents of other children come into view, readers, I suggest, may wonder about a different set of parents: Mary and Joseph. What do they think? How do they feel about what their son is doing? In the same way, Salome's burning and restored hand in the *Proto-gospel of James* points away from itself and toward the unusual mother and child next to her. What does Mary feel when she sees her own body scald the hand of Salome? What does she feel when she sees her baby reverse the harm she has done?

Readers, following the gaze of witnesses in the account, look away from the spectacles and toward the holy family. The violence of the family gospels frames the life of the holy family as its own kind of spectacle—something to be looked at and wondered about. As an analogy, consider depth of field in photography: objects in the background become blurry as the camera focuses on a specific subject. The fear and amazement that envelop the neighbors bring ever more sharply into focus the figures of Jesus, Mary, and Joseph. What kind of pressure did living with the presence of supernatural power put on this family? How did the minds of Mary and Joseph come to grips with what they saw and experienced? How did they deal with these strange events, some of them too astonishing to understand?

The next chapter begins to take up these questions. It focuses on Joseph, the father of Jesus in the *Infancy Gospel*, and Anna, the mother of Mary in the *Proto-gospel of James*. Both are conscientious parents who want what's best for their extraordinary kids. Yet both, in different ways, prove unable to grasp the truth of who their children are and what they will become.

Chapter 3

Wanting What's Best

The boy was trouble.

The *Infancy Gospel of Thomas* includes several classroom stories. In the first one, a teacher writes out the alphabet for Jesus, but the boy remains silent.[1] Angry, the teacher hits Jesus, who finally opens his mouth. What comes out is a dazzling allegory of the first Greek letter. It so baffles the teacher that he wonders aloud whether he ought to retire from the profession. Later Joseph hires a different teacher for his son, and things go from bad to worse. He orders Jesus to recite the letters: "Say alpha." When Jesus refuses, this teacher, like the other one, swats the boy on the head. What follows is unpleasant though not, it must be said, unexpected: Jesus curses the teacher, who collapses, dying or already dead.[2]

For obvious reasons, scholars have focused on the depiction of the child Jesus as a truculent and, as the teachers discover, dangerous student. Some find in it a dramatization of the early Christian resentment of Greek and Roman education.[3] But if we shift the focus away from the pupil, another feature stands out: Joseph's persistence in the face of failure. Despite all that he has witnessed, Joseph continues to seek out teachers for his recalcitrant child. "When Joseph saw his wisdom and understanding, he desired him not to be in lack of letters. So he handed him over to another teacher."[4] Joseph wants his boy to get an education. These stories are not just about the child. They are also about the father and the future that he desires for his son.

Parental hopes likewise come to the surface in the *Proto-gospel of James*. In this account, the destination is the temple of Jerusalem instead of the schoolhouse. When Anna learns that she is pregnant (with the child she will name

Mary), she dedicates the as yet unborn baby to the temple: "I will offer it as a gift to the Lord my God, and it will minister to him its entire life."[5] After Mary is born, Anna turns the nursery into a "sanctuary" and "did not allow anything impure or unclean to pass through her lips."[6] Later Anna does the hardest thing of all: as promised, she says goodbye to her three-year-old daughter and hands her over to the priest, who accepts the toddler into her new home, the house of God. Like Joseph, Anna wants what's best for her child, whatever it takes.

This chapter is about the aspirations of parents. It is also about conflict. What are parents willing to do to realize the dreams they have for their children? What are they willing to give up? And what if the child takes a path other than the one that has cost the parents so dearly? This set of questions may at first seem more promising for the analysis of one family gospel than the other. In the *Infancy Gospel*, the classroom is depicted as a setting for intellectual and social growth. It prepares children for a respectable adulthood. It is easy for readers to understand why Joseph would invest in education on behalf of Jesus. So too it is easy to understand why the son's poor conduct leaves his father disappointed and confused. Nevertheless, Joseph persists in trying to find a teacher for his son. Why doesn't he give up?

A similar dynamic may be found in the *Proto-gospel of James*, but recognizing it takes perhaps more empathy. One must see the temple through Anna's eyes, as the place where her daughter will learn how to fulfill the highest possible calling—that of serving in the house of God for the rest of her life.[7] The temple is thus both a home and a training school for Mary. But nine years after she moves in, Mary is forced out of the sacred precincts. The time for Mary's first period arrives, and the priests fear that her presence will defile the sanctuary. Is Anna, like Joseph, mistaken about the future, about where Mary will live and what she will do?

Why do the family gospels put the conflict this way? My historical argument is that it reflects how classical Greek learning and culture, or *paideia*, was thought of and debated under the Roman Empire. *Paideia* could be viewed as a badge of good taste or as a path to a better future. One of the era's sharpest minds, Lucian of Samosata, recounts his own teenage struggle over how to deal with the burden of family expectations, on one hand, and how to advance socially, on the other. In an essay, *The Dream*, he weighs in the

balance costs and benefits. Here is the portrait of a young man caught between two paths to adulthood: one road leads to becoming a stonemason
(what his father wants), while the other leads to joining the cultured elite
(what Lucian himself wants).

The family gospels, like *The Dream*, depict families thinking about the
future. But where the adult Lucian channels the viewpoint of his childhood,
the family gospels dramatize the struggle and outlook of parents trying to secure a safe future for their children. In this difference of perspective is a larger
point about the limits of human knowing. The parents risk finances, reputation, and, in Anna's case, her only chance at being a mother. On one hand,
Joseph's persistence and Anna's sacrifice show just how much their children
mean to the parents. On the other, their efforts on behalf of their children
show just how little the parents understand about what heaven has in mind
for their offspring. And this is a lesson that the early Christian audience could
appreciate because they knew from the Synoptic gospels that Mary did not
grow old in the temple and that Jesus did not grow up to join the cultured
elite and become a father himself. The lives of Mary and Jesus have a significance that exceeds human comprehension, and this is why their loving parents are unable to see what lies ahead.

Counting the Cost

One way to approach the "classroom" stories of the *Infancy Gospel* is to treat
them as an index of early Christian attitudes to Greek and Roman education.
They can serve as "insider" corroboration of "outsider" complaints about early
Christians. Recall from Chapter 1, for example, the second-century pagan
critic Celsus and his unflattering report of Christian contempt for education.
Is the unruly student Jesus of the *Infancy Gospel*, which dates to around the
same time, a hostile witness to the claims of Celsus?[8] Tony Burke argues that
ancient Christians would have cheered to see the boy turn the tables on the
schoolteacher.[9] Moreover, the account of Celsus corroborates other depictions
of ancient Christians. Lucian, author of *The Dream*, also wrote the *Passing of
Peregrinus*, a satire on the gullibility of Christians. What these sources share is
an image of Christianity as a religion of fools and ne'er-do-wells. A Christian,

skeptics said, was not only possessed of a feeble intellect but also rejected education.

What should we make of such claims? Were most ancient Christians suspicious of pagan teachers and classical learning? Did they encourage children to treat the wisdom of teachers and fathers as "nonsense"? The record of the first three centuries CE is mixed.[10] Some early Christians thought that the apostolic founders of their religion had not needed a formal education to get the message across. As Robert Kaster observes, "The canonical reminder that Peter and John were 'illiterates and laymen' (Acts 4:13) and Paul's claim to be 'ignorant in speech but not in understanding' (2 Cor. 11:6) converged on the powerful model of the illiterate or ill-educated apostle as charismatic teacher, whose truth owed nothing to the conventions and institutions of men."[11] The apostles did not try to persuade with elegant words but spoke only the unvarnished truth.

At the same time, Justin, a highly educated second-century Christian teacher, could demonstrate a sophisticated grasp of Greek rhetoric and philosophy even as he praises followers "who do not even know the letters of the alphabet—uneducated and barbarous in speech, but wise and faithful in mind."[12] Moreover, ancient Christians did very little to challenge the status quo when it came to education.[13] Citing the case of Tertullian, the second-century North African apologist, Mary Ann Beavis notes that "it never occurred even to a rigorist like Tertullian ('What does Athens have to do with Jerusalem?') that Christian children should eschew the schools, or that Christians should set up their own schools."[14] If the thought did not come into Tertullian's black-and-white mind, in other words, it probably did not enter the minds of other Christians. In the eastern half of the empire, where Celsus published his caricature of the religion, Christianity slowly transformed Greek learning "from within," as Beavis puts it.[15]

The attack of Celsus betrays how much Greek-speaking intellectuals cared about *paideia*. Why was Greek learning such an important topic in the Roman era? When the family gospels were written, Rome was identified with the exercise of rule and Greece with that of education. While Greece was held captive under the Roman Empire, a kind of power rested in the allure of Greek learning and knowledge.[16] As Rome was expanding and consolidating its rule from one end of the Mediterranean Sea to the other, conquering not only Greece but also the network of Hellenized cities that dotted the eastern end of the Mediterranean world from Asia Minor to Egypt, Greek authors returned time and again in their writings to the theme of learning and, importantly, to the way of life with which learning was associated, *paideia*.[17] A classicist has recently glossed the term in this way: "*paideia* . . . implies both a body of privileged texts, artworks, values—a culture to be inherited and preserved as a sign of civilization—and also a process of acculturation—education—which 'makes men,' which informs the structures and activities of the lives of the civic elite."[18] Under Rome, education came to be identified with Greek culture and civilization with Greek learning. For this reason, the findings of an authoritative and sweeping account of ancient learning could be summarized with this formula: "Classical education was essentially an initiation into the Greek way of life."[19] Greek *paideia* made the respectable Roman-era man.

Greek learning was something to be possessed, and Romans traveled from the capital city in search of it.[20] The second-century CE biographer Plutarch, in his *Life of Cicero*, describes the midlife crisis of the great Roman politician, Cicero, who journeyed to Greece to receive advanced training from masters who embodied the ideal of *paideia*. Cicero's achievements in language and rhetoric led one of his teachers to observe that, since his Roman pupil had thoroughly conquered Greek learning, there was nothing left for Greeks to claim as their own.[21] The passage is illuminating both for what it says about the magnetic force of Greek culture and for what it reveals about Roman authority. The power of Rome was expressed in what was added to the stock of empire rather than by what was eliminated or destroyed. Greek *paideia* was respected by Roman elites and consumed by them. Meanwhile, the Greek purveyors of *paideia*, such as Cicero's teacher, played a role in maintaining the image of Greek learning as something worth the while of aristocratic Romans. It was a valuable commodity, there for the taking.[22]

From a Roman perspective, this packaging of Greek learning and culture offered a solution to an intractable problem,[23] for Romans of the imperial period considered the Greeks of their own day, as a rule, to be dissolute and immoral. But when understood in terms of acquisition, Greek *paideia* was splendidly free of the taint of contemporary Greek society. It belonged to the classical age of Greece, a glorious product from a bygone era that could be neatly merged with the Roman ideal of manly virtue. Romans sought out *paideia* from Greek teachers and philosophers, authentic purveyors of culture and education, and once they had it, they paraded their sophisticated Greek knowledge around in public.

So widely accepted was this view of Greek *paideia*—that acquiring it would supremely enhance one's public perception and reputation—that it became the subject of parody. Lucian of Samosata mocks the idea of purchasing learning and culture, for example, in *On Salaried Posts in Great Houses*. In it, he describes the upper crust of Rome, strolling about the city, with a Greek philosopher conspicuously in tow.[24] Lucian boils down the scene to its essentials: it is the beard and cloak of the Greek philosopher that are for sale, the "tchotkes of *paideia* for the upwardly mobile Roman," as Laura Nasrallah memorably puts it.[25] All that was required in the competitive world of Roman public life was the appearance of good taste, which could be had, for a price.

But it was not only well-to-do Romans who looked with longing on Greek *paideia*. Since *paideia* was power, education could be empowering for people on the margins—geographical and otherwise—of the Roman Empire.[26] Hailing from regions that had long been dismissed as home to barbarians, some were able to use *paideia* as a pass into the ranks of the cultured.[27] Expansion of the empire brought the prestige of Greek learning and knowledge to new audiences, a facet of imperial life that is evident in the careers of some well-known outsiders.[28]

Lucian, hailing from Roman Syria, was one such outsider.[29] His playful adult recollection of his own childhood in *The Dream* offers what is ostensibly a "child's-eye" view, from the Greek-speaking provinces, on the risks and rewards of Greek education. Lucian begins *The Dream* by recounting his father's decision to put the teenage Lucian on a path to a career in masonry. Father and friends agree that advanced education would take "considerable expense," a burden to the family's "moderate" finances.[30] Up to this point, the boy had been something of a day-dreamer in school. Rather than completing his school assignments, Lucian would create toy animals and people from the wax of writing tablets. For this, Lucian receives "thrashings" from his teachers but praise from members of his family.[31] His father is impressed by Lucian's abilities. Encouraged by this glimpse of talent, Lucian's father cuts a deal with one of the boy's uncles, a sculptor: "Come, take this lad . . . and teach him to be a good stone-cutter, mason, and sculptor, for he is capable of it, since, as you know, he has a natural gift for it."[32] His education brought to a halt, Lucian is suddenly pushed into the different world of masonry.

Things begin well, but soon the beginner's clumsiness of Lucian angers his uncle. At this point in the story, Lucian begins to have second thoughts about masonry. Running back home to seek the comfort of his mother, Lucian falls asleep and begins to dream, for which the essay is named. In the vision, two female figures, a personified *Paideia* and a personified *Technē* (Craft), rise up in the mind of Lucian, each one making the case on behalf of her field of expertise. Craft, dressed in dirty, workshop clothing, tells Lucian that the work will leave him "generously kept" and will give him "powerful shoulders."[33] She also promises stability: Lucian will remain in his native Syria, among the friends and family he has always known. *Paideia*, on the other hand, pledges that if Lucian opts for her over Craft, he will travel the world and attain greatness: "'And you, who are now the beggarly son of a nobody, who have entertained some thought of so illiberal a trade, will after a little inspire envy and jealously in all men, for you will be honoured and lauded, you will be held in great esteem for the highest qualities and admired by men preeminent in lineage and in wealth, you will wear clothing such as this'—she pointed to her own, and she was very splendidly dressed—'and will be deemed worthy of office and precedence.'"[34] *Paideia* promises Lucian the trappings of elite culture and wealth, an open door into the corridors of social power. How could Craft compete with *Paideia*'s vision of Lucian's future—of having "the best seat in the house"?

Seduced by the promise of material comforts and prestige, Lucian opts for *Paideia*. The adult Lucian would go on to exploit the value of "playing Greek," even as he lampooned the cheapening of *paideia* by the snobs of Rome.[35] Is this hypocrisy? Perhaps so. And yet affection for his writings endures because of the author's acute sensitivity to double standards, whether they are someone else's or his own. Lucian's awareness of his own compromised position comes out in his account. Consider how *The Dream* casts learning and training in transactional terms. In *The Dream*, a cost-benefit analysis is shared by the presentations of Craft and *Paideia*. Craft promises Lucian a stable future, surrounded by friends and family. *Paideia* tells Lucian, "You will put on a filthy tunic . . . you will make yourself a thing of less value than a block of stone."[36] And it is not only in the vision that costs are counted. There are other "expenses," too, such as the ones that come in the form of physical punishment. Before he dreams of the personifications of Craft and *Paideia*, the young Lucian has a bruising interaction with his uncle. He broke a slab in a clumsy first attempt at sculpture, so his uncle hit him with a stick.[37] Later in the essay, following his nocturnal encounter with *Paideia*, Lucian casually lets drop that the dream was probably prompted by fear of his uncle's blows.[38] The whipping, perversely and ironically, "knocked some sense" into Lucian. It begets the vision that pushes the boy away from the harsh training of Craft and into the waiting arms of *Paideia* and further to renown and wealth in adulthood.

There is still more irony. *Paideia* was as brutal as craft, as Lucian himself well knew. A schoolteacher, according to the account, administers Lucian's first beating—for the offense of making toys from wax writing tablets. *The Dream* is not a position paper. It does not argue for or against the use of the rod on children. Rather, Lucian seems conflicted, both conceding and disputing the value of educational thumping. Perhaps such ambivalence reflects the tension and compromise built into the acquisition of Greek learning under Rome. Indeed, the ludic sequence of *The Dream* mocks the pretensions of Roman high society. First, a schoolteacher hits Lucian for making toy sculptures, then the sculptor thrashes Lucian, sending him on to *paideia*. The relentless beatings of childhood could be enlisted to poke fun at the ostensibly refined world of adults. Lucian is tossed between *paideia* and masonry and suffers on both paths to adulthood.

In the back and forth over the merits of each option, *Paideia* observes that no matter how much Lucian would be able to achieve as a sculptor, he would still be looked down upon by the snobby members of the upper crust. "You would still be considered a mechanic," *Paideia* asserts, "a man who has nothing but his hands, a man who lives by his hands."[39] The drudgery of manual labor is thrown into relief when *Paideia* offers to Lucian a pair of wings instead of soiled hands. She beckons him into a carriage drawn by "winged horses." Then Lucian suddenly soars above the clouds, taking in a view of the world spread out before him, receiving acclaim from gods and human beings. "I was carried up into the heights," Lucian recalls, "and went from the East to the very West, surveying cities and nations and peoples . . . men, looking up from below, applauded, and all those above whom I passed in my flight sped me on my way with words of praise."[40] Recall that the story of Cicero's journey to Greece for acquiring *paideia* likewise associates learning with travel. Here Lucian surpasses his predecessors. Where Cicero's Greek tour remained confined to the ground, Lucian takes flight. For a moment, everything is illuminated.

Then Lucian returns to earth. Hope and fear meet in *The Dream*, as Lucian is tossed from education to sculpture and back again. An image of unsettled youth, it is also an image of uncertainty. Unlike other Greek authors who saw education as the bright line separating culture and anomie, Lucian recognizes that the pursuit of learning contains elements of both. *The Dream* charts a painful to and fro, raising questions: Of what value is learning? What does one have to do to obtain it? What is one willing to give up to gain knowledge—family, home? And what, in turn, can learning be "cashed in" for? As is so often true of his writings, Lucian poses these serious questions in a subversive way. While *Paideia* wins the contest over Craft, there is equivocation in the final sentence of the essay. He ends *The Dream* with a wink and nod, saying that now, as an adult master of *paideia*, I am "at least quite as highly thought of as any sculptor."[41] Is Lucian here acknowledging the wisdom of his father in trying to steer him toward masonry, a worthy profession? In hindsight, did Lucian's father know best?[42]

Say Alpha

Lucian knows all about the rewards that *Paideia* promises. But his final bon mot suggests that he wonders whether his choice of *Paideia* over Craft was worth it. Do the fine clothes of *Paideia* garner any more respect than the soiled uniform of the sculptor? Lucian's essay is an inventory of costs: the financial burden of literary education, the physical toll of beatings, and, perhaps, the emotional cost of separation from home and family.

It is obvious that the *Infancy Gospel* does not involve *paideia* in the sense of the mature Greek literary culture that would have come to mind for Lucian and his contemporaries. Nor does the family gospel share Lucian's style or wit. Yet, as we shall see, the *Infancy Gospel*, like Lucian's essay, counts the costs. It does so from a different perspective and for a different purpose. Lucian offers readers a child's-eye view and, in doing so, turns his conflict with his father into one of the losses incurred by his choice of *Paideia*. In the *Infancy Gospel*, it is the father, not Jesus, who is attracted to the classroom. Joseph thinks he knows what's best for Jesus. The ensuing conflict exposes the ignorance at the heart of Joseph's good intentions. The classroom episodes are about a parent pushing his son to reach his potential, all the while unaware of who and what his son truly is.

Even so, the family gospels do not discount the value of places of learning. As we shall see, Jesus in the *Infancy Gospel* speaks words of wisdom to people gathered in the classroom, and the temple in the *Proto-gospel of James* serves as the dwelling place of angels. And both Jesus and Mary learn in their respective locations, although this facet of the storytelling has been mostly overlooked by scholars. Jesus recites the alphabet, and Mary learns how to spin thread.

First, we turn to the *Infancy Gospel of Thomas*. The *Infancy Gospel* includes three classroom tales.[43] Thanks to the careful study by Stephen Davis, it is clearer than ever how the schoolhouse scenes of the *Infancy Gospel* reflect educational practices of the Roman era. They also recall some of the details in *The Dream* of Lucian. In all three examples, the Greek terminology suggests professional teachers and settings, as Davis observes. Jesus is led, for example, into a *paideuterion*, a place of instruction separate from home.[44] The teachers of Jesus are referred to as *didaskolos* or *kathēgēthēs*.[45] They are professionals. While the *Infancy Gospel* does not explicitly describe Joseph paying the teachers, the use of these terms implies their hiring.

A transactional element emerges as well in other, less tangible ways.[46] In this first account, the longest of the three, the teacher, one Zacchaeus, offers his services to Joseph: "Come, give him over, brother, so that he may be taught letters, and so he may know all knowledge, learn to love those his own age, honor old age and revere elders, so that he may acquire a desire for children of his own and teach them."[47] If Joseph assigns Jesus to Zacchaeus, he will receive in return a transformed child. Not only will Zacchaeus train Jesus in the basics of literacy, but he will also mold the boy into an upright member of the community. He will teach Jesus to respect adults and be kind to others so that someday Jesus can do the same with his own children. But

Jesus does not wish to be taught, nor will he someday have children of his own. He declares his intention to reverse the flow, to teach to Zacchaeus and Joseph "a *paideia* by me which no other knows nor is able to teach."[48] Then, turning to a crowd of onlookers, Jesus asks, "Why do you not believe the things I said to you?"[49]

The prospects for fulfilling the terms of the deal—for teaching the child Jesus his letters and his proper place in society—seem dim. And this first hostile exchange between the child Jesus and the adults he is supposed to respect may have called to mind for ancient Christian readers another story from the earlier Gospel of Luke, the rejection of the adult Jesus in the synagogue in Nazareth (Luke 4:16–30). In the Lukan account, Jesus reads a passage from the scroll of Isaiah and claims to embody its fulfillment. The people in Nazareth wonder aloud, "Is not this Joseph's son?" (Luke 4:22). Conflict erupts when Jesus, comparing himself to Elijah and Elisha, contends that "no prophet is accepted in the prophet's hometown" (Luke 4:24). The crowd chases him outside to the edge of a cliff, but Jesus escapes (Luke 4:29–30). In this story, the adult Jesus demonstrates reading proficiency; what he lacks is the acknowledgment of his neighbors. If we think of this Lukan image of the adult Jesus as the backdrop to the classroom stories of the child Jesus, it suggests the futility of Joseph's efforts. The child, ancient Christians knew, would not grow up to be the kind of adult that Zacchaeus describes to Joseph.

As a child, Jesus at first resists Joseph's plan, then he yields. Escorted by Joseph, the boy goes to the schoolhouse of Zacchaeus. Joseph remains in the classroom, a point later confirmed when Zacchaeus asks the father to take his son back home. The supporting role of the household in "educating Jesus" is a recurring element of the storytelling. Joseph remains steadfast in his desire to secure an education for his son, despite the difficulties. It is Joseph, after all, who continues to look for teachers for his son. The classroom stories always involve more than a tug-of-war between pupil and tutor. Home life is bound tightly to the experience of the classroom, for good and for ill. When Jesus gets in trouble at school, it follows him back to the household of Joseph and Mary.

It is not long before Jesus is the subject of the corporal punishment of his teacher. Childhood remembrances by authors from Lucian to Augustine attest to the rough treatment meted out by fathers and teachers in the name of learning.[50] Zacchaeus begins the lesson by writing the alphabet, cueing Jesus to say the letters. When Jesus refuses to speak, Zacchaeus strikes Jesus on the head.[51] The reaction of Jesus to the blow is, unsurprisingly, anger. He declares once more his superiority to Zacchaeus: "I wish to teach you rather than be taught by you, for I know the letters you are teaching more accurately and far better than you."[52] And yet, what follows in the wake of this reproach seems to undermine the idea of Jesus' renunciation of the student role. When he finishes his speech and his anger ceases, Jesus recites "by himself all the letters from alpha to omega with much skill."[53] In the middle of rebuking Zacchaeus, Jesus pauses to complete the assignment.

Zacchaeus gets both more and less than he bargained for. Recalling the original deal the teacher strikes with Joseph, we now see that the classroom story offers a menu of different kinds of learning. Zacchaeus pledges to teach Jesus "his letters," respect for authority, and love for neighbor.[54] Three items of learning, and Jesus performs one: elementary literacy. It is, perhaps, missing the point to infer that Jesus knew "his letters" before arriving in the classroom.[55] What the story suggests is cause and effect. Jesus learns the Greek alphabet and practices the knowledge he acquires as a result of the beating he receives at the hand of the angry Zacchaeus.

To elementary literacy, Jesus adds a mystical riff on the letter alpha.[56] "Hear, teacher," Jesus says, "and understand the order of the first element. Pay close attention here how it has sharp lines and a middle stroke, which you see pointing, standing with legs apart, meeting, spread, drawn aside, elevated."[57] Jesus continues in this vein for several more lines. Jesus' articulation of heavenly knowledge overwhelms the teacher, to the degree that Zacchaeus seems unable to recall and recognize the partial success of getting Jesus to recite the alphabet. (Joseph, likewise, does not understand, for later he worries about Jesus' "lack of letters."[58]) Zacchaeus laments the moment as a defeat: "Woe is me! Woe is me! I have been baffled, wretch that I am."[59] He regrets having taken on Jesus as a student: "I have brought shame down upon myself, attracting me to this child."[60] He admits that the tables have turned: "He stupefies me. I cannot follow along in my mind. I have deceived myself, thrice unhappy as I am. I thought to gain a student and I am found having a master."[61] Finally, Zacchaeus pledges to withdraw completely from village life, to accept a social death: "I must be cast out and die or flee from this village on account of everyone, especially after all these people saw that I was defeated by a very small child."[62]

Ancient Greek and Roman biographies often include tales about the precocious childhood of admirable figures. Reports of a superior mind in boyhood may be found throughout Plutarch's profiles, from Solon to Alexander the Great to Augustus. It is part of the checklist of ancient biography. And it was a commonplace of ancient biography to describe the student teaching and surpassing the teacher—a "prophecy of future greatness."[63] Consider Philo's biography of Moses: teachers arrived from Egypt and Greece to dispense their knowledge, but soon the child "devised problems which they [i.e., the teachers] could not easily solve."[64] It is not an act of rebellion against formal education but evidence of inspired ability: "For the gifted soul," Philo affirms, "takes the lead in meeting the lessons given by itself rather than the teacher and is profited."[65] Setting aside for the moment the misery of Zacchaeus, the classroom story could be said to run parallel to Philo's high-minded vision of learning.[66] Indeed, rather than humiliating Zacchaeus, the child Jesus may be showing off what he has learned from the teacher. Jesus' mastery of the Greek alphabet is the foundation upon which he builds the allegory.

But the nature of the storytelling in the *Infancy Gospel* invites us to push beyond the listing of parallels, as important and revealing as some of these may be. It is one thing to show great figures as children exemplifying the traits that would make their adult lives worthy of remembrance, as Greek and Roman biographies do. It is another to string out the depiction of learning over multiple episodes, as the family gospels do, and to describe the interruption and failure of learning. Ancient biography has been put to good use as comparative material to the Christian gospels, especially regarding the art of characterization.[67] But the genre may not yield much in the quest to understand why Jesus fights with his teachers. Why, for example, once they decided to put Jesus in the schoolhouse, did Christian storytellers make him into such a pill? And why does Joseph keep asking for trouble by hiring more teachers?

Jesus has the teacher's number. Zacchaeus, by contrast, remains mystified: "What great thing he is—god or angel or whatever else I might call him—I do not know."[68] Zacchaeus tells Joseph to take Jesus back home. The story draws a boundary between the divine mind of Jesus and the limited

understanding of Zacchaeus. In light of what Zacchaeus says, it is understandable why scholars construe the episode as an all-or-nothing contest that
shows that Jesus does not have anything to learn.[69] But is it? To my mind, it
also suggests a crossing of that boundary, for teacher and student come together, albeit briefly, when Jesus recites the Greek alphabet. Moreover, elsewhere the child Jesus shows himself to be a creative and eager learner outside
the classroom. Much of this learning extends what readers encounter in the
opening scene: there Jesus molds toys from the mud, an act that may remind
us of Lucian's play with wax tablets. Jesus collects water for his mother and
gathers fuel for a fire for her baking.[70] So too he helps his father to farm.[71]
Most intriguing, perhaps, given the contrast of masonry and *paideia* in *The
Dream*, Jesus helps his father in his carpentry.[72]

But inside the schoolhouse, the student Jesus remains a problem. In the
second classroom story, Joseph resolves once again to hire a teacher: "So he
handed him over to another master. The master wrote the alphabet for him
and said, 'Say alpha.'"[73] Jesus refuses to do so and throws down the gauntlet:
"First tell me what is the beta and I will tell you what is the alpha."[74] The scene
begins, then, as a replay of the earlier classroom episode. On cue, the anonymous teacher hits Jesus. But where the blow of Zacchaeus leads to a performance of learning on the part of Jesus, the beating of the second teacher
rebounds onto the teacher himself. Jesus curses the teacher, who immediately
falls dead to the ground. Jesus walks away from the scene.[75] Because Jesus kills
his teacher in the second story, it can be difficult to appreciate the similar
structure of the pair of episodes. Zacchaeus, we will recall, describes his defeat
as a kind of mortal blow: "I must be cast out and die." What may be the most
striking difference, then, is not what happens to the teachers but the presence
and absence of the learning of Jesus. In the first, Jesus makes the alphabet his
starting point for teaching a divine lesson. In the second, Jesus withholds
learning and instead issues a curse. In the first, learning is acquired and put on
display. In the second, Jesus keeps to himself what he knows.

There is finally a third shared element: family drama. When Jesus returns
home after killing the second teacher, Joseph, evidently at wit's end, turns to
Mary and commands "her not to let him out of the house so that those who
make him angry may not die."[76] Joseph decides to cut off his child from society. Out of this turn of events emerges a set of parallels. Like Zacchaeus, Jesus

suddenly becomes a pariah. And like Zacchaeus, Joseph does not know what to do with Jesus.

Given the drastic measures that Joseph takes in the second classroom story, it may come as a surprise to encounter a third teaching story immediately following it. A vague reference—"after some days"—serves to measure the time between the death of the second teacher and the third classroom account.[77] Another teacher agrees to take Jesus, once again promising to teach Jesus "his letters." This time Joseph does not have to escort his son: Jesus gladly trots off to school, holding hands with the instructor. Chastened perhaps by the misfortune of prior tutors, this instructor does little more than watch. The boy walks into the schoolhouse, finds a scroll, and begins to speak: "He took the book but did not read what was written in it, but, opening his mouth, he spoke awe-inspiring words, so that the teacher sitting opposite listened to him very gladly and encouraged him so that he might say more."[78] What are the book's contents? Since Jesus does not actually read from it, the audience is kept in the dark about its precise contents. Perhaps, as some manuscripts suggest, it is scripture or, as others suggest, it is not.[79] Grasping but not reading the book, the image of the child Jesus is one of being "in between." He is an un-educable prodigy who, nevertheless, sometimes demonstrates learning in the schoolhouse.

Unlike the previous episode, the tale of the third teacher has a happy ending. Like the others, it includes a subtext of family drama. Shifting from close-up to wide angle, the narrator pans around to take in an admiring crowd: "the crowd standing there were astonished at his holy words."[80] Joseph, who is not part of the crowd but somewhere else nearby, overhears the clamor and rushes to the scene, "suspecting that this teacher too was no longer inexperienced and that he may have suffered."[81] Joseph fears the worst and arrives too late to hear any of his son's words, which have electrified the audience. But the teacher lavishes praise on the boy: "Please know that I accepted this child as a student, but already he is full of grace and wisdom."[82] The teacher has acquitted himself well, and the result is a show of benevolence: "Since you have spoken and testified rightly," Jesus says, "that other teacher who was struck down will be healed."[83] Here the public recognition of the boy's greatness—specifically, the teacher's praise of his lesson—triggers a reversal of past harm. Life is restored to the dead teacher of the second classroom story.

What would Zacchaeus think about this final classroom episode? We do not know. He is not mentioned again after the first schoolhouse incident. He might be proud of Jesus for demonstrating key social lessons: respect for elders and kindness to others. One scholar has recently noted an "evolving pattern of the portrayal of a more socially conditioned Jesus, who learns to live within the constraints of the human world."[84] A similar proposal describes the *Infancy Gospel of Thomas* as a story of growing maturity. When Jesus acts out as a child, he is shown to be acting like a child or, at least, childishly, lacking in self-control. The *Infancy Gospel of Thomas* goes on to describe the "slow transformation" of Jesus, his gradual maturation "from boy to man."[85] It is an attractive theory, in part because the cursing diminishes as the gospel unfolds. In the third classroom story, congeniality reigns. The teacher yields the floor immediately to Jesus, and later, speaking to Joseph, he speaks highly of the student.

All is well. It must be said, however, that Jesus' self-control is not truly put to the test in this scene. What would Jesus have done if this teacher, like the second one, had hit him on the head? Rather than a sign of Jesus' emotional development, the episode can be viewed as a lesson in conflict avoidance. If experience is the best teacher, this is the lesson: flatter Jesus and get out of his way.

But I would suggest a different meaning. What binds the last story to the others is incompleteness. Jesus holds the book but does not read from it. Moreover, the third teacher sends Jesus home with Joseph without having ever taught the boy "his letters," which is why Joseph hired the teacher in the first place. The third story is an inverse reflection of the first story: Jesus learns either his letters or good manners but not both at once. For this reason, I have doubts about a model of evolution or a linear development in the classroom stories. I would suggest instead a triptych, on whose panels are depicted three iterations of the classroom scene. Across the images, Jesus accepts some bits of knowledge while refusing others and, each time, leaves the classroom before the lesson has been completed. Perhaps these scenes of interrupted learning are designed to remind readers of the rushed exit of the adult Jesus from the synagogue in Nazareth (Luke 4:16–30). If so, ancient Christians also would have been reminded that they knew the end of the story in a way Joseph could not. Joseph, unable to comprehend who or what Jesus is, keeps bringing Jesus back to the classroom, imagining for his son a future that will not come to pass.

Sacrifice, Interrupted

Teachers and classrooms do not figure into the *Proto-gospel of James*. Yet, this gospel, like the other accounts we have discussed, shows a parent who dreams up a future for a child. More specifically, it shows what a mother, Anna, is willing to give up to see her child, Mary, live out the dream. What does it cost Anna? What will she *sacrifice* on Mary's behalf? And what does it mean that Anna's vision of Mary's future does not come to pass?

The young Mary does not astound the adults of her village with precocious intelligence.[86] She nevertheless charms the neighbors in the playful, slightly irreverent way that only children are allowed to get away with. When she turns three, her parents, Joachim and Anna, bring their daughter to the temple. Mary is received by the priest, who declares a benediction: "Through you will the Lord make known his redemption to the sons of Israel at the end of time."[87] He sets the toddler down on the third step of the altar, and little Mary does the most adorable thing: "She danced on her feet, and the entire house of Israel loved her."[88] Mary basks in the glow of public acclaim. Such is not the case in much of the *Infancy Gospel of Thomas*. Receiving compliments about their son is something the parents can only dream of.

As a toddler, Mary is hailed as an apocalyptic messenger, someone who will announce God's "redemption" to the people of Israel at the end of time.[89] The quest for revealed heavenly truth is an important feature of the *Proto-gospel of James*. Before and after this scene are episodes about humans seeking answers from above. Many examples involve the temple, which, like the classroom of the *Infancy Gospel*, is a setting for acquiring knowledge. Priests and laypeople visit the sacred precincts looking for heavenly insight.[90] But unlike the *Infancy Gospel*, which depicts an uneasy relation between heavenly and human learning—think of the allegory of the letter alpha that Jesus uses to stump Zacchaeus and the book that Jesus takes up but does not read in the classroom—the two are intertwined in the *Proto-gospel of James*.

The most striking example of human and divine learning coming together involves Mary. The temple serves as a training school for Mary, for it is there that Mary learns how to spin thread.[91] Now spinning thread can be dismissed as a rather ordinary sort of learning. And it can be overshadowed by the dramatic instances of revealed heavenly information elsewhere in the family gospel. But it should not be ignored. Not only does Mary's spinning have heavenly origins, since she learns how to do so from angels in the temple, but it is also put to use in a divine task: the creation of the curtain in the temple. It is also, as we shall see, important as a reminder of an unfulfilled or interrupted promise. Anna, Mary's mother, believes that Mary's future consists of dwelling in the temple. When an angel tells Anna that she will conceive a child, Anna responds by making a vow: "I will offer it as a gift to the Lord my God, and it will minister (*leitourgōn*) to him all the days of its life." The Greek term *leitourgōn* expresses the liturgical aspect of Anna's vow: she sees Mary, like the high priest Zacharias, who describes himself as a "minister" (*leitourgos*), as playing a role in the formal worship of the temple.[92] Anna gives up the chance to watch her child grow up under her own care in order to uphold the terms of the vow. She believes that she is giving Mary the best of all possible worlds. But Anna, although she wants what's best for her child, is mistaken about the future: her daughter will be forced to leave the temple. Heaven has other plans for Mary.

Before we can understand Anna's attempt to secure a future for Mary, we must look at how she and her spouse, Joachim, try to make sense of the past, specifically, why for so many years they have been unable to have a child. This is one of three set pieces, all of which patrol the boundaries of human perception and knowledge. The first involves the conception of Mary, which brings an end to the childlessness of Anna and Joachim. The second involves priestly worry over the problem of Mary getting her period in the temple. A solution leads to Joseph being chosen to take Mary away from the temple to his own house. A surprising turnaround is the subject of the third example: having been forced to leave the temple, Mary is called back and asked to use her skill at spinning thread.

The *first moment* of learning involves the conception of Mary, which is modeled on the biblical account of the birth and childhood of Samuel (1 Sam 1:1–4:1).[93] Following the biblical template, the story of the *Proto-gospel of James* begins with a childless couple, Joachim and Anna. Joachim is a wealthy man of Israel.[94] He is also generous, giving twice what is expected. But his ostentatious gift seems to rankle some onlookers. When Joachim goes up to offer his sacrifice, another man, Reuben, blocks his way. "You are not allowed to offer your gifts first," Reuben says, "since you have not produced any offspring in Israel." When Joachim's plan stalls, he leaves behind Reuben in order to consult an authority about his situation.[95] He turns to the "[Book] of the Twelve Tribes of Israel," a reference to some unknown archive.[96] There Joachim learns that "everyone who was righteous" had offspring. The dispute between Reuben and Joachim is thus about the latter's integrity. Why doesn't Joachim have any children? Is it a punishment for some unseen wickedness? But Joachim is not defeated. He "remembers" Isaac, the son born to the righteous Abraham in his dotage. Joachim's story remains unfinished. He decides to retreat into the wilderness, abandoning his wife, Anna. There he prays for divine aid, staying put "until the Lord my God pays me a visit."[97] Joachim's self-imposed exile is an act of defiance against Reuben's interpretation.

So too Anna must contend with others over the meaning of this state of affairs. The question is posed again in the ensuing scene, when Anna gets into a fight with her slave, Judith.[98] The catalyst for the argument is obscure. As the "great day of the Lord" approaches, Anna is in mourning "twice over," both for not having children and over the absence of her husband. Judith, in what might at first be seen as kind gesture, urges Anna to change into more festive clothing and offers to give Anna a "headband" to wear.[99] But Anna finds the offer tantamount to an accusation of loose living. She scolds Judith, saying, "Go away from me. I did none of these things and yet the Lord God has severely humbled me. For all I know, some scoundrel has given this to you, and you have come to implicate me in your sin." Like her husband, Anna rejects the notion that her childlessness is retribution for her own sinful acts. "I did none of these things," she protests. Judith, undaunted, clings to the theory, insisting that God is responsible for the closing of Anna's womb.[100] To Judith, the situation is obvious: Anna is in denial.

The problem of how to interpret the childlessness of the couple moves into a new arena when an angel appears separately to Joachim and Anna to announce the news of Anna's pregnancy. Importantly, the angelic announcement does not refer to sin: "Anna, Anna, the Lord has heard your prayer. You will conceive a child and give birth, and your offspring will be spoken of throughout the entire world."[101] The angel likewise tells Joachim to return home, for "the Lord God has heard your prayer."[102] But sin is on Joachim's mind when he decides, the next day, to go up to the temple to offer a sacrifice.

There, he believes, looking into the "the leaf of the priest," likely some kind of mirror, he will learn whether or not he is blameworthy.[103] On his way up to the altar, he peers into the glass and sees a pure reflection. Sin is absent.

Does the glass confirm the suspicions of Reuben and Judith?[104] Or does it do just the opposite and show that sin was not a factor in the childlessness of Joachim and Anna? Reuben and Judith do not appear again in the story, so we do not know how they and other naysayers react to news of Anna's pregnancy. Joachim, for his part, believes that the mirror shows the grace of God, that whatever his sins, they have been forgiven. By contrast, the restoration of so-cial respectability is the main theme of Anna's take on events. For her part, she believes that the birth of her daughter has, once and for all, exposed as baseless the whispered gossip of misdeeds. "I will sing a holy song to the Lord God," Anna declares, echoing the victory cry of the biblical Hannah, "for he has visited me and removed from me the reproach of my enemies."[105] To this, she adds a personal rebuke of one of the couple's accusers: "Who will report to the sons of Reuben that Anna is now nursing a child?"[106]

In the temple, the knowledge of heaven is disclosed. Discerning its mean-ing is left up to human beings. If the opening set piece establishes the temple as a place of learning, so too it illustrates the economy of sacrifice. Joachim's offering on the altar—before he searches the priest's mirror—suggests a trans-action, not unlike that of Joseph's hiring of teachers for the child Jesus in the *Infancy Gospel*. So too consider that upon receiving the news that she will conceive, Anna proposes an exchange: "As the Lord God lives," she prays, "whether my child is a boy or a girl, I will offer it as a gift [*dōron*] to the Lord my God, and it will minister to him its entire life."[107] As Lily Vuong has re-cently emphasized, Anna has vowed to deliver Mary to the temple as a *dōron*, the Greek term routinely used for sacrifice in the Septuagint.[108]

The gift of Mary is also the sacrifice of parents.[109] She and Joachim give to God all they have to give: Mary, their only offspring. What Anna wants in return is for Mary to grow up and grow old in the temple. The vow turns the infant Mary into a resident alien in her own home from the moment of her birth. Not surprisingly, Anna and Joachim both put off meeting their obliga-tions for a few years. In the meantime, Anna pledges to create a sanctuary in her own home.[110] Once Mary turns three, Joachim and Anna act to fulfill the vow. They worry that little Mary will lose heart and become "homesick for her father and mother" on her way to the temple. To ease the transition, Joachim and Anna arrange to have the "undefiled virgins of the Hebrews" line the path with torches ablaze. And as Mary travels between the home and temple, she walks down the illuminated path.[111]

Anna's sacrifice is a cost. The fulfillment of the vow means breaking up the family. Is it worth it? For a long time, everything unfolds according to the terms of Anna's vow. Mary passes nine uneventful years in the temple, a period of time summarized in one brief sentence: "Mary was in the Temple of the Lord, cared for like a dove, receiving her food from the hand of an angel."[112] Mary's life in the temple is heaven on earth.

But then a crisis erupts, and this leads to the *second moment* of learning. Mary, now twelve, approaches puberty, and the priests start to worry about ceremonial purity and the possibility it will be defiled by Mary's first period. Because of the condensing of nine years into one sentence, the arrival of the crisis is sudden and abrupt. Has something gone wrong? Didn't the priests anticipate this maturing of Mary when they admitted her to the temple?[113] The priests gather to work on the problem. Zacharias, the high priest, enters the Holy of Holies, the most sacred space in the temple, seeking an answer.[114] An angel appears in the temple and prescribes a ritual for resolving the problem of Mary's growing up. Gather the widowers of Israel, the angel tells Zacharias, and look for a sign, for Mary "will become the wife of the one to whom the Lord God gives a sign."[115]

The ritual of selection requires a new sacrifice, one less tangible than Anna's gift of Mary. Zacharias, following the angel's prescription, calls the widowers of Israel to the temple. Singled out by the casting of lots, Joseph is instructed to take Mary "into his safekeeping."[116] Joseph immediately objects. Reminding the priest that he is an old man, he refuses because it risks his reputation: "I do not want to become a laughingstock to the sons of Israel."[117] The priest trumps this worry with a threat of divine repercussions. Remember, he tells Joseph, what the Lord did to Dathan, Abeira, and Korah for their disobedience: they were swallowed up by the earth (Num 16:1–33). "Now, Joseph, you should be afraid of this happening to you."[118] Joseph, sacrificing his dignity and reputation, relents and takes Mary to his own home. At the same moment, the terms of Anna's vow are suddenly vacated.

The crisis in the temple exposes the limits of human perception. Mary, under Joseph's care, is now cut off from the temple. And her role as a gift, a sacrifice, is interrupted, similar to the way that the student role of Jesus repeatedly comes to an abrupt halt in the *Infancy Gospel*. But Mary, in a *third moment* of learning, has brought with her to Joseph's house the skill of spinning thread—manual dexterity that she acquired at the temple—and it will lead to a restoration. Spinning, of course, resonates with one of the best-known images of "women's work" in the Greek world: the nightly unraveling of the cloth of Penelope, the long-suffering wife of the paradigmatic traveler, Odysseus. In the *Proto-gospel of James*, it is the spinner, Mary, who is forced to leave her home in the temple.[119] And it is spinning that brings her back to the temple, something that neither the priests nor the vow of Anna's anticipate.

In Chapter 11 of the *Proto-gospel of James*, the priest Zacharias sends out servants to collect the "undefiled virgins" of the "tribe of David" to spin thread for the curtain.[120] When he does so, he remembers that Mary is also from this tribe, and "the servants went out and led her back." While her tribal identity makes her eligible for the work, it is her acquired skill that receives more attention. We are not told where the other virgins learned to spin thread, but in Mary's case, there is only one possibility: she learned to spin in the temple, while being "cared for like a dove and fed by the hand of an angel." The sacred character of her own learning is confirmed in another priestly ritual designed to disclose heavenly knowledge. Lots are cast once again, and Mary is selected to spin the royal threads of scarlet and true purple.[121] She returns home to complete the task.[122]

The depiction of Mary as a spinner may be a riposte to the attacks of Celsus, whom we encountered earlier in the chapter.[123] In the *True Doctrine*, Celsus launches an ad hominem assault on the family background of Jesus. The marriage of Joseph and Mary was a sham, he contends, and the child of Mary is illegitimate. Mary herself was obviously a woman of loose morals, he maintains, because she sought employment in spinning cloth. The *Proto-gospel of James*, by contrast, puts Mary's quiet labor in the best possible light: hers is the work of the kingdom of God.

What begins as a series of moments that reveals information about Mary—about her parents, about her conception, about her life in the temple, and about how she met Joseph—culminates in the image of Mary using her own acquired learning. It is spinning thread that allows Mary to continue to "minister" after her expulsion from the temple, and it allows at least a partial restoration of Anna's vow. What Anna wanted for her child has both come to pass and not. When Mary finishes the work, she takes the threads back to the temple, where the priest receives her with a blessing: "Mary, the Lord God has made your name great; you will be blessed among all the generations of the earth." She receives the blessing happily, "full of joy."[124] What she has created will now be installed in the temple. Mary remains bound to the temple, even after she is forced to live outside its walls.

At the same time, the reunion would have served as an ironic reminder to an early Christian audience of the limits of human understanding. They would have known from the Synoptic gospels that the curtain of the temple, sewn from threads that Mary joyfully spun, would be torn in two later when Mary's grown-up son, Jesus, hung dying on the cross.[125] And there is yet another dark irony, for by the time the *Proto-gospel of James* was composed, the temple in Jerusalem was no longer standing.[126]

*   *   *

In the family gospels, the promise of the future matters, or this at least is what drives the parents. When Joseph sends Jesus to the schoolhouse and when Anna sends Mary to the temple, the parents are trying to set their children on a path to an adulthood of dignity. That Joseph and Anna are willing to sacrifice so much to realize these dreams bespeaks their good character and loving devotion. But it also implies a reckoning of costs and benefits, one that may reflect wider debates under the Roman Empire about the worth of Greek education and culture. If Lucian offers a teenager's perspective of the choices before him and the risks entailed, then the family gospels give us an idea of what parents go through under similar pressures. Indeed, just as *The Dream* can bring to the surface dynamics in the storytelling of the family gospels, the family gospels can do the same for Lucian's essay. Although Lucian recalls his father sending him to study masonry under an abusive uncle, we can wonder if he was motivated to do so by the same hope for a respectable future that, in the stories of the family gospels, fills the hearts of Joseph and Anna.

Jesus learns his letters, while Mary spins thread for the temple curtain. What remains elusive is the precise meaning of these images. For example, how should we interpret interruptions in the learning process? Jesus tangles with a teacher and quickly leaves the classroom before the lesson is completed. Mary is dedicated to a lifetime of service in the temple but then, amid a crisis of ritual purity, she is sent away. What is the significance of these breakdowns? And what is the point of having Jesus and Mary return to schoolhouse and temple to leave once again? Between home and schoolhouse, on one hand, and between home and temple, on the other, Jesus and Mary are displaced, unsettled. And if the student Jesus is "in-between," then so too is Joseph. He is in the middle of something that he does not understand. As we shall see in the chapters that remain, Jesus, Mary, and Joseph often find themselves poised between possible futures in the family gospels.

Conflict and the limits of human understanding remain important themes of the chapters that follow. In them we dig more deeply into the fraught, interpersonal relationships of Joseph, Mary, and Jesus, taking up first the *Proto-gospel of James* and next the *Infancy Gospel of Thomas*. Here we will see more examples of a point shared by both accounts: that the life of a family touched by God must nevertheless confront unknowns. Will the members of this small, holy family be able to overcome doubt and recriminations, or will the household instead come apart at the seams?

Chapter 4

Carnal Ignorance

How did Mary meet Joseph?

The gospels of the New Testament do not say. Their engagement is an accomplished deed in the Gospel of Matthew: "When his mother Mary had been engaged to Joseph, but before they lived together, she was found to be with child by the Holy Spirit" (Matt 1:18). The Gospel of Luke includes a similar passage: "In the sixth month the angel Gabriel was sent by God to a town in Galilee called Nazareth to a virgin engaged to a man whose name was Joseph, of the house of David" (Luke 1:26–27). Both Matthew and Luke include a genealogy of Jesus: Matthew's runs in descent from Abraham (Matt 1:1–17) and Luke's in ascent from Joseph back to Adam, "son of God" (Luke 3:23–38). Beyond this, neither the earliest gospels nor any other writing of the New Testament describe the lives that Mary and Joseph led prior to their engagement. We do not know if theirs is a first marriage, second marriage, or something else. We do not learn anything about the households they come from. Who are their parents? Do they have siblings? We are not even told how old they are.

The *Proto-gospel of James* tackles many of the questions that the earliest gospels leave unanswered. It reports on Joachim and Anna, the pious parents of Mary. We find out that Anna's conception of Mary involved divine intervention. And we learn more here than elsewhere about Joseph, an elderly widower.[1] When the account begins, Joseph is much older than Mary. He has already been married (at least once) and has fathered children. Most important, the family gospel tackles the question that all couples, it seems, are required to answer at some point: how did the two of you meet?

"When Mary met Joseph" is not a romantic scene in the *Proto-gospel of James*. Joseph's unhappiness is the first sign of trouble. According to the *Proto-gospel of James*, Joseph is selected by lot in the temple to take in Mary, a twelve-year-old girl. He is unhappy about it and only submits to the arrangement when the high priest threatens Joseph with a punishment of biblical proportions. Are these two really meant for one another? What motivated the author of the *Proto-gospel of James* to "fill in the gaps" of earlier accounts, to create a backstory in this way? Studies of this question usually focus on what the account says about Mary and how it illustrates her holiness. What if, however, the heart of the book lies elsewhere—not in the characterization of Mary but in the story of the entwining of her life with Joseph's?

"Entwining" may be too strong a word for what happens between Mary and Joseph in the *Proto-gospel of James*. A recent study describes the bond between Mary and Joseph as "extremely ambiguous."[2] I agree and will argue that this ambiguity relates to the problem of knowledge. Sex is a particular kind of knowing that comes under scrutiny in the *Proto-gospel of James*. Mary and Joseph do not have sex and so they share in "carnal ignorance." As the account unfolds, moreover, the meaning of carnal ignorance expands to encompass more than sex. This chapter investigates this theme in three stages. First, I discuss the scope of carnal ignorance in the *Proto-gospel of James*. This will involve framing the family gospel as a tale of bedtrick. Bedtricks are stories about sex that feature masquerade and mistaken identity, such as the dodgy marriage of Jacob and Leah in the book of Genesis (29:15–30).[3] Second, the chapter takes up three key events in the *Proto-gospel of James*, all of which take Joseph by surprise and highlight how much he does not understand. Third, we turn to the juxtaposition of Mary and Joseph's carnal ignorance with the sometimes violent and always nosy forms of public investigation into private matters.

The theme of this chapter is ignorance. Its argument is about the significance of choices in the narrative. In the face of uncertainty, Joseph and Mary must make decisions, choices that will determine the future of their relationship. This chapter on the *Proto-gospel of James*, like the next one on the *Infancy Gospel of Thomas*, investigates these choices. Will the pressure of public scrutiny break apart the fragile, strange relationship of Mary and Joseph? Or will they together press on, despite what they do not know? Will they, in other words, choose to be a family? By framing *family* as a matter of choice in the face of uncertainty, the family gospels propose a distinct model of the household, different from the patriarchal and ascetic models that other ancient Christian authors were championing at the time. To the welter of competing definitions of the household, the family gospels offer yet another model: in it, familial life is beset by imperfect knowledge of self and other. In the family gospels, the household is not a setting for acquiring knowledge but a place of confusion and misunderstanding. Acts of loyalty and love require boldness and courage under such conditions.

The *Proto-gospel of James* follows Mary and Joseph as they try to find a path together through a thicket of uncertainties. The drama of not knowing finally builds to a crescendo in a single decision of Joseph. When he chooses to face death in the water ordeal rather than betray the young, pregnant Mary, we catch a glimpse of the deep well of courage inside the elderly man as well as his true affection for the frightened girl. The *Proto-gospel of James* may not be a romance. Yet, against all expectations, it is a love story.

Bedtricks and Other Kinds of Ignorance

One of the things readers will notice in the *Proto-gospel of James* is the expanded role given to Joseph when compared to earlier gospels. In the Gospel of Matthew, Mary is found to be pregnant *before* she and Joseph live together (Matt 1:18).[4] Joseph is above suspicion in the matter since he has had no opportunity to sleep with Mary. In the *Proto-gospel of James*, by contrast, Mary conceives *after* she has moved into Joseph's house. It provides a scandalous opportunity for sexual activity where the Gospel of Matthew allowed none. Now readers of the *Proto-gospel of James* know that Joseph is not the father, but the family gospel leaves him vulnerable in a way that the Synoptic gospels do not. It becomes the basis for ensuing accusations against and investigations into the couple.

Within the narrative world of the *Proto-gospel of James*, Joseph's struggle to come to terms with events is just as important as Mary's. Joseph may play a minor, supporting role in the earlier gospels; in the family gospel, he is a co-star, and without him, the tension of the storytelling dissipates. Using the character of Joseph as the prism through which to see what is important in the family gospel can be dismissed as special pleading. It may also be criticized for neglecting the focus on Mary's body, which raises a set of clearly important issues around purity and boundaries in the *Proto-gospel of James*. Some things are lost when Joseph is brought to the fore. What is gained is a deeper appreciation of how at least some early Christians thought about the uncertainty of human relationships and the mystery of God. What the figure of Joseph offers, moreover, is a degree of character development. This claim runs contrary to the vast majority of treatments of the *Proto-gospel of James*: most see the characters, Mary in particular, as "one-dimensional."[5] But this is underreading. Joseph develops, even matures. Rather than living in dread of future humiliation, he learns to accept a strange, new present.

I concede that Joseph is not the most sympathetic character. He whines and complains. While Mary, an adolescent, may be forgiven for not understanding her purpose and significance, Joseph, a full-grown adult, seems singularly unperceptive. Despite heavenly reassurances and signs of divine providence, he turns on Mary at the first moment of crisis. Yet, the *Proto-gospel of James* does not simply hold up Joseph to ridicule. His perplexity advances a theological point about the difference between divine omniscience and the ignorance of human beings. So too it gives Joseph a chance at redemption, and he seizes the opportunity. In so doing, Joseph binds his own life to Mary's.

Joseph's weaknesses and strengths are illuminated through his time with Mary. To peer into the strange relationship of Mary and Joseph, to watch as they respond to the pressure of God having taken an interest in them—such are the driving concerns of the *Proto-gospel of James*. Heir to both the Synoptic nativity accounts and the Jewish scriptures, the family gospel casts sexual intercourse as a specific form of knowing and then uses it as a platform for examining the limits of human understanding. In the Bible, the term for "knowing" is a quasi-euphemism for sexual intercourse.[6] Adam "knew" Eve, for example, and conceived a son, Cain, after being expelled from the garden of Eden (Gen 4:1). In the same way, the absence of *eros* is described as not knowing in both of the Synoptic accounts. Matthew and Luke both report that Mary and Joseph "did not know" one another (Matt 1:25; Luke 1:34).[7]

Biblical narrative typically gives the active role to men: men are knowers, women are known. At the same time, as literary critics have pointed out, biblical examples can sometimes pivot on the fraught question of who knows whom. Women may know far more about the sexual encounter than men, as in the example of Jacob and Leah. Promised Leah's younger sister, Rachel, in exchange for seven years of work, Jacob finally completes his service and beds his new wife. The next day, Jacob is shocked to discover that he has been mistaken: "In the morning, it was Leah!" (Gen 29:25). Jacob believes he had sex with one person only to learn upon waking that he was with someone else. Why could he not tell that he held Leah in his arms? Why did he not know the difference? As Wendy Doniger observes, "The bedtrick is an exercise in epistemology."[8] And such stories inevitably connect the dots between other and self: "But the more pertinent question, coded in the story and relevant not just to incestuous bedtricks but to all bedtricks, is perhaps 'How is it that you do not know who is in bed with you?' Or 'How is it that you do not know that you do not know who is in bed with you?' Or better, 'Who are you who do not know that you do not know who is in bed with you?' Or, finally, 'How is it that you do not know who you are?'" What begins as a question of ignorance, "How is it that you do not know who is in bed with you?" evolves into a question of identity, "How is it that you do not know who you are?"[9] Tales of bedtrick, biblical and otherwise, raise basic questions about what kinds of knowledge and ignorance pass between self and other.

Like other stories of divine-human coupling, the Synoptic accounts of Mary's pregnancy have been taken as a species of bedtrick, echoing not only the world of biblical narrative but also the love stories of Greek and Roman mythology.[10] But the laconic storytelling of the Synoptic nativity stories leaves so much unsaid that such a connection will seem tenuous, even to sympathetic minds. Is it fair to suggest that the Joseph of Matthew feels tricked by Mary? Is it fair to call what happens to the pair in the Synoptic gospels a sexual masquerade?

The *Proto-gospel of James*, by contrast, spells out what may be found only between the lines of the Synoptic source material. It will not come as a shock to anyone that an early Christian book denies Joseph and Mary a robust sex life. But the *Proto-gospel of James* does something more. It dwells on and intensifies the ignorance of Mary and Joseph in a way that recalls biblical accounts of bedtrick. Joseph does not know how it happened, nor does Mary. In this way, the *Proto-gospel of James* picks up on and expands a claim that is stated outright in only two places in the Synoptic accounts: Mary and Joseph do not make love and thus do not "know" one another. Unlike Matthew and Luke, which do not spend any time exploring the epistemological depths of this pun, the *Proto-gospel of James* amplifies the usage of the Greek verb for "knowing" (*ginōskō*). The carnal ignorance of Joseph and Mary is not just about sex. It is doubled, affecting body and mind.

Mary and Joseph do not know one another sexually. Nor do they know one another in any other sense. What does the stacked ignorance of the *Proto-gospel of James* mean to its depiction of Mary and Joseph? We have already seen that questions about the relationship of Mary and Joseph lead to dramatic truth tests: think of the test of the "bitter waters" and Salome's failed digital inspection. Now we turn to the heart of the matter—the not knowing that threatens to break apart the couple-hood of Mary and Joseph before it begins.

Three Surprises

Does the *Proto-gospel of James* merely "fill in the gaps" of earlier Synoptic accounts? If so, then the process could be compared to adding pieces to an already furnished room. But the analogy does not capture the more radical approach of the *Proto-gospel of James*. While the family gospel inhabits the same room as the nativity stories, it rearranges the furniture, even replacing some pieces. It constructs, for instance, a different timeline of events for when Mary becomes pregnant. It combines details from Matthew and Luke in surprising ways. Mary places Jesus in a manger, a detail from Luke (2:7), in order to hide the infant from Herod's bloodthirsty soldiers, a detail from Matthew (2:16–18). And it omits altogether the holy family's "Flight to Egypt" (Matt 2:13–15), which preserves the infant Jesus from Herod's "Massacre of the Innocents." Above all, the *Proto-gospel of James* adds confusion to the early relationship of Mary and Joseph. Angels visit the pair in the Synoptic accounts, delivering messages. In turn, Mary and Joseph are enlightened about their circumstances. Not so in the *Proto-gospel of James*, which states that Mary "forgets" the heavenly secrets that she has been let in on, and shows that Joseph refuses to accept divinely ordained outcomes.

Because it is a consistent theme of the *Proto-gospel of James*, the confusion of Joseph warrants close attention. Following Joseph attunes us to the way that the family gospel creates sympathy around his ignorance—*sympathy*, because what Joseph does not see coming, what takes him by surprise, are events that readers likewise may not anticipate.[11] Three events come as a surprise to Joseph: being selected to take care of Mary, her pregnancy, and finally the public discovery of Mary's compromised state.[12] There is a pattern in these examples. First, a crisis emerges; next, a resolution to the crisis seems to fall into place; finally, the resolution is upended, leading to another iteration of the crisis. Time and again in these examples, Joseph finds himself in the awkward position of resisting the authority of priests and, perhaps, the designs of heaven.

First Surprise: Joseph Wins the Lottery

Before Joseph comes on the scene, the *Proto-gospel of James* describes a crisis in the temple, one that we discussed briefly in Chapter 3. Here I present it in more detail. At the age of three, Mary had been welcomed into the temple for life. Now, with the coming of her twelfth birthday, her residency is in jeopardy as the onset of menstruation threatens the purity of the temple.[13] A council is assembled; the single item on the agenda is Mary: "See, Mary has become twelve years old in the Lord's Temple. What then shall we do with her, to keep her from defiling the sanctuary of the Lord?"[14] Prayer is the next step: the council advises the chief priest, Zacharias, to seek an answer from heaven. Zacharias withdraws into the most sacred area of the temple, the Holy of Holies, and there seeks out divine assistance. Prayers do not go unanswered for long in the *Proto-gospel of James*, and Zacharias soon receives instructions from the angel of the Lord: "Zacharias, Zacharias, go out and gather the widowers of the people, and have each of them bring a rod; she will become the wife of the one to whom the Lord God gives a sign."[15] The solution to the problem of Mary is to marry her off, thus removing her from the temple.

Widowers are summoned, and Joseph, a carpenter, is among them. When he hears the trumpet, he "flings aside" his ax and sprints to the temple.[16] The chief priest collects staffs from the widowers for the lottery and goes inside to pray. Afterward, the priest returns the staffs, and following the angel's advice, begins to look for a sign. A dove flies out of Joseph's staff and alights on his head.[17] Presumably, this is the sign. The priest says, "You [Joseph] have been chosen to take the Lord's virgin into your safekeeping."[18] Joseph objects and begins to list the reasons why it is a bad idea: "I already have sons and am an old man." Besides, she's still "a young girl." Plus, he complains, "I'll be the laughing-stock of Israel."[19] How different is the postlottery hesitation from his former display of ax-flinging obedience! Faced with refusal, the priest threatens Joseph with the grim tale of the biblical Dathan.[20] One wonders if the priest overplays his hand. Once the bird lands on his head, Joseph's leverage shrinks to nothing. He has been selected by a divine sign. That he wants to "fight the future" anyway says something perhaps about Joseph's stubbornness or his capacity for denial or both.

Problem and solution: a pattern of crisis and (apparent) resolution emerge in this first example of surprise. Yet, important questions remain open. What is the nature of the relationship between Joseph and Mary? For some, the scene suggests a lawful marriage, and for others, the point of the episode is the opposite—that a lawful marriage does not take place.[21] Within this murkiness, the only beacon of certainty is the old age of Joseph. The Synoptic gospels do not mention the age of Joseph. In this sense, the *Proto-gospel of James* "fills a gap," but to what end? Some think it is intended "to suggest the improbability of sexual contact between the two of them."[22] But this theory is flawed, for later in the *Proto-gospel of James*, Joseph is accused of having sex with Mary, of having "defiled" her and "stolen her wedding rights."[23] Joseph's age does not shield him from the suspicion of sexual activity.

In the wake of the lottery, Joseph seems embarrassed by the appearance of impropriety. The priestly resolution to the crisis is temporary. Joseph wants nothing to do with Mary. Joseph takes Mary back to his house and immediately abandons her, saying, "Mary, I have received you from the Temple of the Lord. Now I am leaving you in my house, for I am going out to construct some buildings; later I will come back to you."[24] He adds in conclusion, "The Lord watch over you."[25] Anyone can see that the match is terrible. Joseph is an old man; Mary is an adolescent. And Joseph believes that the pairing puts his reputation at risk. In these details, the family gospels add layers of problems to the Synoptic portrayals of the relationship of Mary and Joseph. In the earlier sources, readers are not given any reason to think that the pair is ill-matched. Factors such as age and social background are left out. In the *Proto-gospel of James*, Joseph is ashamed by the pairing. He already has sons, moreover, and thus the passing on of wealth and social values has been settled. Joseph treats with disdain his relationship with Mary because there is little incentive to do otherwise.

Erotic literature of the era, to which the *Proto-gospel of James* is sometimes compared, is preoccupied with the question of match-making. What makes a good couple? Is it a given—a question of background, wealth, status? Is it something achieved through tests of fidelity? How important is one's surroundings? Consider the second-century romance of Achilles Tatius, *Leucippe and Clitophon*, which tells the story of two young, well-heeled lovers separated by shipwreck, pirates, and other disasters. Their fidelity to one another is threatened throughout the story. Surviving these tests is important, but what gives the romance a happy ending is their wedding in Byzantium, a flourishing Greek city. The romance is about going home, about returning to a haven of stability in a dangerous and uncertain world. Joseph, by contrast, does not want to go home. He leaves at the first opportunity rather than stay and risk calling attention to his association with a twelve-year-old girl. With Mary now dwelling there, it is no longer a safe harbor but doubtful and risky.

Second Surprise: Mary Is in Trouble

From the start, the relationship of Joseph and Mary, whatever it is, seems poised on the brink of dissolution. Joseph refuses to stay under the same roof as Mary, which is why he is not present when Mary receives life-changing news of her own. An angel appears to her at a well and declares, "You will conceive a child from his Word."[26] Mary asks, "Am I to conceive . . . and give birth like every other woman?" The angel replies, "The power of God will overshadow you. Therefore the holy one born from you will be called the Son of the Highest."[27] This language from the Gospel of Luke would likely have been familiar to an early Christian audience. The Synoptic story of the annunciation almost certainly was. What is different in the *Proto-gospel of James* is its focus on how Joseph reacts to the news.

Mary mostly takes things in stride, so much so that she travels to see her relative, Elizabeth. And then confusion sets in. When Elizabeth spots Mary, she exclaims, "How is it that the mother of my Lord should come to me?"[28] The greeting puzzles Mary because, as the *Proto-gospel of James* reports, "Mary forgot the mysteries that the archangel Gabriel had spoken to her."[29] Like Luke, the *Proto-gospel of James* describes the annunciation and the conception of Mary as an exchange of knowledge. Mary will be "overshadowed" or known by the power of God. At the same time, Mary receives knowledge. She learns from Gabriel that she has found favor with God. She learns that her son will be holy, a son of the highest, and that he will save his people from their sins. But the knowledge that Mary acquires does not remain with her. For as soon as she visits Elizabeth, she forgets Gabriel's message. Mary's amnesia is hard for some commentators to accept. One argues, "Mary only 'forgets' to communicate her mystery."[30] Another insists that "Mary does indeed comprehend her situation."[31] But later episodes indicate the opposite. Mary is unable to explain the circumstances of her pregnancy because she no longer can recall them. Alarmed by her expanding midsection, Mary scurries home to hide "in fear."[32] And it is there, in Joseph's house, that the wheel of drama begins to turn, and a new crisis erupts.

The crisis is evident: Mary is pregnant, and she does not know how it happened. Six months later, Joseph finally returns home from work: "As he came into the house he saw that she was pregnant."[33] Joseph's reaction does not redound to his credit. He flings himself upon the ground—as he did with the ax—and begins to cry.[34] He lashes out at everyone and no one: "Who has done this wicked deed in my home?" He wallows in self-pity: "Has not the entire history of Adam been summed up in me? For just as Adam was singing praise to God, when the serpent came and found Eve alone and led her astray, so too has this now happened to me."[35] Joseph's histrionics seem to drive Mary from the room. When Joseph rises from the floor, he must call her back.[36] Then he berates Mary for her condition: "Why have you done this? Why have you humiliated your soul—you who were brought up in the Holy of Holies and received your food from the hand of an angel?"[37]

Before moving to the apparent resolution, we should linger for a moment over Joseph's allusion to Adam and Eve. Ancient interest in the account of the Garden of Eden (Gen 3) by Christians and Jews serves as context to Joseph's harangue in the *Proto-gospel of James*.[38] In the second and third centuries, debates about the meaning of the story were widespread among Christians. As Elaine Pagels observes, Clement of Alexandria "rejects, above all, the claim that Adam and Eve's sin was to engage in sexual intercourse—a view common among such Christian teachers as Tatian the Syrian, who thought that the fruit of the tree of knowledge conveyed *carnal* knowledge."[39] Earlier writings describe the union of Adam and Eve as a "great mystery" (Eph 5:31–32).[40] Jewish interpreters took a different view, observes Daniel Boyarin: "According to the Rabbis, there was no Fall into sexuality in the Garden of Eden. On the rabbinic readings, Adam had had intercourse with Eve from the beginning." In Genesis Rabba 18:6, the snake becomes "inflamed with lust for Eve because he saw Adam and Eve having intercourse with each other."[41] The background for understanding Joseph's allusion is thus deep and wide.[42] The biblical story of Adam and Eve evokes a set of issues around sex, knowledge, and self-understanding. And Joseph's interpretation of the story as a bedtrick—that Adam was an innocent victim, unwittingly caught up in Eve's deception—poses sharply the problem of not knowing. While he was away, Joseph suggests, Mary got in bed with another man. What follows this accusation is more doubt and confusion.

In tears herself, Mary replies to Joseph, "I am pure and have not known any man."[43] The phrase is lifted directly from Luke, where Mary asks Gabriel how she will become pregnant: "How will this happen, since I have not known any man?" (Luke 1:34).[44] In the *Proto-gospel of James*, Mary's statement is transformed. She does not utter it in wonder before the angel but in desperation in the face of her husband's attacks. Joseph refuses to yield, repeating the question, "How then?" Mary admits the full scope of her ignorance: "As the Lord my God lives, I do not know how it got inside me."[45] She "weeps bitterly" as she puts up the defense, leaving both of them despairing and afraid.

Mary's denials gesture to the different kinds of doubt and ignorance that the couple shares. One, Mary and Joseph do not know each other sexually. And, two, they do not know each other in any other sense. In six months of acquaintance, this is only the second time that Mary and Joseph have been together in the same place. And there is a third level of ambiguity: Mary does not know *herself*, which is to say, she does not know how she has conceived a child. Mary has forgotten her encounter with the angel, which means that Joseph's interrogation can only leave him exasperated and, like Mary, "afraid."

When Joseph accuses her of adultery, Mary fights back, protesting her
innocence. "I have not known any man," she tells Joseph. This identical statement, as was noted, appears in the Greek text of the Gospel of Luke (1:34),
where it is Mary's response to the angel Gabriel's announcement of her impending pregnancy. In Luke, Mary's claim refers to a state of virginity.[46] In the
Proto-gospel of James, "I have not known any man" refers to far more. In the
family gospel, Mary addresses Joseph rather than the angel Gabriel. Her denial in the face of Joseph's accusations, I propose, expresses a sense of alien-
ation. Joseph does not know her, and she does not know him. That Mary and
Joseph do not have carnal knowledge of one another serves as a platform for
presenting a deeper problem. It goes beyond the mechanics of reproduction
and summons up a picture of the chasm between self and other.

Mary does not know any man, including and especially the one standing
in front of her. Nor does Joseph know her. I have suggested that Mary's claim
means something different in the *Proto-gospel of James* than it does in the Gospel of Luke. As already noted, the addresses are different: in Luke, it is the
angel Gabriel; in the *Proto-gospel of James*, it is Joseph. Her protest of innocence is at the same time a confession of ignorance. She may be puzzled by the
fact of the pregnancy, unaware of the mechanism by which she has conceived.
But Mary is also ignorant in a broader sense. She does not know men. (Her
knowledge of other women is also limited to a specific class: the temple virgins.) She has been raised by angels in the temple, and whatever interactions
she has had with the opposite sex have been brief. Even when she is paired off
with Joseph and given the opportunity to get to know him, the chance quickly
dissipates as he promptly abandons her. It is not only that Mary can claim
ignorance in the "biblical sense"; so too she can claim it in every other sense.
She really does not know any man.

The *Proto-gospel of James* next gives Joseph a turn as Hamlet. In a solilo-
quy, Joseph weighs his options: "If I hide her sin, I will be found fighting the
Law of the Lord; if I reveal her condition to the sons of Israel, I am afraid that
the child in her is angelic [or holy], and I may be handing innocent blood
over to a death sentence. What then should I do with her? I will secretly divorce her."[47] Joseph's churning inner life becomes a multiverse of causes and
effects: hide her sin or turn her in. Joseph opts for a third way: a secret divorce. Here the *Proto-gospel of James* follows the cue of Matthew: "Her hus-

band Joseph, being a righteous man and unwilling to expose her to public disgrace, planned to dismiss her quietly" (Matt 1:19). Some have argued that the Synoptic passage implies the prospect of "honor killing"; if so, the threat is latent in Matthew.[48] In the *Proto-gospel of James*, it is manifest: Joseph worries about handing Mary over to a death sentence.

Having reached a decision, Joseph decides to sleep on it. In his dreams, a solution takes shape. An angel appears, bringing a message of comfort: "Do not be afraid of this child. For that which is in her comes from the Holy Spirit."[49] At first, the visitation seems to settle the issue. The couple is rescued from danger. When Joseph awakes, he praises God and finally does what he was originally charged with doing by Zacharias: Joseph "watches over" Mary.[50] But tranquility lasts only a few hours. Then there's a knock at the door, and Joseph, this time without the benefit of divine counsel, is faced once again with a difficult decision.

Third Surprise: The Nosy Neighbor

"But Annas the scribe came to see him, and said, 'Joseph, why have you not appeared before our council?' Joseph replied, 'I was tired from my journey and rested on my first day back.'"[51] Annas turns and sees that Mary is pregnant.[52] His timing is impeccable. Of all the surprises in the *Proto-gospel of James*, the unannounced visit of Annas wins the prize for verisimilitude. He is the nosy neighbor who shows up at exactly the wrong instant. It upends the angelic resolution to the problem and throws Joseph back into crisis management mode. He withholds crucial information from Annas, blaming his absence on fatigue.[53] This may not be a lie, but is it the whole truth? Regardless, Annas does not fall for the misdirection. He takes one look at Mary's belly and goes to report to the high priest, accusing Joseph of "defiling" Mary and stealing her "wedding rights."[54] This accusation is of course strange, given the earlier lottery that assigns Joseph to Mary.

The investigation unfolds like a police procedural, as the high priest interviews one suspect and then the other. He asks Mary, "Why have you humiliated your soul . . . You who were brought up in the Holy of Holies and received your food from the hand of an angel?"[55] The question is nearly identical to Joseph's earlier one. Mary, sobbing, reasserts her earlier oath and denial: "As the

Lord my God lives . . . I am pure before him and have not known any man."[56]
The priest next turns to Joseph, asking, "Why have you done this?" Now Joseph swears a denial: "As the Lord my God lives . . . I am pure toward her."[57]
Dissatisfied, the priest invokes the Decalogue: "Do not bear false witness, but
speak the truth." "And Joseph," the gospel reports, "kept his silence."[58] A life-
and-death purity ordeal looms ahead for the couple.

Studies of the *Proto-gospel of James* often remark on patterns of repetition,
pointing out parallels of biblical childlessness and the story of Mary's parents.
Some speak of a "law of duplication" (*Zweiheitsgesetz*) and contend that repetition is designed to connect the extracanonical gospel to the Septuagint.[59]
Recent studies tend to refer more often to intertextuality and midrash, mounting a similar case while making room for flexibility and irony. I want to suggest another purpose: narrative suspense. The priestly interview recapitulates
the scene of Joseph's harsh questioning of Mary and hence recalls not only
that painful interaction but also the anxious reflection that follows. The questions remain the same, but Joseph's role is transformed. Earlier he was in
charge; now he must submit to hieratic scrutiny. Will he break under pressure? The multiverse, momentarily banished from view by angelic reassurance,
suddenly rematerializes, and we are reminded of the choices that Joseph earlier entertained. One of them—"hide her sin"— is no longer on the table. The
priest gives Joseph the chance to change his story—that is, to "turn her in."
Joseph refuses this dark possibility, even though he is overwhelmed by events
and plagued by uncertainty. He opts instead for a third way by keeping his
mouth shut and facing the ordeal with Mary.[60]

Let us dwell for a moment longer on the narrative dynamics of the scene.
The priest's question bridges back to Joseph's sotto voce deliberations; so too it
builds suspense. Bear in mind that the author of the *Proto-gospel of James* is
not rigidly bound to the Synoptic source material. We could easily imagine
another scenario: Joseph could have turned in Mary and watched the "drink
test" from the sidelines. His mind would change once he saw Mary divinely
vindicated. At every moment of decision, storytellers have an array of plot-
lines to follow. There is an openness to the scene that carefully raises the possibility of multiple futures; at the same time, there is an assurance in the
notion that no matter what happens, no matter what Joseph decides to do,
Mary will one way or the other give birth to the baby Jesus. Ancient Chris-

tians, reading for divine mystery, learned in the family gospel about the designs of God—about how the omniscience of heaven anticipates and outmaneuvers the limited perception and power of human beings. Readers may not know what Joseph will choose to do, but they do know that, no matter what, the will of God will be accomplished in the fullness of time.

In so doing, the *Proto-gospel of James* is biblesque, harkening back to the Jewish scriptures. It throws readers into the "ordeal of interpretation," as Meir Sternberg calls it, an ordeal that nevertheless takes hold under relatively safe conditions.[61] Sternberg's poetics lays out the competing forces of suspense and antisuspense in biblical narrative. On one hand, "suspense would dovetail with the biblical line of making our hypothesis-construction run parallel to the characters.'"[62] Uncertainty about the future, suspense, is perhaps the most effective tool in the writer's kit for establishing "continuity between the human condition inside and outside the world of the text."[63] Joseph does not know what to do, and we do not know what Joseph will do. Suspense thus "universalizes the ordeal of interpretation."[64] Against this, however, is the author's "overriding need to publish his [God's] supremacy," and "the generation of suspense throughout the tale would militate against our sense of the divine control of history."[65] Hence, "the attractions of demonstrating the human state of ignorance are at odds with the need to demonstrate superhuman knowledgeability."[66] In lesser hands, the desire to do both—to build suspense and to show order, to entertain and to prove—would result in storytelling that was neither fish nor fowl and thus disappointing. In the case of biblical narrative, and in examples of biblesque, like the *Proto-gospel of James*, the tension between these two modes offers an engaging give-and-take. We know some things and not others, and thus our viewpoint mirrors that of the intratextual characters.

The ensuing purity ordeal suddenly takes on new meaning. For the first time, Mary and Joseph face the same future. The priest orders both Mary and Joseph to drink the "water of refutation." They do so—Joseph first, then Mary—and, to the astonishment of all, they both survive. What holds true for Joseph holds true for Mary. The priest lets them go: "If the Lord God has not revealed your sin, neither do I."[67]

A bond between Mary and Joseph is cemented, not by surviving the water ordeal but in the moments before it is carried out, when Joseph discovers his true feelings for Mary. Recall that when Joseph first finds out about Mary's pregnancy, tears of anger and regret separate him from Mary, and when Mary cries, Joseph's rage is the cause. But later, during the priestly interrogation leading up to the ordeal, Joseph cries again. Here his sorrow reflects something else—a selfless and protective worry over Mary. The priest commands Joseph to "hand over the virgin." Sensing the grave peril of the "death sentence" awaiting Mary, he begins "to weep bitterly."[68] Where Joseph had earlier shed angry tears over finding Mary pregnant, now he weeps at the thought of losing her. Although he may not know why or how, Joseph has fallen in love.

Beyond the Reach of a Nosy Empire

The *Proto-gospel of James* depicts Joseph as a man repeatedly taken by surprise. To what end? On one level, the answer is plain: surprise is a technique for involving the reading audience. It creates sympathy with and for characters. Like Joseph, we cannot always see what is coming. I have argued that a pivotal moment of the family gospel occurs when Joseph is most in the dark. What at first appears to be the resolution of the crisis—the angelic reassurance Joseph receives about the child Mary carries—turns out to be only a stopgap when a neighbor knocks on the door. Faced with the threats of the high priest, Joseph decides to stick with Mary, although he does not know whether he is making the right choice. Given the opportunity to turn in Mary, Joseph silently refuses. Thus, the larger purpose is achieved: Mary and Joseph may not know what the future holds, but they will face it together because of choices they have made.

As the *Proto-gospel of James* continues to unfold, the not knowing of Joseph and Mary comes into even sharper relief against the backdrop of larger forces looking for the holy family. The Roman emperor Augustus and the client-king Herod the Great, figures kept separate in the Synoptic birth narratives, are brought together in the family gospel. As we have already seen, the *Proto-gospel of James* is fond of doubles. So too are the Synoptic gospels. There are, to begin with, two accounts of the events surrounding the birth of Jesus and two distinct genealogies. In Luke, the most obvious set of doubles is the parallel of Jesus and John the Baptist.[69] The in-tandem conceptions and births of the two boys organize and frame the narrative.

The *Proto-gospel of James* adds new sets of doubles. The story of the parents of Mary, Anna and Joachim, doubles the Lukan story of Elizabeth and Zechariah. Anna and Joachim likewise serve as doubles of Mary and Joseph. To these, the *Proto-gospel of James* presents a doubling of ruling authorities. What is kept separate in the Synoptic accounts is joined together in the family gospel: the seemingly benign Augustan census from Luke is followed immediately by Herod's brutal investigation, the gruesome "Massacre of the Innocents," from Matthew. While the couple at the heart of the story shares in carnal ignorance, they are pursued in the final chapters by powers that seek to know it all.

The pursuit begins after the water ordeal, when Joseph and Mary travel to Bethlehem to register for the imperial census. The counterpoint to the couple's surrender to uncertainty is the depiction of the Roman appetite for meticulous recordkeeping and classification.[70] Rome's was an empire of knowledge, and the Gospel of Luke depicts it as bent on collecting information from all corners.[71] Unlike Luke's worldwide event, the *Proto-gospel of James* restricts the enrollment to "everyone from Bethlehem of Judea." At the same time, the *Proto-gospel of James* goes a step further than Luke, for it summons up the ambiguity of Mary and Joseph's relationship in the family gospel. Joseph wonders, "How should I enroll her? As my wife? I would be too ashamed. As my daughter? The sons of Israel know that she is not my daughter. This day of the Lord will turn out as he wishes."[72] Questions about the relationship have vexed Joseph from the start. The difference here is that Joseph perceives a divine purpose in familial ambiguity. The holy household remains mysterious. Neither Joseph nor Mary fills conventional roles, and the boxes on the census form cannot be neatly ticked off.

As the couple travels further on, emotional bonding and carnal ignorance are again put on display. On the way to Bethlehem, Mary is "gloomy" one moment and laughing the next. Joseph guesses that the baby is causing discomfort and asks, "Mary, what's bothering you?" Mary explains that she's had a vision of "two peoples"—one in mourning, the other rejoicing.[73] As if to stress the point, in the very next line, Mary asks Joseph to help her down, for "the child inside me is pressing on me to come out."[74] Is Joseph wrong or right? Joseph may misread the source of the mood swings, but his show of

concern is genuine. Joseph's lack of insight into Mary's interior life underscores the portrait of the couple as not knowing.

Joseph finds Mary a safe place, a cave, to deliver the baby and then goes
in search of a midwife—not abandoning her, as before, but giving his sons to
Mary for support. In Chapter 2, we discussed the foiled examination of Salome. Prior to this, Joseph encounters a different midwife who begins to interrogate Joseph about the identity of the woman in the cave. Still unclear
himself about the nature of the relationship, Joseph replies, "My betrothed."[75]
The midwife says, "Is she not your wife?" Perhaps Joseph hears a hint of disap-
proval in the question, for he finally gives up on withholding information and
lays out the whole story for the midwife: "She is Mary, the one who was
brought up in the Lord's Temple, and I received the lot to take her as a wife.
She is not, however, my wife, but she has conceived her child by the Holy
Spirit."[76] Prior to the interview and ordeal, Joseph was troubled by not knowing. When he finds Mary pregnant and thinks he has fallen victim to a
bedtrick, Joseph comes undone over a relationship that he has refused to be a
part of. Now he accepts what he does not understand. Rather than fight the
future, he settles into the fluidity of his present circumstances. His relationship to Mary is the question mark in the middle of Joseph just as the pregnancy is the question mark in the middle of Mary.

Augustus wants to know. The midwife wants to know. In this context,
Josephus's persistent wondering about his role (is he husband, father, something else?) and Mary's (daughter, wife, something else?) poses an epistemological challenge. He takes Mary to a cave outside of Bethlehem, beyond the
reach of the Augustan census. Without Rome there to count its inhabitants,
to enforce familial roles, the roles of "husband" and "father" are ambiguous.
Mary is his wife and she is not his wife. Joseph is her husband and he is not.

While the curiosity of the midwife or the census of Augustus might appear neutral or benign, the final regime of surveillance is anything but. Herod
sends his soldiers out both to kill infants and to find the baby John. The
agents of Herod arrive at the temple and interrogate Zacharias, the father of
John, the husband of Elizabeth.[77] The *Proto-gospel of James* conforms to the
Lukan portrayal of Zechariah in some ways, but here it diverges. The death of
Zacharias, father of John, which is not mentioned in the Synoptic gospels, is
a key difference.[78] In the wake of Herod's anger at being duped by the Magi,

Herod sends out soldiers to search and destroy infants. They confront Zacharias, the high priest. He denies knowing the whereabouts of his wife and infant son: "How should I know? I am a minister of God, constantly attending his temple."[79] As it turns out, Elizabeth and John have found a haven inside the mountain of God, which miraculously opened a cleft for their escape.[80] Zacharias may or may not know to where they have fled, and perhaps he chooses not to know. He declares that he is dying as a martyr, and thus the spectacle immediately becomes part of the symbolic universe of Jewish and Christian martyr accounts. In such accounts, the death of the martyr is not a defeat but a victory, a transformation confirmed by miracles.[81] The soldiers kill Zacharias, and his blood turns to stone as it spills over the altar.[82] Zacharias's self-professed ignorance results in an expression of divine power and knowledge.

Christians of course have this kind of body language at the core of their tradition.[83] The apparent victory of the persecutor is suddenly overturned. The earliest narrative accounts of the passion of Jesus contest the meaning of Roman punishment. The canonical gospels still afford readers a glimpse of the perverse play in the crucifixion of Jesus. In the canonical gospels, the crucifixion of Jesus is one part irony and one part parody.[84] Jesus is dressed in purple and given a crown of thorns by soldiers. When Pilate condemns Jesus as the "King of the Jews," he is poking fun at the Jews under his control. But for Christians, the suffering of the cross becomes a sign of truth and power.[85] "I preach Christ crucified," Paul wrote to his followers in Corinth, "a stumbling block to the Jews and foolishness to Gentiles" (1 Cor 1:23). Spectacles of violence, as we saw in Chapter 2, left meaning up for grabs. In the second and third centuries, the relationship between truth and flesh emerges as a common theme of early Christian martyr accounts.[86] Zacharias's death, at first a scene of death and defeat at the hands of Herod's henchmen, is a sign of the power of God. The designs of heaven are illuminated by the replacement of Zacharias, Simeon, who, in the Gospel of Luke, comes to the temple when Mary and Joseph bring their newborn baby to Jerusalem for naming and circumcision (2:25–35).

In the Gospel of Matthew, Herod's "Massacre of the Innocents" threatens the family of Jesus. But Joseph is warned by an angel to take his family and flee to Egypt. The "Flight to Egypt" is omitted in the *Proto-gospel of James*. The most widely subscribed to theory for this omission is that the author of the *Proto-gospel of James* was aware that the association of Jesus with Egypt was a source of controversy and fodder for anti-Christian polemic. Opponents argued that the miracles of Jesus were nothing more than magic tricks, which he learned as a boy in Egypt.[87] Here I want to suggest an alternative theory—that the *Proto-gospel of James* omits the "Flight to Egypt" in order to tell a different story that illustrates the courage of Mary. The holy family does not flee. Rather, making creative use of details from the Synoptic accounts, the *Proto-gospel of James* reports that Mary hides Jesus in a cattle manger.[88] Earlier, an angel appeared to Joseph to allay his fears about Mary's pregnancy. Here, angelic counsel is absent, and Mary must act to save her baby.

*   *   *

Mary and Joseph's relationship does not model conjugal harmony. It is awkward, at once ordinary and extraordinary.[89] Rather than perfect harmony or oneness, the family gospel offers a series of doubles. First, there is the doubling of the pun on "knowing." Mary and Joseph do not know each other sexually, nor do they know each other in any other way. This failure of understanding creates the most powerfully intimate moments of the account, when the couple must survive Joseph's own doubts and suspicions about Mary. His fear of being caught in a humiliating bedtrick nearly separates the couple forever. Second, there is a doubling of the search for knowledge. The seemingly benign census of Augustus is paired with the cold-blooded investigation of Herod's massacre. The writer of the *Proto-gospel of James*, inheritor of stories that are found separately in the gospels of Matthew and Luke, recognized in them a common problem. Zacharias's ignorance of his family's whereabouts echoes Joseph's uncertainty about his relationship to Mary. And Mary's bold and clever idea to hide Jesus in a manger from Herod's soldiers runs parallel to Zacharias's courage in resisting them.

Amid these doubles, certainty gives way to uncertainty. The problem of Mary's virginity is in service to a larger concern about human beings and the use of sexual knowledge to construct difference, such as the difference between husband and wife, father and child, knower and known. Incomplete knowledge of other and self undermines hierarchies and the "given-ness" of markers such as husband-wife and parent-child. Interpersonal conflict and confusion, remarkably, gives Mary and Joseph room to maneuver. The relationship between Mary and Joseph is something that cannot be known by Augustan imperial counting.

But uncertainty does not weaken the bond between Mary and Joseph. In the *Proto-gospel of James*, the nature of the relationship between Mary and Joseph remains vague but rich in emotion. Together they brave doubt, scandal, and a potentially lethal ordeal. Their bond is forged in a crucible of miracle and courage, and their fidelity to one another scrapes away at expectations about what constitutes conjugal intimacy. For all of the problems that bedevil the relationship of Mary and Joseph, the *Proto-gospel of James* remains a story of family ties. It would not have mapped easily onto the hierarchical family model favored by some Christians or onto the model of chastity favored by others. It is an account of two people thrown together by forces beyond their control and comprehension. Although Mary and Joseph cannot understand it, God is in control of the events that they witness and in which they participate. Human perception is limited; omniscience is a divine quality.

The *Proto-gospel of James* is not an "infancy gospel" after all. It is a story about a family—a strange household, fashioned by chance and angels, and frustrating to ruling powers that want to know it all. Recently, Kate Cooper has also remarked on the "comic nosiness" of the *Proto-gospel of James*. Of course, I think Cooper is right: Rome is nosy; the priests are nosy; the neighbors are nosy. But I take issue with Cooper's mild disparaging of the *Proto-gospel of James*, which she says lacks the "emotional realism" and "moral courage" of the Lukan infancy narrative.[90] The *Proto-gospel of James* paints a rich and moving portrait of family life, one that can be said to expand on those qualities that Cooper admires in the earlier gospel. Joseph's teary and silent "declaration" of loyalty to Mary in the *Proto-gospel of James* is a subtle and poignant depiction of courage in the face of the unknown.

Chapter 5

Parents Just Don't Understand

He was going to be a superstar.

As a boy in first-century Jerusalem, he took education seriously. His dedication to the life of the mind soon attracted attention. The leading men of Jerusalem sought him out. They admired the boy's love of learning and put to him questions about the Jewish law. Who is this child? Some readers may guess that it is Jesus, the twelve-year-old prodigy whose insight "amazes" the teachers in the temple of Jerusalem. But this profile in childhood smarts does not belong to Jesus. It comes from a firsthand recollection by Yosef ben Mattityahu, the man known to most historians as Josephus. He gives the following account of his childhood in *The Life*: "While still a mere boy, about fourteen years old, I won universal applause for my love of letters; insomuch that the leading men of the city used constantly to come to me for precise information on some particular in our ordinances."[1]

Modesty may not be one of Josephus's virtues, but he should not be judged too harshly for adopting a self-regarding pose. For one thing, Josephus wrote *The Life* as a defense against critics.[2] For another, childhood, as it is defined in ancient biography, is the time when great people, mostly men, begin to show what they were made of. Luminaries of the classical Greek past, Plato and Aristotle, were, as children, quick witted and eager to learn. Philo, the Greek-speaking Jewish philosopher of Alexandria, encouraged his readers to see Abraham and Moses, the great ancestors of the Jewish people, in a similar way. That Josephus remembers himself as a child of precocious intelligence is in keeping with the spirit of the genre of ancient biography.

I begin this chapter with Josephus because this nugget from his childhood calls to mind the childhood story about Jesus in the temple in the Gospel of Luke (2:41–52). Equally important, a rendering of the Lukan story forms the conclusion to the *Infancy Gospel of Thomas* (17.1–4). Like Josephus's account, the story about Jesus illustrates the superior intelligence of the youth. That it takes place in the temple of Jerusalem is another intriguing point of contact with *The Life*. If Rome is depicted as obsessed with collecting information about the subjects of empire in both the Gospel of Luke and the *Proto-gospel of James*, the city of Jerusalem serves as the destination for those who seek truth in both *The Life* of Josephus and the *Infancy Gospel of Thomas*.[3]

But is the childhood story only about the wisdom of the twelve-year-old Jesus? Is this the sum of its meaning? The Christian story as it appears in both the Gospel of Luke and the *Infancy Gospel of Thomas* differs from *The Life* in the foregrounding of family dysfunction. The young Josephus wins "universal" acclaim for himself, to the delight of family and friends alike. The adolescent Jesus, as we shall see, causes his parents distress and seems to dispute Joseph's claim of paternity. It is an account of the breakdown of communication and comprehension between a child who is a riddle and parents that just don't understand. Where the young Josephus basks in the glow of admiration, the performance of the child Jesus baffles the two people who are closest to him.

The contrast with *The Life* reveals flaws in recent proposals about the *Infancy Gospel*. One is the notion that the *Infancy Gospel* "improves" the Gospel of Luke by bringing it in line with the conventions of ancient biography.[4] The claim is that ancient readers expected to encounter childhood stories in the lives of great men. Absent such tales, the Gospel of Luke, a kind of ancient biography, would have been viewed as deficient.[5] The *Infancy Gospel* adds childhood stories to address the lack. "Improvement" is of course in the eyes of the beholder, but even if we grant improvement in this case, the idea does not bring us any closer to understanding why the *Infancy Gospel*, from beginning to end, depicts familial strain. Other scholars contend that the tales send a positive message about Mary and Joseph and that they gradually come to understand their child.[6] Still others suggest that the *Infancy Gospel* is designed to respond to critics of the Christian faith by presenting the anger and aloofness of the child Jesus in "justifiable" terms.[7] All of these proposals miss the mark because they do not account for the anxiety and confusion of the parents in the conclusion to the *Infancy Gospel*.

Like the last one, this chapter proposes that confusion and ignorance serve as the framework for a choice. If Jesus was hard to parent as a twelve-year-old, what were things like when he was younger—at five, eight, and ten years old? This chapter will discuss both the feats of the child Jesus and the ways that these signs are missed, ignored, and not understood—especially (but not exclusively) by his parents. It will further suggest that instances of unknowing in these family stories likewise were disquieting moments for early Christian readers. They, like Mary and Joseph, are brought close to demonstrations of divine power only to be confounded by it. The *Infancy Gospel* presents a family in distress, and the cause of the turmoil is the unpredictable child Jesus. By including other strange stories about the childhood of Jesus, the *Infancy Gospel* offers a new perspective on the decision that lies before the members of the holy family when, after being separated, they reunite in the temple precincts. Will the parents accept what they do not understand about this strange child? Will Jesus opt to stay in the temple, doing "the things of his father," or will he choose instead to return with Mary and Joseph—the two people who know him the best, which is to say, not at all. Will they choose, in other words, to be a family?

Because so much of the argument of this chapter depends upon seeing the *Infancy Gospel* as an elaboration of questions hinted at in the Lukan account of the twelve-year-old Jesus, it begins there. An important point is how Luke 2:41–52 stands at odds with what precedes it, a tension that, as we saw in Chapter 1, early Christian interpreters like John Chrysostom sought to resolve. In the Lukan infancy narrative, a series of miracles together reveal and confirm for Mary and Joseph the significance of their newborn baby. These earlier episodes suggest that miracles teach human beings about divine purpose. Yet, when they confront the twelve-year-old Jesus in the temple, Mary and Joseph cannot understand what he is doing there or why he is doing it. The second section turns to the nearly toxic brew of harmful and benevolent wonders in the *Infancy Gospel of Thomas* to show how these tales amplify the familial strain depicted in its source material. These unpredictable demonstrations of power inevitably distance the child Jesus from neighbors, friends, and family. All of this confusion adds weight to the choice that lies before the members of the holy family. In the end, the parents choose to remain with the child, and he chooses to remain with them.

Parental Undersight

The Gospel of Luke dedicates most of the first two chapters to the events surrounding the birth of Jesus. At the tail end of the Lukan infancy narrative comes the account of a twelve-year-old Jesus. His intellect amazes the religious experts of the great temple of Jerusalem:

> Now every year his parents went to Jerusalem for the festival of the Passover. And when he was twelve years old, they went up as usual for the festival. When the festival was ended and they started to return, the boy Jesus stayed behind in Jerusalem, but his parents did not know it (*ouk egnōsan*). Assuming that he was in the group of travelers, they went a day's journey. Then they started to look for him among their relatives and friends. When they did not find him, they returned to Jerusalem to search for him. After three days they found him in the temple, sitting among the teachers, listening to them and asking them questions. And all who heard him were amazed at his understanding and his answers. When his parents saw him they were astonished; and his mother said to him, "Child, why have you treated us like this? Look, your father and I have been searching for you in great anxiety." He said to them, "Why were you searching for me? Did you not know (*ouk ēdeite*) that I must concern myself with the things of my father?" But they did not understand (*ou synēkan*) what he said to them. Then he went down with them and came to Nazareth, and was obedient to them. His mother treasured all these things in her heart.
>
> And Jesus increased in wisdom and in years, and in divine and human favor.[8]

Synopses and commentaries sometimes refer to the episode as the "Finding of Jesus in the Temple" because Mary and Joseph lose track of where he is.[9] It begins with a family pilgrimage. Mary and Joseph take Jesus to Jerusalem for Passover. After the observance, Mary and Joseph turn back for home. Jesus decides to stay behind in Jerusalem, without asking permission: "but his parents did not know it" (2:43).[10] When Mary and Joseph realize what has happened, they begin the search. "After three days" they find Jesus, safe and sound, in the great temple of Jerusalem (2:46).[11] There he sits among the elders, asking questions and amazing all with his "understanding" (2:47).[12] Reproaching her son, Mary asks, "Child, why have you treated us like this?" She and Joseph have been worried sick, searching for Jesus "in great anxiety" (2:48).[13] "Why were you looking for me?" Jesus replies. "Did you not know that I must concern myself with the things of my father?" (2:49).[14] His questions confuse Mary and Joseph: "But they did not understand what he said to them" (2:50).[15] The family returns to Nazareth, where Jesus "was obedient to them" (2:51), a noteworthy detail in a story that seems to recount a mildly wayward moment from Jesus' youth.

Three times in eleven verses Mary and Joseph are exposed as having some degree of ignorance (Luke 2:43, 49–50). The Greek text employs three different terms for "knowing" and "understanding" and adds to them the negative Greek particle.[16] Mary and Joseph do not know many things about their child. In this case, they do not even know his whereabouts. Jesus meets his mother's reprimand with a reproach of his own: "Did you not know?"[17] The implied response is, no, Mary and Joseph do not know. They do not know that the twelve-year-old had earlier made up his mind to stay behind in Jerusalem or that he is now preoccupied with "the things of my father," whatever that may mean.[18] Mary may "treasure" what has happened in her heart, but she does not understand the events.[19] If this is what the domestic situation was like, it is little wonder that the earliest gospels mostly skip over the growing-up years of Jesus. In the coda, Jesus returns to Nazareth, remains obedient to his parents, and increases in wisdom (Luke 2:51–52).

What is the point of this story? Is it to show off precocious intelligence of the twelve-year-old Jesus? Or does it lie elsewhere, in the breakdown of communication between parents and child? If nothing else, Luke 2:41–52 is a story about a family trying and failing to understand one another. There is a palpable tension in the relationship between Jesus and his parents. Domestic harmony is upset. The teachers of the temple recognize the genius of the boy, while his parents are left in a state of uncertainty. If a divine lesson is being taught to Mary and Joseph, they seem unable to grasp what it is (much less learn the lesson for themselves).[20] Does he understand them? Meanwhile, readers acquainted with the biblical reports about the otherworldly nature of the birth of Jesus might also be confused by the strange ignorance of Mary and Joseph. Why, twelve years later, should Jesus' remark about the "things of my father" fly over their heads? What does Jesus mean by "the things of my father"?

Parents just don't understand: the message is loud, but the meaning is unclear. Luke's tale of conflict between a willful twelve-year-old Jesus and his parents marks one of the most jarring transitions in the New Testament. Much of the first two chapters of Luke features Mary and Joseph as thoughtful recipients of information about Jesus. Prior to the "Finding of Jesus," Mary is present for multiple predictions of her son's future greatness. Gabriel and other angels visit her, and relatives and strangers prophesy about the child. When Gabriel gives Mary the news that she will soon conceive, the angel alludes to "future greatness": "Do not be afraid, Mary, for you have found favor with God. And now, you will conceive in your womb and bear a son, and you will name him Jesus. He will be great, and will be called the Son of the Most High, and the Lord God will give to him the throne of his ancestor David. He will reign over the house of Jacob forever, and of his kingdom there will be no end" (Luke 1:30–33). Mary's initial reaction is skepticism: "How will this happen," she asks Gabriel, "since I have not known any man?" (Luke 1:34).[21] Gabriel reassures her, declaring, "For nothing will be impossible with God" (Luke 1:37), and Mary accepts her fate. "Here am I, the servant of the Lord," she says to Gabriel, "let it be with me according to your word" (Luke 1:38).

If Mary has any lingering doubts, they are soon overcome. Elizabeth, Mary's relative, feels the child in her own womb leap when she greets Mary. "Blessed are you among women," Elizabeth says to her cousin, "and blessed is the fruit of your womb" (Luke 1:42). Mary sings about the miracle in what is now known as the Magnificat: "My soul magnifies the Lord, and my spirit rejoices in God my savior, for he looked with favor on the lowliness of his servant. Surely, from now on all generations will call me blessed; for the Mighty One has done great things for me, and holy is his name" (Luke 2:46–49). A choir of angels appears over Bethlehem when Jesus is born; one of the host speaks to a gathering of shepherds: "I am bringing you good news of great joy for all the people; to you is born this day in the city of David, a Savior, who is the Messiah, the Lord" (Luke 2:10–13). The shepherds pay a visit to the holy family and report to Mary and Joseph what they had heard and seen (Luke 2:17). When the time comes to name the child, the parents obey the command of Gabriel and choose the name Jesus (Luke 2:21; see 1:31). Events unfold according to a heavenly blueprint in Luke 1–2, and Mary and Joseph seem content to stick to the plan.

Two other unusual figures confirm the importance of the newborn. Soon after naming and circumcising their child, Mary and Joseph bring the baby to the temple in Jerusalem (Luke 2:22–24). There they meet Simeon, a prophet, who for years has been waiting this day to come: "It had been revealed to [Simeon] by the Holy Spirit that he would not see death before he had seen the Lord's Messiah" (Luke 2:26). Taking Jesus in his arms, Simeon cries out to God, "Master, now you are dismissing your servant in peace, according to your word; for my eyes have seen your salvation" (Luke 2:29–30). Mary and Joseph's reaction to Simeon is hard to pin down: "And the child's father and mother were amazed at what was being said about him [i.e., Jesus]" (Luke 2:33). "Amazed" translates *thaumazō*, a term that suggests astonishment, even shock.[22] Are they pleased by what they hear, or are Mary and Joseph stunned by the words of Simeon? More ambiguity follows in Simeon's aside to Mary: "This child is destined for the falling and rising of many in Israel, and to be a sign that will be opposed so that the inner thoughts of many will be revealed— and a sword will pierce your own soul too" (Luke 2:34–35). A moment later, another prophet, Anna, spreads the news about the baby's significance: "[She] began to praise God and to speak about the child to all who were looking for redemption in Jerusalem" (Luke 2:38).

Years later, what would Mary and Joseph have remembered from this first trip as a family to Jerusalem? Did they remember the "amazing" words of Simeon and Anna? Did they recall the morbid spectacle of a stranger talking about his own death while holding their newborn baby? What about earlier events—did they remember the remarkable circumstances of their baby's conception and birth? These are questions left open by Luke's narrative, and without any clues, they are unanswerable. But the prophecies of future greatness (and future tragedy) in the first trip to Jerusalem, I think, linger in the mind when one, just a few transitional verses later, comes to the story of the second trip to Jerusalem.

For many commentators, the strange "Finding of Jesus" episode (2:41–52) undermines any claim of narrative coherence in Luke 1–2. Given all of the signs and wonders that attend Mary's pregnancy, how is it possible that Mary and Joseph would later be puzzled by the speech and behavior of their twelve-year-old son? "Such a failure is surprising," Raymond Brown dryly observes, "after the annunciation to Mary in 1:26–38, after the prediction of Simeon in 2:21–40."[23] Some, like Brown, have cautiously accepted the hypothesis of a pre-Lucan source for 2:41–52.[24] An episode about the clueless parents of Jesus from a different source was spliced onto the infancy narrative of Luke 1–2. This result is an uneven narrative that includes both "a multitude of the heavenly host" and what seems to be a bout of amnesia twelve years later in the temple of Jerusalem. In other words, clumsy editing takes the blame for the strange ignorance of Mary and Joseph. Luke, in adopting the source, fails to reconcile the strange ignorance of the parents with earlier moments in which they are showered with information about their unusual child. Yet, this solution runs headlong into an obstacle, as Brown himself concedes: "If there was a pre-Lukan story, one must recognize that Luke has thoroughly rewritten it."[25] The vocabulary and structure of the story bear all of the hallmarks of Lukan composition. Why would Luke throw his back into revising the story and not also "fix" the forgetfulness (or sudden obtuseness) of Mary and Joseph? Whatever the reason, one is left with a strange narrative arc. In one chapter, Mary sings the Magnificat, while in the next, she is bewildered by her adolescent son's sense of purpose.

The confusion of the parents is confusing, a state of affairs that at first may not strike many readers as much of a problem. Friends and family regularly misunderstand and underappreciate Jesus across the canonical gospels. Still, the multiple references to parental unknowing in the "Finding of Jesus" invite scrutiny. Even the coda of the pericope, which may at first glance seem to resolve the familial tension, is ambivalent. According to Luke, the twelve-year-old Jesus returns home to Nazareth and was "obedient" to Mary and Joseph (Luke 2:51). Commentators typically greet this verse with relief, pointing out that Jesus, like a good boy, fulfills the commandments.[26] But why, we may ask, does the twelve-year-old Jesus show such brazen disregard for the authority of his parents in the first place? And why, afterward, does Jesus go on to submit to the interfering adults who interrupt his service to "the things of my father"?

The Gospel of Luke sets the agenda for the *Infancy Gospel* not only by what it leaves out—that is, gaps in the childhood of Jesus—but also by including the extraordinary story of Jesus and his parents in the temple. The "Finding of Jesus" is the hinge that joins the *Infancy Gospel* to its Lukan source material.[27] The *Infancy Gospel of Thomas* includes a longer version of this story as its conclusion. I am of course not the first to suggest that it was the Lukan pericope that inspired the *Infancy Gospel*. Raymond Brown argues, "The unknown period of his boyhood could best be filled in through a creative use of what was known from his ministry. I contend that this same instinct has been at work in Luke 2:41–52; and it is no accident that, at the end of his sequence of apocryphal 'hidden life' stories about Jesus, the author of the *Infancy Gospel of Thomas* presented an adaptation of Luke 2:41–52. He has recognized kindred material."[28] Brown's good point about the "kindred material" of Luke 2:41–52 and the *Infancy Gospel* nevertheless skirts around the problem of unknowing in the "Finding of Jesus," the "surprising failure" of Mary and Joseph. Rather than projecting adult activities back into the childhood of Jesus, the *Infancy Gospel* gathers together stories that create a context for understanding the dysfunction of the "Finding of Jesus" episode.

I contend that the childhood tales of the *Infancy Gospel* anticipate the crisis triggered by the twelve-year-old in the temple in Jerusalem. Viewed in this light, the *Infancy Gospel* appears as a narrative organized around two questions: what did the parents of Jesus know about him, and when did they know it? As we saw in Chapter 1, early Christian interpreters were drawn to these same questions. Irenaeus, in his dispute with the "Marcosians," rejected both their use of "apocryphal and spurious writings" and their interpretation of the "Finding of Jesus," namely, that the twelve-year-old Jesus taught Mary and Joseph about the "unknowable God." What did Irenaeus himself think about the story? For all of his contempt for the Marcosians, he does not offer an alternative interpretation.[29]

A century and a half later, John Chrysostom would fill in the space left open by Irenaeus. Is it credible to think that Jesus was raised in obscurity? That even his family shrugged off the angelic fireworks in Bethlehem and went on with their lives as if nothing extraordinary had happened? Yes, it is credible, according to John Chrysostom. It took the Baptist's declaration about the adult Jesus at the Jordan River to bring him to the attention of the public. Those that lived closest to him, including and especially Mary, saw an ordinary boy. His low profile was due to the *absence* of childhood wonders, which, in turn, was part of a deliberate strategy of secrecy on the part of young Jesus. All of a sudden, at the age of thirty, Jesus outgrew the need for withholding: he performed the miracle of changing water into wine at the wedding in Cana, and his reputation exploded. It was no longer plausible to deny the power and status of Jesus. Prior to the performance of the adult Jesus in Cana, there was nothing. The "Finding of Jesus" episode, according to John Chrysostom, was a single blip on the radar.

Although they differ in their interpretations, Irenaeus, the "Marcosians," and John Chrysostom share an interest in questions about what Mary and Joseph did and did not know about their child. To this network of interpretation of the childhood of Jesus, add the *Infancy Gospel of Thomas*. The *Infancy Gospel* extends the ambiguity of the Lukan childhood story and, in so doing, offers a compelling interpretation of the holy household, one that finds meaning in familial strain. Against the background of other early Christian readings—from the Marcosians to John Chrysostom—we can see that the *Infancy Gospel* implies a distinctive theory of household dysfunction: Mary and Joseph do not understand their child because he is hard to understand— ambiguous in speech, deed, and identity. The narrative enactment of this theory in the *Infancy Gospel* represents the opposite of John Chrysostom's approach. If his sermons try to close the door to thinking with the childhood of Jesus, then the *Infancy Gospel* lets it swing wide open.

In the *Infancy Gospel*, readers learn why Mary and Joseph (not to mention all of the neighbors) are so confused by the twelve-year-old Jesus. The family gospel responds to the Gospel of Luke by anticipating the familial dysfunction of the "Finding of Jesus." Consider Mary's question to her son: "Child, why have you treated us like this?" (Luke 2:48). For the author of the *Infancy Gospel*, Mary's question is not, as the Marcosians had it, meant to imply an unknowable deity. Nor is it, as John Chrysostom believed, the by-product of an economy of deniability, put in motion by the absence of childhood wonders, Mary's lack of confidence, and Jesus' self-veiling. It is instead evidence of how little the parents understood about their child. Rather than solving the riddle of the "Finding of Jesus," the *Infancy Gospel* shows the events that led to Mary's heartbreaking question. In so doing, the *Infancy Gospel* turns on its head John Chrysostom's theory of an absence of childhood wonders. Instead of an absence of wonders, the *Infancy Gospel* includes an abundance. What if, the family gospel asks, Jesus had performed miracles as a child? Would they have been understood by those closest to him? Or would they have left even Mary and Joseph in a state of confusion?

Nearness and Knowledge

All great literature involves conflict: tradition against innovation, gods against humans, men against women, or a woman against herself. While no one would mistake the *Infancy Gospel* for great literature, the conflict is easy to spot: everyone who meets Jesus either hates or misunderstands him. The *Infancy Gospel* begins with a story of Jesus at play. "The child Jesus was five years old and, after a rain, he was playing at the ford of a rushing stream."[30] The idyllic scene is quite unlike anything in the gospels of the New Testament. In those books, every word and deed is swollen with portent, and there is no time for play. By contrast, in the *Infancy Gospel*, Jesus plays like any other five-year-old. But charm gives way to demonstrations of unusual power. The river is silty, and Jesus miraculously makes the water pure. No one else in the text sees this marvel; the reader alone is invited to picture the scene and, in the light of unfolding events, to recognize the allusion to the accounts of creation in the book of Genesis. Next, Jesus shapes twelve sparrows from the dirt. An onlooker, offended, goes and confronts Joseph: "Behold your boy is at the ford of the stream and has taken mud and fashioned (*eplasen*) twelve birds with it, and so has violated the Sabbath." When Joseph scolds his son—"Why are you doing these things on the Sabbath?"—Jesus responds with a second miracle. The boy claps his hands, and the clay sparrows turn into real birds and fly away.[31]

This brief episode has at least three noteworthy aspects. First, it relates the stories of the *Infancy Gospel* to the Jewish scriptures. Second, it shows the power of the child. Jesus' miracle of creation repeats, playfully, the creation of Adam.[32] Third, we see that Joseph does not understand his son. From the start, then, the *Infancy Gospel* decouples not only miracle and knowledge but also nearness and knowledge. Should not the people closest to Jesus know him the best? Joseph may live with Jesus, but he does not or cannot grasp the whole truth about his son.

For all of the serious aspects of the story, we should not overlook the humor of the scene. When Jesus is accused of violating the Sabbath in earlier gospels, the atmosphere is tense. In the *Infancy Gospel,* a burst of comedy changes the climate. The *Infancy Gospel* not only shows Jesus at play but is also a playful account. Most will chuckle when Jesus, like any other child, tries to cover up his mistake. The story is told with a wink and a nod, adding a ludic "second accent" to the serious portrait of Jesus in the Synoptic tradition. Daniel Boyarin has recently traced a "second accent" alongside the serious "first accent" of Hellenistic philosophical traditions. This intellectual legacy was both embraced and interrogated in surprisingly similar ways by Greek-speaking satirists (such as Lucian) and the compilers of the Talmud. "Menippean satire," a rather amorphous style dedicated to the combination of incongruous elements, of first and second accents, is the name that Boyarin gives to this form of inquiry.[33] In the broadest sense, the *Infancy Gospel* acts as a Menippean satire of the Synoptic storytelling that it absorbs and extends. Similar to other examples, the *Infancy Gospel* develops a "seriocomic" (*spoudogeloion*) tone and purpose.[34] In the rough play of the child Jesus, inherited practices and claims of knowledge come under scrutiny.

Along with comedy, the *Infancy Gospel* adds uncertainty to the Synoptic tradition, a sense of confusion that grows not despite but because of Jesus' childhood acts of power. As soon as one is ready to tag these stories as lighthearted, the mood darkens. In the following scene, the son of Annas (a religious expert) drains the water that Jesus had gathered into pools. Jesus lashes out, "Your fruit shall be without root and your shoot dried up like a branch scorched by a strong wind."[35] Immediately, the son of Annas withers, and Jesus returns home. Next a boy runs past Jesus, banging him in the shoulder.[36] In response, Jesus curses the child to death: the boy's parents beg Joseph either to take his family and leave or, at least, "teach him to bless and not to curse; for we have been deprived of our child."[37] Joseph's second rebuke of Jesus is more urgent, even desperate: "Why do you say such things? They suffer and hate us." Jesus does not yield: "Since you know wise words, you are not ignorant of where your words come from."[38] When Joseph, detecting sassiness in these words, grabs Jesus by the ear, the boy sounds an ominous warning: "Let it be enough for you to seek and find me, and not, in addition to this, torment me by having a natural ignorance. You have not seen me clearly, why I am yours. Behold! You know not to upset me. For I am yours and have been handed to you."[39]

Not only does Jesus reject Joseph's admonishment, but he also underscores how little Joseph knows about the most basic familial elements. Whatever Joseph thinks is the nature of his relationship to Jesus is wrong. Is he Jesus' father? Is Jesus his son? What is the meaning of all this? The conflict raises the problem of knowing. When Joseph questions his son, we see a father trying to act on what he knows—biblical precepts about the day of rest and honoring one's parents.[40] Joseph does what he is supposed to do. Meanwhile, Jesus' childlike reenactment of Genesis, while telegraphed to the reader, is missed entirely by the father. The contrast of what the reader sees, on one hand, and what Joseph fails to see, on the other, seems crucial to the *Infancy Gospel*. It must be by design that Joseph, at the beginning of the *Infancy Gospel*, asks the same question that Mary will ask at the end: "Why?" Joseph and Mary do not understand the boy, nor does anyone else.

If we neglect the back and forth of knowing and not knowing, the early stories of the *Infancy Gospel* can seem all too predictable: the fight between the "son of Annas" and the son of Joseph "is meant to foreshadow Jesus' later meeting with the High Priest himself."[41] This is likely at least part of the purpose. Yet, to reduce events in the *Infancy Gospel* to mere childhood prototypes of adult episodes does not do justice to the narrative.

Let us consider a different episode from the Gospel of Luke as a comparison rather than as a kind of foreshadowing: the story of Zechariah, priest and father of John the Baptist (Luke 1:5–80). Here again the strain is between fathers and sons, and the conflict turns on the axis of epistemology. When the angel Gabriel announces the pregnancy of John the Baptist, Zechariah scoffs at the plan: "How will I know [*gnōsomai*] that this is so? For I am an old man, and my wife is getting on in years." "I am Gabriel," the angel replies, "I stand in the presence of God, and I have been sent to speak to you and to bring you this good news. But now, because you did not believe my words, which will be fulfilled in their time, you will become mute, unable to speak, until the day these things occur" (Luke 1:18–20). The angel Gabriel curses Zechariah, leaving him mute, and the people are left to wonder why. Once the child is born,

Zechariah expresses conviction and belief by writing down the name of the boy, John—the name commanded by Gabriel. The curse is lifted and Zechariah is again able to speak. Here is a contrast between the sweeping nature of divine vision and the limited perspective of Zechariah.[42] He suffers for a lack of imagination, believing that his advanced age will keep him from becoming a father. Even so, Zechariah and the readers learn from his suffering.[43]

We might speculate that the *Infancy Gospel* pursues the same goal: to magnify divine knowledge at the expense of feeble-minded humans. Yet, even if the promise and proof of divine power is apparent to readers, the blindness of characters remains unsettling. By contrast, the reason for Zechariah's punishment is unmistakable: how dare a mortal question the designs of God! The *Infancy Gospel* goes a step farther, giving with one hand while taking away with the other. The reader may know more about Jesus than Joseph does—he or she has seen the child playfully mimic the creation of the world—and yet be left, like his parents, in the dark about the meaning of Jesus' curses and declarations.

Without guidance from the characters, the audience must on their own contemplate the riddle of the child's intentions. When Zacchaeus, the first teacher of Jesus, admits defeat, he asks, "What kind of belly bore him? What kind of womb nourished him?"[44] Readers know to whom the belly and womb belongs; they also know that the parents are no less confused than Zacchaeus. The child's deeds and, in this case, his words seem only to drive a wedge between himself and others. The *Infancy Gospel* invites reflection on differences in knowing: the difference between what Jesus knows and others do not, the difference between what the audience knows and the characters do not, and the difference between what the audience knows and what it does not know. The *Infancy Gospel* takes delight in jolting turnabouts: the son corrects his father; the student teaches his teacher. Moreover, the *Infancy Gospel* also involves the audience in the drama, sometimes confirming assumptions but just as often confounding expectations. It is a kind of parallel play that teaches about epistemological boundaries. Caught up in narrative gaps and ambiguity, in surprises and suspense, readers become aware of the limits of human perception.[45]

Then, as if to trip up an audience already on the wrong foot, things change. After Jesus raises Zeno from the dead, the wonders of Jesus in the second half of the family gospel lead (mostly) to reconciliation and harmony. Jesus catches spilled water in his cloak to give to his mother and helps his father with a carpentry project by stretching a piece of wood to match it up with another board. Joseph exults, "Blessed am I, for God gave me such a child."[46] The villagers also witness miracles: when a young man splits open his foot chopping wood and dies, Jesus, a hometown hero, pushes his way through the onlookers to heal and restore the victim to life. Hope overcomes the fear of the "first-half" stories, and the crowd's cry rings out: "For he saved many souls from death. And he will continue to save all the days of his life."[47]

The transition of neighbors and parents from contempt and fear to admiration of the child Jesus has been an important question in recent studies of the *Infancy Gospel*.[48] Is the change in the behavior of Jesus or in the perception of those around him? The single blip in the convivial mood of the second half of the *Infancy Gospel* suggests the latter. A brutal schoolhouse episode leaves the teacher dead, but in the very next chapter, a different tutor wisely yields the floor to the pupil, and Jesus, standing at a lectern with a book on it, utters "awe-inspiring words" to an appreciative crowd. The teacher lavishes praise on Jesus—"he is full of much grace and wisdom"—and thus earns a reward: "Because you spoke rightly and testified rightly," announces Jesus, "on account of you the one struck down also shall be saved."[49] In light of this splendid act of restoration, Tony Burke suggests that the "real transformation in the narrative is made in those around Jesus, not Jesus himself. . . . In IGT [*Infancy Gospel of Thomas*] this means that people should respond to Jesus not with incredulity or violence, but with belief and praise . . . it is Jesus' teachers, neighbors, and parents who have a lesson to learn here."[50] So too Reidar Aasgaard argues, "Audiences—both individuals and groups—gradually realized the greatness of Jesus."[51] Aasgaard applies this conclusion with equal force to the "increasing insight" of the parents of Jesus. In the first half of the gospel, Jesus drives his parents up the wall; in the second half, father and son together assemble furniture like a well-oiled machine.

This proposal about "increasing insight" circles back to the problem with which we began: Mary and Joseph's failure to understand Jesus. While the second half of the *Infancy Gospel* is brightly optimistic, some shadows of doubt linger. When Joseph returns to collect Jesus from the third teacher, he finds a crowd gathered around the classroom. He assumes that Jesus has acted out once again: "And Joseph quickly ran to the classroom, suspecting that this teacher too was no longer inexperienced and that he may have suffered."[52] As it turns out, Joseph's worry proves to be unwarranted, as teacher and crowd praise the child. But the father's anxiety is a reminder that the son remains an unknown quantity.

Moreover, if we lay too much stress on the cheerful atmosphere of the second half of the *Infancy Gospel*, we risk overlooking the domestic trouble that persists in the concluding chapter, a retelling of the canonical "Finding of Jesus." As in the Gospel of Luke, Jesus remains in Jerusalem without his parents' consent: "And his parents did not know."[53] When Mary and Joseph arrive at the temple, Jesus' role is accentuated: more than ask questions, as in Luke, Jesus also "explained the main points of the law and the riddles and the parables of the prophets."[54] But Jesus' virtuoso performance does little to lessen the parents' confusion. The *Infancy Gospel* even amplifies Mary's worry, adding another term to Luke's "great anxiety": "Child, what have you done to us? See, we have been looking for you in great anxiety and distress."[55] As in the Lukan version, the reply of Jesus in the *Infancy Gospel* hangs in the air, leaving matters unresolved: "Why were you looking for me? Did you not know that I must be in the place of my father?"[56]

At this point, the *Infancy Gospel* distinguishes itself from the canonical source by eliminating the Lukan verse: "But they did not understand what he said to them" (Luke 2:50). In its place, the *Infancy Gospel* inserts a benediction from the "scribes and the Pharisees" in the temple: "Blessed are you, because the Lord God has blessed the fruit of your womb. For we have never before seen nor heard such wisdom of praise and such glory of virtue we have never seen nor heard."[57] It is a blessing that gives and takes away: they recognize greatness, although they cannot fully comprehend it. It is, I suspect, a kind of feint. The perception of the learned figures is cast in playfully negative terms: the experts were ignorant before—"we have never seen nor heard"—and so they prove themselves again when they conspire to destroy the adult Jesus in the Lukan passion narrative. Still, whether one reads it as straightforward or ironic, the praise of the temple experts does not tell the reader anything about the parents. Jesus is unprecedented, and so is the set of domestic relationships to which he belongs.

Reidar Aasgaard takes the omission of Luke 2:50—"But they [i.e., Mary and Joseph] did not understand what he said to them"—as a sign of the purpose of the *Infancy Gospel*: to show the "growing insight" of the parents into the mission of their child.[58] The "omission" of Luke 2:50 from the *Infancy Gospel*'s version of the story is not unimportant, but I do not think that the absence alone can support the weight of Aasgaard's proposal. Rather than parental understanding, the reader of the *Infancy Gospel* is left with a doublet of unyielding interrogatives: first, Mary's reproach and then the cutting rejoinder from the twelve-year-old: "Why were you looking for me? Did you not know?" No, Mary and Joseph did not know. The question-and-question format implies precisely the opposite of "growing insight."

In the *Proto-gospel of James*, the temple is a site of knowledge and carnage. Meanwhile, Joseph and Mary resist the surveillance of Rome and hide from Herod's brutal investigators. In the *Infancy Gospel*, the temple is a place of recognition. But it is also a place of confusion. Some people in the *Infancy Gospel* recognize and understand the wisdom of the child Jesus, but these people do not include his parents. Jesus is confronted with a choice: stay in the temple, among those who understand, or return to live with parents who do not.

The parents remain mystified by this child, and the reader may feel the same way. But now, at least, the reader understands why Mary and Joseph *do not* understand their son. Mary knows the blessings and curses, the good and the bad that her strange child can do, and the combination has left her, like the reader, at a loss. Mary's own reproach of Jesus becomes in context a moment of sincere and reflective probing, a knowing question about not knowing: "Child, what have you done to us?" It also echoes the father's earlier interrogation of his five-year-old son: "Why do you say such things?"[59] The result, I submit, is a complex and sympathetic rendering of the parents in the "Finding of Jesus." As the *Infancy Gospel* tells it, Mary and Joseph arrive at the temple, hearts filled with anxiety, minds filled with questions about Jesus' disruptive childhood. They hope for the best and fear the worst.

Will Jesus, Mary, and Joseph remain a family? It is composed of a father who is not quite a father, a mother who is not quite a mother, and a son who is not quite a son. When Jesus denies Mary and Joseph their claims as parents by appealing to "the things of his father," he also disavows his place in their family as son. Each member of the trio stands askew of stable roles of father, mother, and son, which is why the move that the *Infancy Gospel* makes here, the way that it alters its source material, is crucial. Only here, in the *Infancy Gospel*, do scribes and Pharisees arrive to ask Mary the key question—the only one that matters: "Are you the mother of this child?" Mary, who had been rebuffed by Jesus only a moment earlier, steps into the void: "I am," she replies.[60]

Mary makes her choice. She will remain his mother. What will Jesus choose? Like the Gospel of Luke, the *Infancy Gospel* reports, "Then Jesus rose from there and followed his mother and was obedient to his parents."[61] The twelve-year-old Jesus, so recently prepared to abandon Mary and Joseph and live instead in the house of God, his father, suddenly turns about. When commentators discuss the parallel verse in the Lukan version (Luke 2:51), they focus on the "obedience" of the child. But what about the return home? In the Gospel of Luke, the prior family life of Jesus is not reported, so readers are left on their own to imagine what it might have once entailed and how it could be different after the scene in the temple. The *Infancy Gospel*, by contrast, fills in the space. It shows the good and the bad that took place during the previous seven years. What kind of home life awaits this family when they travel back to Nazareth? More of the same, or will things be different?

*   *   *

It is tempting to find something timeless in the Lukan story of the "Finding of Jesus." If François Bovon succumbs, he does so thoughtfully and humanely: "He does not do what his parents expect; he does what they do not wish. This makes them suffer, and women, above all, can identify with Mary's question: 'Child, why have you treated us (ἡμῖν) like this?' Like an adolescent, Jesus does not give in. He asserts his opinion with absolute matter-of-factness. As often in generational conflicts, the parents do not understand their children at the close of the argument, and, as often in such cases, the father remains silent."[62] This is a poignant reading of a tense moment of familial strain that is usually underappreciated in the rush to explicate Jesus' reference to "the things of my father." Sometimes, to be sure, the truth of human experience breaks through in the canonical gospels, and Luke 2:41–52 may be one of those moments. But Bovon's attention to some possibilities neglects other aspects of the story, especially the rhetorical drumbeat of parental failure. The ignorance of Mary and Joseph is more than typical—it is spectacular.

The *Infancy Gospel* offers readers the prelude to this confrontation in the "Finding of Jesus," anticipating but not resolving domestic misunderstanding. As such, the *Infancy Gospel* resists a didactic approach that would find in the childhood stories a straightforward lesson about Jesus or the faith of the readers.[63] The gospel is characterized instead by ambiguity and suspenseful gaps, reminding readers of what human beings do not know. In the face of acts of divine power and expressions of divine knowledge, mortal understanding reaches its limits. The family of Mary, Joseph, and Jesus, tested by these limits, accepts uncertainty and chooses to remain together. It is a tense and sometimes dysfunctional household, but a household nonetheless. This depiction of family life is not in line with the rigid definitions of a patriarchal hierarchy espoused by the Pastoral Epistles. But neither is it consistent with the "apostolic love triangle" of the Apocryphal Acts, which denies the worth of spousal and parental relationships. The *Infancy Gospel*, which portrays and seems to accept the static on the lines between members of the household, puts a fair amount of distance between it and other early Christian models of family life.

Why? Because we know so little about the specific historical circumstances of the writing and telling of the *Infancy Gospel of Thomas*, answers to this question must remain incomplete. In this chapter, I have suggested that it has something to do with ambiguity in the Lukan childhood account. So too it reflects what can be spotted in biblical narrative, another important source of storytelling for the family gospels, in the contrast between divine omniscience and human ignorance. It may also articulate a sense of the fragile position of Christianity, a new and strange religion, amid more time-tested claims of religious knowledge.[64] In skillful hands and before a sympathetic audience, incomprehensibility could be turned to advantage. The religion about "Christ crucified," Paul insists, is "a stumbling block to the Jews and foolishness to the Greeks" (1 Cor 1:23). In other words, the story of Jesus does not make sense, and that proves that it is true. Perhaps this is why the Lukan image of a clueless Mary and Joseph first captured the imagination of the author of the *Infancy Gospel*. The twelve-year-old Jesus, touched by heaven and thus mysterious, was a puzzle—even to, especially to, his parents.

Afterword

Together Again

If we did not have to live our lives amidst a fog of uncertainty about a whole range of matters that are actually of fundamental interest and importance to us, it would no longer be a human mode of existence that we would live. Instead we would become a being of another sort, perhaps angelic, perhaps machine-like, but certainly not human.

—Rescher, *Forbidden Knowledge and Other Essays*

Is not this Jesus, the son of Joseph, whose father and mother we know?

—John 6:42

All books about the canonical gospels must answer the question, Why add to the shelf another study of the Gospel of Matthew or the Gospel of John? All books about extracanonical gospels must answer a different question: Why add to the shelf a study of writings that were ultimately left out of the Christian biblical canon? Why spend time on writings that were excluded from the Christian scriptures? Doesn't this indicate the unimportance of such books—not only to the Christian religion but also to history? Some may attempt to rise above such questions by maintaining that all evidence from the past is precious. But scholars who study marginal texts ignore the "why" question at their peril. At a time when biblical scholars often lament the immense number of studies—so many that no individual could ever hope to read them all in the course of a single lifetime—it is important to reiterate why the present book deserves an audience.

The first chapter of this book sets out to answer the "why" question as clearly as possible. The *Infancy Gospel of Thomas* and the *Proto-gospel of James* are important and relevant to the study of early Christianity because they are about family. And family is a leading theme of scholarship on ancient Christians. The first Christians met in households, as Paul's letters show. He attempts to intervene in the affairs of Philemon's household, and he urges followers in Corinth to "remain unmarried as I am" since "the present form of this world is passing away" (1 Cor 7:8, 31). Apocalyptic fervor waned as the decades passed, but Christian authors continued to seek to shape notions of family life. The Pastoral Epistles, by an author writing in Paul's name, view the patriarchal household as the ideal setting for Christian teaching. Still, others explored theological issues through metaphors of domestic life: the relationship between Christ and his followers, according to the author of Ephesians, while a mystery, could be compared to the bond between husband and wife (Eph 5:31).

Leap forward to the second and third centuries and family life remains a crucial theme of early Christian literature. In the popular Apocryphal Acts, apostles find ways to break up conjugal matches. In martyr accounts, mothers give up the care of their newborn children, opting instead to join their Christian "brothers and sisters" in the arena. Rather than live with her baby under the care and protection of her pagan father, Perpetua chooses to die. To do otherwise would be to betray her loyalty to her Christian savior and spiritual family.[1]

Early Christian fascination with family life is the background for understanding the *Infancy Gospel* and the *Proto-gospel of James*. Having established this context, the rest of the book explores the contents of the *Infancy Gospel* and the *Proto-gospel of James*, focusing on the different kinds of family drama that emerge in the storytelling. The depiction at the heart of these stories belongs somewhere between or to the side of opposite poles. The holy household is rather chaotic, a far cry from the rhetoric of patriarchal order in the Pastoral Epistles. At the same time, the life of this family is at some remove from accounts of apostles breaking up couples in the Apocryphal Acts. When external or internal crises threaten to tear apart the trio, time and again Joseph, Mary, and Jesus affirm their familial bonds. Family ties persist in the family gospels even as the stories raise questions about household roles. Joseph is not quite a father or a husband, Mary is not quite a wife or a mother, and Jesus is not quite a son or, for that matter, even a child.[2] Yet together they make a family, or as I have argued, they *choose* to be a family over and over again.

So much for the main argument of this book. If it has provoked readers to look again at these accounts and to think of them as "family gospels" rather than as "infancy gospels," then I will count it a success. Readers may also wonder about a "how" question: how did the family gospels survive?[3] This is a good question but one that carries with it assumptions about the canon of the New Testament. Asking about the survival of the family gospels or any other volume in the vast library of early Christian parabiblical literature implies that a certain kind of process produced the New Testament. It was the end result of a "survival of the fittest." Such a view does not account for the continuing Christian interest in the life of the holy family. In the next section, we will look at an example of storytelling about the family of Jesus in the *History of Joseph the Carpenter*, an account dated to sometime in the fourth to sixth centuries. It betrays an acquaintance with the family gospels and features Jesus at the bedside of his 111-year-old father. In it we find a reflection of enduring Christian fascination with how much and how little the parents of Jesus understood about their unusual child.

A Loss in the Family

If Christian claims about texts and authority in the second and third centuries were fluid, the fourth century witnessed a hardening of lines for the Christian religion. Historical factors can be enlisted to explain the difference. Uncertainty was not one problem among many; it was the enemy: emperors and clergy had decided to work together to fashion creeds that would define, once and for all, the Christian God. At the same time, influential bishops began to insist on a closed canon of "New Testament" writings.[4] A high fence was built around the four canonical Gospels. Athanasius, bishop of Alexandria, put it this way in 367 CE: "In these books alone, the teaching of piety is proclaimed.

Let no one add to or subtract from them."[5] Athanasius envisioned "an irrefutably stabilized order of books."[6]

The family gospels are not included in Athanasius's "order of books," and we may wonder why. The dismal portrait of Jesus is routinely cited as the reason why the *Infancy Gospel of Thomas* was left out of the Christian canon.[7] While this may be one factor, it is not the only one. When we look for commentary on the family gospels or the *Infancy Gospel* in particular, the character of Jesus is not even an important factor. There is hardly unified opposition to the childhood stories about Jesus. From the perspective of John Chrysostom, childhood miracles of Jesus would contradict the Gospel of John's reporting of the "first miracle." In the same century, however, other Christian authorities were sanguine about the possibility of childhood stories. Epiphanius, a different fourth-century bishop, argues that Jesus "ought to have childhood miracles too, in order to deprive the other sects of an excuse to say that it is from the time of the Jordan that 'the Christ,' meaning the dove, came to him."[8] For Epiphanius, childhood miracles would prove that Jesus was divine from birth and not, as some Christian interpreters maintained, adopted by God at his baptism. If two fourth-century authorities could not agree on whether to accept the authenticity of childhood stories, there was some wiggle room for accounts such as the family gospels among Christian readers in that century and beyond. Perhaps the *Infancy Gospel of Thomas* and the *Proto-gospel of James* did not just barely escape the closing jaws of orthodoxy. On the contrary, for some arguments, childhood stories about Jesus may have come in handy.

John Chrysostom's objection to stories like those in the *Infancy Gospel* may have had as much to do with the ambiguity of the storytelling as it did with breaking the "first miracle" rule. For the portrayal of the ignorance and misunderstanding of Joseph and Mary, hinted at in the earlier gospels and elaborated upon in the family gospels, raises a disturbing question: can human beings ever truly understand anything about divine affairs? A troubling question for someone like John Chrysostom, perhaps, and yet he was willing to entertain the thought in his discussion of what Mary did and did not know about her child. The relationship of mother and child gave John Chrysostom the opportunity to advance points about divine power, the limits of human knowing, and familial affection.

These are the same issues explored by the family gospels, and they echo through the centuries in other Christian accounts. The exclusion of the family gospels from Athanasius's fourth-century canon did not impede the continuing fascination that ancient Christians had with the early family life of Jesus. The *History of Joseph the Carpenter*, a Coptic text that has been variously dated between the fourth and sixth centuries, is cited by specialists as a witness to the transmission of the family gospels.[9] The narrative framework of the account places the adult Jesus, on the Mount of Olives, teaching his disciples. Jesus begins to relate to them the story of the death of his father, Joseph. Like the book of Tobit, it is an example of the popular genre of "testament" literature. The *History of Joseph the Carpenter* begins by relating details that are familiar to readers from the *Proto-gospel of James*: that Joseph had a prior marriage and that Mary lived in the temple until she was twelve years old. Jesus also recalls details from the Synoptic accounts: the doubt of Joseph and the reassuring message of Gabriel, as well as the flight of the family to Egypt. And, in what is perhaps a repudiation of the more troubling aspects of the *Infancy Gospel*, Jesus says, "I called Mary my mother and Joseph my father, and I obeyed them in everything they told me. I never contradicted them, but I loved them dearly."[10]

Even so, the account does not erase entirely the memory of tensions between father and son. When Jesus turns to recalling father's finals hours, he begins by quoting Joseph's lament. It is a litany of physical aches and pains.[11] Jesus responds by going to his bedside to comfort him. Joseph's reaction is to praise Jesus as "truly God."[12] Then Joseph begins to confess to his own doubts and misunderstandings as a husband and father. First, he admits, "I did not understand, my Lord, nor do I know the mystery of your incredible birth; nor did I ever hear that a woman had conceived without a man, or that a virgin bore a child while sealed in her virginity."[13] All of this could be implied in the Synoptic infancy narratives. But I wonder if Joseph's "reminiscence" of serial doubts reflects both the Synoptic gospels and the *Proto-gospel of James*, in which he arrives at the cave in time to witness a strange series of events: first cloud cover; then a bright light; then, suddenly, an infant at the breast of Mary; and, finally, the examination of Salome.[14] Next, the dying Joseph recalls a moment from the childhood of Jesus, one that combines details from the *Infancy Gospel*, including the healings of Jesus and the skepticism and hostility provoked by his spectacles of power:

I remember also the day when the asp bit a boy and he died. His people surrounded you in order to deliver you to Herod. Your mercy laid hold of him: you raised him, even though they falsely charged you that it was you who killed him. And there was great joy in the house of the one who had died. I immediately took you by the ear and spoke with you saying, "Be prudent, my son!" You rebuked me at once and said, "If you were not my father according to the flesh, surely I would tell you what you did to me!"[15]

Joseph goes on to admit that he worries that his present suffering is the result of revenge for the way he treated the child Jesus: "Now then, my Lord and my God, supposing that you have settled accounts with me for that day and caused these fearful signs to fall upon me, I beseech your goodness not to bring me to your judgment."[16] Jesus, for his part, is moved by what he hears: "As my father Joseph was speaking, I could not refrain from shedding tears, and I cried, watching as death held sway over him and listening to the words of misery he was speaking."[17] He breaks down in tears. Mary, whom Jesus describes as "my beloved mother Mary, whose name is sweet to my mouth," sits nearby. She asks her son, "Woe to me, my beloved son. Is he perhaps going to die . . . your beloved and honorable father according to the flesh?"[18]

In some ways, the *History of Joseph the Carpenter* is quite unlike the family gospels. Joseph, for example, here seems to express a clearer understanding of the significance of Jesus than he does in the family gospels. As one scholar observes, in the *History of Joseph the Carpenter*, Joseph "recognizes the divine nature of his son."[19] In other ways, however, there is a convergence. The "deathbed confession" of Joseph shows not only the possibility of redemption and forgiveness but also that some Christians of the fourth century and beyond continued to think of the early family life of Jesus as a time of turmoil and confusion. This is why Joseph, as he lays dying, must ask his son's forgiveness. So too, like the earlier family gospels, the *History of Joseph the Carpenter* shows Joseph, Mary, and Jesus clinging to the ties that bind. Jesus may be in this account "truly the Son of God and son of man at once," but he is also, for a moment at least, a member of a family, weeping for his father and with his mother.

*   *   *

Neither the *Infancy Gospel of Thomas* nor the *Proto-gospel of James* is found in the New Testament shared by the major branches of the Christian religion—Roman Catholic, Orthodox, and Protestant. And yet some of the authoritative ideas of the faith, such as the notion of the perpetual virginity of Mary and the names of Mary's parents—embraced by many Catholics and Orthodox Christians—are found first in the storytelling of the family gospels.[20] Orthodox Christians include readings from the *Proto-gospel of James* on September 8, the day on which Mary's birth is celebrated in worship. The *Infancy Gospel of Thomas* has not enjoyed the same level of success in the mainstream of either Roman Catholic or Orthodox traditions. Yet, it remains intensely popular and authoritative among Ethiopic Orthodox Christians, embedded in a collection of stories known as the *Miracles of Jesus*.[21]

There are many other signs of the influence of the family gospels. The *Infancy Gospel of Thomas* shares at least one episode with the Qur'an: the story of a child Jesus turning toy birds into live ones.[22] A robust tradition about the holy family resting in their travel to Bethlehem is central to the historical veneration of Mary.[23] There is also the *Piacenza Pilgrim*, an account from the sixth century that describes the sacred sites of holy land pilgrimage. In it, the pilgrim describes a synagogue in Nazareth in which "there is kept the book in which the Lord wrote his ABC."[24]

But this book has been about the earliest readers. And I remain convinced that what was appealing about the family gospels for ancient Christians is their depiction of human relationships. The *Infancy Gospel* and the *Proto-gospel of James* suggest that if readers want to grasp the difference between human beings and the omniscient God they worship, they need look no further than the persistent misunderstanding that plagues human communication and interaction—what Andrew Solomon describes as "the terrifying, profound unknowability of even the most intimate human relationship."[25] This would be a message of deep despair if not for another facet of human existence, one that is also suggested by the family gospels: that, in this life, it is possible to stumble arm in arm with family and friends through the "fog of uncertainty" that blankets human minds. And this is why, for me, the lingering image from all of these stories is that of Joseph, Mary, and the twelve-year-old Jesus, reuniting at the temple and returning home, together.

That's some kind of family.

Notes

PREFACE

1. Mary Dzon discusses the image in the context of medieval storytelling about Jesus and Joseph ("Joseph and the Amazing Christ-Child," 135–36 n. 3).

2. *Inf. Gos. Thom.* 13.3.

INTRODUCTION

1. An exception is Allen, "The 'Protoevangelium of James' as an 'Historia,'" esp. 510, 512–15.

2. Some argue that this reflects the oral transmission of the gospel. See Aasgaard, *Childhood of Jesus*, 14–34, and Davis, *Christ Child*, 26–35.

3. The view that curiosity alone—that is, a desire to "fill in the gaps" of canonical narratives—was the impetus for these childhood stories restricts their significance. See, e.g., Ehrman, *Lost Christianities*, 206. Helmut Koester remarks on the "biographical" interest that prompted the stories (*Ancient Christian Gospels*, 312). It is not hard to find contempt for the *Infancy Gospel of Thomas* in the literature: "Crudely sensational" (Elliott, *The Apocryphal New Testament*, 68); "tasteless" (Enslin, "Along Highways and Byways," 84).

4. Burke, *De infantia Iesu.*

5. Davis, *Christ Child.*

6. Aasgaard, *Childhood of Jesus.* See too Bovon on the "curiosité des enfants" ("Évangiles canoniques et évangiles apocryphes," 25).

7. Glancy, *Corporal Knowledge,* and Vuong, *Gender and Purity.*

8. See Voicu, "Ways to Survival," 402–17.

9. For a succinct discussion of critical questions and evidence, see Gamble, "The New Testament Canon," 272–94.

10. Mussies, "Reflections on the Apocryphal Gospels," 597. Ronald Piper, more persuasively, contends that "the fourfold gospel had begun to achieve widening recognition as authoritative" ("The One, the Four, and the Many," 271).

11. As Reed notes, when Irenaeus argues for the "four-formed gospel," he "does not describe a 'Canon of Christian Scriptures' in any later sense of those terms. These texts are

not yet the literary guarantors of the sacred tradition, merely its special guardians" ("Εὐαγγέλιον: Orality, Textuality, and the Christian Truth," 45). Cf. Kellhoffer, " 'How Soon a Book' Revisited," 1–34.

12. See Davis, *Christ Child*, 20–21.

13. See Arnal, "Collection and Synthesis of 'Tradition,' " 193–215. See too Lieu, *Christian Identity*, 37–45.

14. Gamble, "New Testament Canon," 273.

15. Although it is likely that ancient Christian commentators did confuse the two. For discussion and sources, see Burke, *De infantia Iesu*, 38–41.

16. Brakke, "Scriptural Practices in Early Christianity," 263–80. See too Bovon, "Beyond the Canonical and the Apocryphal Books," 125–37. A good case for putting canonical and extracanonical on a level playing field has been made by Kazen, "Sectarian Gospels for Some Christians?" 561–78. See too Mitchell, "Patristic Counter-Evidence," 36–79.

17. On the difference between scripture and canon, see Sundberg, "Toward a Revised History," 452–61. See too Dungan, *Constantine's Bible*, 1–10.

18. Brakke, "Scriptural Practices," 275–76.

19. Brakke, "Scriptural Practices," 273.

20. Brakke illustrates this mode with an unlikely pairing: the "heretical" Marcion and Eusebius, the "orthodox" historian. They shared a methodology when it came to scrutinizing the authority attached to certain texts. Both approached Christian texts with a scholar's eye, each assessing the truthfulness of the writing at hand. See too Bovon, "The Reception and Use," 289–306.

21. As Brakke observes, "It is simply anachronistic to ask of writers of the second century which books were in their canon and which not—for the notion of a closed canon was simply not there" ("Scriptural Practices," 266).

22. François Bovon sees a similar relationship—"midway between the use of Luke as a source and the use of Luke as normative Scripture"—implied by the *Didache* and the *Apocalypse of Peter* ("The Reception and Use," 300). See too Mussie, "Reflections on the Apocryphal Gospels," 597–611; Burke, "Completing the Gospel," esp. 109–13.

23. Voiçu, "Ways to Survival," 401–17.

24. See Hock, *The Infancy Gospels*, 4, 84–85.

25. On the pseudonymous authorship of the family gospels, see Hock, *The Infancy Gospels*, 8–11, 90–91. The first chapter of the *Infancy Gospel of Thomas* attributes the account to "Thomas the Israelite," but this chapter is not found in the earliest versions of the text, leading scholars to conclude that it is secondary (Aasgaard, *Childhood of Jesus*, 40; see too Burke, *De infantia Iesu*, 205–6).

26. On the epilogue of the *Proto-gospel of James* (25.1), attributing the book to James (presumably the brother of Jesus, although this is not stated explicitly), see Vuong, *Gender and Purity*, 31–34.

27. Lily Vuong argues for a Syrian provenance of the *Proto-gospel of James* (*Gender and Purity*, 213–39).

28. Most scholars would accept these parameters on the basis of several factors,

including manuscript evidence and allusions in early Christian writings. For discussion of the *Infancy Gospel of Thomas*, see Burke, *De infantia Iesu*, 3–44, 201–5. Cf. Stephen Davis's argument for a later dating of the written account (*Christ Child*, 40–42). For the *Protogospel of James*, see Foster, "Reception of the Canonical Gospels," 284–88.

29. It is unlikely that either of the family gospels was familiar with the other one.

30. See Sim, "Matthew's Use of Mark," 176–92.

31. Boyarin, *Carnal Israel*, 14. See too Steven Weitzman's remarks about Jewish storytelling in the ancient world: "Storytelling did not act directly on the world, but it did help Jews to develop certain options and to keep them open, describing the world in ways that made it seem possible to shake off the yoke of foreign rule, or evade its notice or manipulate the king's power to one's own advantage" (*Surviving Sacrilege*, 32). Averil Cameron contends, "We still lack an analysis of late antique Christian writing that would do justice to its social dynamism and intellectual and literary force" (*Dialoguing in Late Antiquity*, 5). I would add that insights from postcolonial studies can illuminate subtle aspects of cultural negotiation found in ancient sources. Particularly important for my own thinking are Burrus, "Mimicking Virgins"; Jacobs, *Christ Circumcised*; and Nasrallah, *Christian Responses to Roman Art*.

32. Sternberg observes, "By the narrator's art, the historical texts applied to the fathers in the world [of biblical narrative] are perpetuated in the discourse addressed to the sons as a standing challenge to interpretation" (*Poetics of Biblical Narrative*, 48). Characters misunderstand things and thus enact a problem of interpretation, and the audience recognizes themselves in the enactment.

33. Sternberg's proposals have been subjected to sharp criticism: Fewell and Gunn, "Tipping the Balance," 193–212. See too Sternberg's equally sharp retort, "Biblical Poetics and Sexual Politics," 463–88. For a critical and constructive overview of strengths and weaknesses in Sternberg's approach, see Berlin, "Narrative Poetics in the Bible," 273–84.

34. Sternberg, *Poetics of Biblical Narrative*, 199–222, 235–37. See too Weitzman, "Before and After *The Art of Biblical Narrative*," 191–210.

35. Sternberg, *Poetics of Biblical Narrative*. Sternberg offers a few remarks on the difference between narrative in the Tanakh, which presumes a low "threshold of intelligibility," and narrative in the canonical gospels, which elevates mystery and secrecy and thus creates an exclusive class of "insiders" (48–49). "Nothing is more alien to the spirit of biblical narrative than discourse fashioned or meaning hidden across the sea [cf. Jesus telling parables on a boat in Mark 4], than speaking in riddles, than the distinction between spiritual insiders and carnal outsiders" (49). This view on the canonical gospels, as Sternberg admits, is wedded to Frank Kermode's brilliant but flawed analysis of the Gospel of Mark (*The Genesis of Secrecy*).

36. Nor do I ask readers to assume later Trinitarian and Christological propositions in reading the family gospels. Early Christian audiences believed that the figure of Jesus was possessed of supernatural power and authority. Ante-Nicene (no less than later) Christians argued about the scope of this claim. That said, our concern is not Christological propositions but storytelling about crises in the household of Mary, Joseph, and Jesus.

37. Canonical in Catholic and Orthodox bibles but not Protestant ones.

38. On the worth of parabiblical writings, see Reed, "Afterlives of New Testament Apocrypha," 401–25. See too Stephen Shoemaker's remarks on recent efforts to "remove the early Christian apocrypha from the shadow of the New Testament writings" ("Early Christian Apocryphal Literature," 521).

39. Kraemer, "Jewish Mothers and Daughters," 92.

40. Schellenberg, "Suspense, Simultaneity, and Divine Providence," 316.

41. See, e.g., Foster, "Reception of the Canonical Gospels," 289.

CHAPTER I

1. Matt 10:36 includes "and one's foes will be members of one's own household."

2. See Mark 13:12; cf. Matt 24:21; Luke 21:16. Rejection of family members can be found in other passages: "Whoever comes to me and does not hate father and mother, wife and children, brothers and sisters, yes, and even life itself, cannot be my disciple" (Luke 14:25; cf. Matt 10:37–38; see too Luke 9:59–60; cf. Matt 8:21–22).

3. Clark, "Antifamilial Tendencies in Ancient Christianity," 356–80. See too Cooper, "Approaching the Holy Household," 131–42.

4. All we know of *The True Doctrine* comes from quotations embedded in the Christian response of Origen, composed some seventy years later. For discussion, see Martin, *Inventing Superstition*, 140–59, esp. 147, 156. See too Frede, "Origen's Treatise *Against Celsus*," 131–55, esp. 134.

5. Origen, *Against Celsus* 3.55 (SC 136:130, ed. Borret; trans. Chadwick, 165–66, modified).

6. Origen, *Against Celsus* 3.44 (SC 136:104, ed. Borret; trans. Chadwick, 158).

7. On Christians as a threat to Celsus's vision of society and, specifically, on pagan worries about the "infiltration of family life," see Francis, *Subversive Virtue*, 131–79.

8. On adoption in Paul's letters to the Galatians and Romans, see Johnson Hodge, *If Sons, Then Heirs*. See too Peppard, *Son of God in the Roman World*, 134–48.

9. Wayne A. Meeks famously connects mobility and the resultant "status inconsistency" to the spread of Pauline Christianity (*First Urban Christians*, esp. 19–23, 190–92). See too the evocative and still useful sketch of MacMullen, *Roman Social Relations*, 88–120. Peter Garnsey and Richard Saller sound a note of caution (*Roman Empire*, 123–25).

10. Frilingos, "For My Child, Onesimus," 91–104. On familial metaphors, see Lassen, "Roman Family," 115. Michael Penn's study of the ritual of kissing illuminates the early Christian conception of a "kinship of faith" (*Kissing Christians*, esp. 31–37).

11. *Acts of Paul and Thecla* 5 (trans. Elliott, 365).

12. *Acts of Paul and Thecla* 43 (trans. Elliott, 372).

13. For an illuminating discussion, see Cooper and Corke-Webster, "Conversion, Conflict, and the Drama," 169–83.

14. *Acts of Thomas* 12 (trans. Elliott, 452).

15. *Acts of Thomas* 12 (trans. Elliott, 452).

16. As Judith Perkins observes, "By advocating universal chastity, they implicitly proposed an end to the social structure" (*Suffering Self*, 29). See too Cooper, *Virgin and the Bride*, 55.

17. Perkins, *Suffering Self*, 41–76. Virginia Burrus discerns a far more ironic and ambivalent perspective on identity in a comparison of ancient pagan, Jewish, and Christian novels ("Mimicking Virgins," 49–88).

18. Jacobs, "Family Affair," 105–38.

19. Jacobs, "Family Affair," 125.

20. On the "apostolic love triangle," see Cooper, *Virgin and the Bride*, 51–56. See too Schroeder, "Embracing the Erotic," 123–37.

21. *Acts of Thomas* 12 (trans. Elliott, 452).

22. *Acts of Thomas* 13 (trans. Elliott, 452).

23. *Advice to the Bride and Groom* (trans. Russell, 5–13). On Plutarch, see Jacobs, "Family Affair," 115–17. Cf. Cooper, *Virgin and the Bride*, 5–11.

24. For a recent sociohistorical study of Roman-era expectations in marriage, see Caldwell, *Roman Girlhood*, 134–65.

25. For discussion of scholarship and sources, see Osiek and MacDonald, *A Woman's Place*, 118–43.

26. See MacDonald, "Beyond Identification of the Topos," 65–90. MacDonald contends that "the codes appear to actualize or articulate conventional arrangements in household church communities that were probably always present in the Pauline churches alongside challenges to traditional family structures through various forms of asceticism and the allegiance to church groups of subordinate members of non-believing households" (78). For a different perspective, which argues for mimicry and the "empire-renouncing logic" of Colossians, see Maier, "Sly Civility," 323–49.

27. MacDonald, *Legend and the Apostle*.

28. As Harry O. Maier observes, "The Pastorals drew on the vocabulary and commonplaces associated with [*homonoia*] to articulate the ideals and values addressees are to pursue" (*Picturing Paul in Empire*, 171–72).

29. As Margaret Y. MacDonald contends, under the Roman Empire, "[n]otions of civic rule are closely tied to the dominion of the *paterfamilias*" ("Beyond Identification of the Topos," 66).

30. On "pictures of harmony" in Roman imagery, see Maier, *Picturing Paul in Empire*, 73. For the late Republic, see Dixon, "Sentimental Ideal of the Roman Family," 99–113.

31. On the Augustan portrayal of empire as an affectionate and disciplined *domus*, see Lacey, "Patria Potestas," 121–44.

32. Ando, *Imperial Ideology and Provincial*, 206–75.

33. For discussion of the legislation, see Treggiari, *Roman Marriage*, 60–80; see too Hopkins, *Death and Renewal*, 78–97.

34. Brown, *Body and Society*, 16.

35. Gibson, "Ephesians 5:21–33 and the Lack," 162–77.

36. Carolyn Osiek argues that Jesus extends but does not abolish family values ("Family in Early Christianity," 1–24). See too Elliott, "Jesus Movement Was Not Egalitarian," 173–210.

37. Horsley, *Liberation of Christmas*, 23–38.

38. On "conflicting details," see Brown, *Birth of the Messiah*, 33–37.

39. Burrus, "The Gospel of Luke," 133–55.

40. On household and family in the infancy narratives, see Moxnes, *Putting Jesus in His Place*, 32–38.

41. NRSV, modified.

42. NRSV, modified. My translation follows that of De Jonge, "Sonship, Wisdom, and Infancy," 317–54. In the genealogy of the Gospel of Luke, the claim of Joseph's paternity is ambiguous: "He was the son (as was thought) [ἐνομίζετο] of Joseph" (3:23).

43. On the "Marcosians," see Davis, *Christ Child*, 121–25.

44. Irenaeus contends that the Marcosians "falsely fit to that standard some of the things put in the Gospel [ἐν Εὐαγγελίῳ]" (*Haer.* 1.20.2 [SC 264:290], ed. Rousseau and Doutreleau; trans. Unger, 76).

45. "Apocryphal and spurious writings" (ἀποκρύφων καὶ νόθων γραφῶν; *Haer.* 1.20.1 [SC 264:288], ed. Rousseau and Doutreleau; trans. Unger, 76).

46. "That he alone knew the unknowable" (ὡς αὐτοῦ μόνου τὸ ἄγνωστον ἐπισταμένου; *Haer.* 1.20.1 [SC 264:289], ed. Rousseau and Doutreleau; trans. Unger, 76).

47. *Inf. Gos. Thom.* 13.1–3 is discussed in Chapter 3. Not only the Marcosians appreciated this story, which they take as being about the alpha privative (expressing negation in Greek). The contemporaneous *Epistula Apostolorum* includes a report of the same story in its opening summary of Jesus' activities (*Ep. Apos.* 4 [trans. Elliott, 559]).

48. *Haer.* 1.20.2 (SC 264:290, ed. Rousseau and Doutreleau; trans. Unger, 76, modified). Origen, meanwhile, fastens on the image of the parents searching for Jesus and turns the story into an invitation to Christians to search the scriptures for truth (*Homilies on Luke* 18.2–3, 19.4–5).

49. *Haer.* 1.20.3 (SC 264:294, ed. Rousseau and Doutreleau; trans. Unger, 77).

50. See Blake Leyerle's study of children in John Chrysostom's scriptural commentaries and adult "problems of cultural reproduction" ("Appealing to Children," 243–70, at 270).

51. See Burke, *De Infantia*, 6.

52. "Childhood deeds" (παιδικά; *Hom. Jo.* 17.3 [PG 59:110], trans. Goggin, 167).

53. Aasgaard, *Childhood of Jesus*, 178.

54. Cf. John 6:42: "They were saying, 'Is not this Jesus, the son of Joseph, whose father and mother we know? How can he now say, I have come down from heaven?'"

55. Quotations are from John Chrysostom, *Hom. Jo.* 21.2 (PG 59:130; trans. Goggin, 205–6, modified).

56. "Implanted in her the suspicion" (ἐνέθηκε τὴν ὑπόνοιαν).

57. See Brown, *Birth of the Messiah*, 480–81.

58. "He was quickly overshadowed" (ἐξέφηνεν ἑαὐτον συνησκίασε; *Hom. Matt.* 10.3 [PG 57:186], my trans.).

59. "Things which the Jews had never seen nor heard": a striking parallel to language in *Inf. Gos. Thom.* 17.3. Günther Schmahl suggests that this notion is already incipient in the Lukan story ("Lk 2,41–52 und die Kindheitserzählung," 249–58, at 252).

CHAPTER 2

1. On *virginitas in partu* prior to the fourth century, see Hunter, *Marriage, Celibacy, and Heresy*, 171–87. See too Lillis, "Paradox *in Partu*," 1–28.

2. *Prot. Jas.* 20.1.

3. *Prot. Jas.* 20.2.

4. *Inf. Gos. Thom.* 4.1. Here my translation follows the wording of Jesus' curse in the vast majority of witnesses to the text. Gs, on which Burke's edition is based, is the only witness to include the phrase "Cursed be for you and your leader." See n. 21.

5. *Inf. Gos. Thom.* 4.2.

6. On intratextual and extratextual audiences, see Bartsch, *Decoding the Ancient Novel*, 3–40.

7. On Christian spectacles of violence, see the classic essay of Davis, "The Rites of Violence," 152–87. In a study of the potency of "tableaux of perversion" in religious history, David Frankfurter argues that descriptions of "monstrous" outsiders throw audiences of insiders into a cycle of disavowal and participation (*Evil Incarnate*, 129–67).

8. On the persuasive power of early Christian storytelling, see Averil Cameron's claim: "The better these stories were constructed, the better they functioned as structure-maintaining narratives, and the more their audiences were disposed to accept them as true" (*Christianity and the Rhetoric*, 93). Cf. Morgan, "History, Romance, and Realism," 221–64, esp. 222.

9. *Inf. Gos. Thom.* 2.3.

10. *Inf. Gos. Thom.* 3.1.

11. *Inf. Gos. Thom.* 3.1.

12. *Inf. Gos. Thom.* 3.2.

13. *Inf. Gos. Thom.* 3.3.

14. On the cursing of holy figures, see Burke, *De infantia Iesu*, 276–81. See too Walter Rebell on the child Jesus as a "trickster" figure (*Neutestamentliche Apokryphen und Apostolische Väter*, 134–36). On childhood as a symbol for peace in early Christian literature, see Bovon, "The Child and the Beast," 369–92.

15. Matthew does not remark on whether it was the season for figs (21:18–22). On a parallel between the "fig tree" pericope and the withering of the son of Annas in the *Infancy Gospel*, see Davis, *Christ Child*, 90.

16. "Without having done him any harm" (μηδὲν βλάψαν αὐτον; Luke 4:35).

17. See Hock, *Infancy* Gospels, 109, n. on 3.2. For examples of retributive curses, see Gager, *Curse Tablets and Binding*, 175–99.

18. *Inf. Gos. Thom.* 4.1.

19. See Davis, *Christ Child*, 64–91.

20. "Tore into" (διερράγη; *Inf. Gos. Thom* 4.1).

21. Davis appeals to one version of the wording of the curse, which is unique to Gs: "Cursed be your ruler [ὁ ἡγεμών σου]!" The story thus is an "agonistic scene—one that dramatizes the fate of a young soul whose hegemon failed to provide sound guidance and who therefore had become a threat to others" (*Christ Child*, 87 and 265, n. 60). But it is Jesus who clearly poses a threat to others in the *Infancy Gospel*. On the increasing Christian interest in divine guides in the third and fourth centuries, see Muehlberger, *Angels in Late Ancient*, 89–118.

22. See variants in Burke, *De infantia Iesu*, 306 n. 3.

23. *Inf. Gos. Thom.* 4.1.

24. *Inf. Gos. Thom.* 4.2.

25. *Inf. Gos. Thom.* 5.1.

26. Cf. Burke, *De infantia Iesu*, 307 n. 9.

27. *Inf. Gos. Thom.* 5.1–2. A different set of manuscripts (Ga) includes here "Every word he says," they say, "good or bad [εἴτε καλὸν εἴτε κακόν], has become a deed and wonder."

28. Cameron, *Christianity and the Rhetoric*, 76.

29. Cameron, *Christianity and the Rhetoric*, 78–79.

30. "Theatricalization of death" is Steven Weitzman's phrase (*Surviving Sacrilege*, 154).

31. See Kathleen Coleman's discussion of Martial, *Liber spectaculorum* 8 ("Fatal Charades," 63).

32. In addition to Coleman, "Fatal Charades," see Bartsch, *Actors in the Audience*, and Barton, *Sorrows of the Ancient Romans*.

33. On Johannine irony, see the classic sociological reading of Wayne A. Meeks in "Man from Heaven," 44–72.

34. Gleason, "Mutilated Messengers," 84.

35. Josephus, *Jewish War* 5.450 (trans. Thackeray, 341). Quoted by Gleason, "Mutilated Messengers," 82.

36. Gleason, "Mutilated Messengers," 51.

37. On parental grief in Plutarch, see Keith Bradley, "Images of Childhood," 183–96, esp. 183–85. See the still valuable assessment of Mark Golden, "Did the Ancients Care?" 152–63. Golden dismantles the idea that widespread infanticide somehow inured parents to the death of offspring, arguing that exposure "could coexist with, and even be caused by, care for other children" (159). For a similar perspective, see Wiedemann on Fronto (*Adults and Children*, 97), and Nasrallah, "Grief in Corinth," 109–40. Note Gleason's apt observation on the importance of empathy in spectacles of bodily violence: "such spectacles would affect the spectators' behavior only to the extent that they felt connected to the body of the victim," forcing them to see "what they would rather not see" ("Mutilated Messengers," 81–82, 90).

38. *Inf. Gos. Thom.* 4.2.

39. *Inf. Gos. Thom.* 5.1.

40. *Inf. Gos. Thom.* 8.1.

41. *Inf. Gos. Thom.* 8.2. Tony Burke sees in this passage an "appreciation of Johannine thought" (Chartrand-Burke, "Authorship and Identity," 35).

42. *Inf. Gos. Thom.* 8.2.

43. *Inf. Gos. Thom.* 8.2.

44. *Inf. Gos. Thom.* 9.1.

45. *Inf. Gos. Thom.* 9.2.

46. *Inf. Gos. Thom.* 9.3. Gs adds, "Jesus said to him: 'Fall asleep!' "

47. Meir Sternberg defines *suspense* this way: "In art as in life, suspense derives from incomplete knowledge about a conflict (or some other contingency) looming in the future" (*Poetics of Biblical Narrative*, 264).

48. Gleason, "Truth Contests and Talking," 287–313.

49. Gleason, "Truth Contests and Talking," 294.

50. Apuleius, *Metamorphoses*, 2.20–30 (ed. and trans. Hanson).

51. *Acts of Peter* 12 (trans. Elliott, 408–9).

52. Gleason, "Truth Contests and Talking," 297–302. See too Jeremy Schott's remarks on oracles and forensic oratory ("Language," 64–71). On child oracles in antiquity, see Johnston, "Charming Children," 97–117.

53. Ramsay MacMullen observes, "Common or not [i.e., judicial savagery], depending on time and place, pictures of brutal routines of law in action were no doubt stored away in the memory of every citizen" ("Judicial Savagery in the Roman," 207). See too Potter, "Performance, Power, and Justice," 129–59.

54. On *Prot. Jas.* as an *encomium*, see Hock, *Infancy Gospels,* 16.

55. See Vuong, *Gender and Purity* (52–54), for a survey of scholarship on this problem. See too Andrew T. Lincoln's recent evaluation of the *Proto-gospel of James* (*Born of a Virgin?* 93–94). On the *Toledot Yeshu,* Celsus, and Celsus's Jewish informant, see Gager and Ahuvia, "Some Notes on Jesus," 997–1019.

56. H. R. Smid describes the claim of virginity as "empirically proved" (*Protevangelium Jacobi,* 142). Clement of Alexandria notes that Mary's virginity was examined (*Stromateis* 7.16.93).

57. See David G. Hunter: "Mary's sole merit, according to the *Protevangelium,* is her sexual purity, and the sole purpose of the narrative is to exalt and defend that purity" (*Marriage, Celibacy, and Heresy,* 178). See too Lily Vuong's argument that the "characterization of Mary as pure involves not her sexual purity and therefore her moral purity, but also a concern for her ritual, menstrual, and even geneaological purity" (*Gender and Purity,* 243).

58. On Mary as a model of asceticism, see Klutz, "The Value of Being Virginal," 71–87.

59. See Glancy, *Corporal Knowledge,* 106. Glancy does not treat *Prot. Jas.* in isolation but as part of a network of early Christian writings, from the *Odes of Solomon* to the *Ascension of Isaiah* to Tertullian, dedicated to the constructing the body of the virgin Mary.

60. See Glancy, *Corporal Knowledge*, and Vuong, *Gender and Purity*.

61. "I do not know how it got inside me" (οὐ γινώσκω πόθεν ἐστὶν ἐν ἐμοί; *Prot. Jas.* 13.3, modified).

62. On the tests, see Vuong, *Gender and Purity*, 171–89.

63. *Prot. Jas.* 15.1–4.

64. *Prot. Jas.* 16.1.

65. *Prot. Jas.* 16.3. Does the phrase betray literary dependence on the disputed *pericope adulterae* (John 8:1–11)? See Petersen, "OUDE EGŌ SE [KATA] KRINŌ," 191–221, esp. 214–15.

66. See Foskett's overview (*A Virgin Conceived*, 74–122). Cf. Burrus, "Mimicking Virgins," 49–88, esp. 49–54.

67. Chew, "Achilles Tatius and Parody," 64. See too Morales, *Vision and Narrative in Achilles*, 206–7, 220–26.

68. On *Scheintod* ("apparent death") in the Greek novel, see MacAlister, *Dreams and Suicides*, 23–33. See too Perkins, "Fictive *Scheintod*," 396–418.

69. *Prot. Jas.* 19.2.

70. *Prot. Jas.* 19.2. Mary breastfeeds immediately, while Anna waits until the end of a period of purification (*Prot. Jas.* 5.8). On this difference, see Glancy, *Corporal Knowledge*, 112–14.

71. *Prot. Jas.* 19.3.

72. *Prot. Jas.* 20.1.

73. On ancient models of female sexual anatomy, see Foskett, *A Virgin Conceived*, 33–36, and now Lillis, "Paradox *in Partu*," 8–16. On the lack of evidence for Roman-era procedures of inspecting female "intactness," see Caldwell, *Roman Girlhood and the Fashioning*, 63.

74. *Prot. Jas.* 20.1.

75. Salome watching her burning hand is a popular theme in early Christian art (Cartlidge and Elliott, *Art and the Christian*, 90–94, 4.11–13). Romans told a story of a legendary hero, Mucius Scaevola, who watched his own hand burn; see Barton, "Savage Miracles," 41–71.

76. See Glancy, *Corporal Knowledge*, 117, and Vuong, *Gender and Purity*, 188–89.

77. Glancy observes, "Her virginity, her body, is untouchable" (*Corporal Knowledge*, 117). See too Vuong, *Gender and Purity*, 182–90, and Foskett, *Virgin Conceived*, 36–44.

78. *Prot. Jas.* 20.2. Hock remarks on the *Proto-gospel of James*'s "bookish acquaintance" with Judaism and midrash (*Infancy Gospels*, 10–11). See too Allen, "The 'Protoevanglium of James' as an 'Historia,'" 513.

79. Is Salome a "Jewish informant" for an early Christian audience? On the figure of the Jewish informant in early Christian writings, see Jacobs, *Remains of the Jews*, 56–100. Alternatively, Salome's aggression may reflect a violent anti-Jewish stereotype; see Matthews, *Perfect Martyr*, 3–26.

80. On images of Jews and Judaism in second-century Christian texts and the contrast to a more fluid reality "on the ground," see Lieu, *Image and Reality*. A complementary

analysis of image and reality, reaching deeper into late antiquity, may be found in Boyarin, *Border Lines*.

81. *Prot. Jas.* 20.3.

82. On the "haunting sensuality" of the nursing Mary, see Brown, "Notion of Virginity," 438–39.

CHAPTER 3

1. *Inf. Gos. Thom.* 6.1–4.

2. *Inf. Gos. Thom.* 13.1–3.

3. Burke, *De infantia Iesu*, 287.

4. *Inf. Gos. Thom.* 13.1.

5. "Minister" (λειτουργῶν; *Prot. Jas.* 4.1).

6. "Sanctuary" (ἁγίασμα; *Prot. Jas.* 6.1).

7. *Prot. Jas.* 5.1. Lily Vuong remarks on "the continued power and importance of the Temple and its priesthood" in the *Proto-gospel of James* (" 'Let Us Bring Her Up,' " 425). See too Horner, "Jewish Aspects of the Protevangelium," 313–35.

8. See Aasgaard, *Childhood of Jesus*, 79–82 and 206–7, citing Origen, *Against Celsus* 3.55.

9. On the "cathartic release" of such stories, see Burke, *De infantia Iesu*, 316 n. 2.

10. An overview may be found in Jaeger, *Early Christianity and Greek Paideia*, 36–46.

11. Kaster, *Guardians of Language*, 77.

12. Justin Martyr, *First Apology* 60 (trans. Hardy, 281). On Justin, see Lyman, "The Politics of Passing." See too Laura Nasrallah's discussion of the second-century trio of Tatian, Lucian, and Justin (*Christian Reponses to Roman Art*, 51–84).

13. Beavis, "Pluck the Rose," 411–23. Whether Christians should be schoolteachers is a different question. Beavis discusses the evidence of Tertullian and the more "lenient" Hippolytus in the *Apostolic Tradition* 16 (416–17).

14. Beavis, "Pluck the Rose," 416. See too Clark, "The Fathers and the Children," 1–28.

15. Beavis, "Pluck the Rose," 422.

16. On "symbolic capital" and the Hellenistic intellectual tradition, see Whitmarsh, *Greek Literature*, 19.

17. Tim Whitmarsh observes, "The centrality of education to cultural definition is of course definitively Greek and definitively postclassical; *paideia* is a primary marker of civilized Hellenism" (*Beyond the Second Sophistic*, 221).

18. Goldhill, "Introduction," 17. See too Watts, *City and School*, 6–7.

19. Marrou, *History of Education*, 99. See too Thomas Wiedemann's remark: education was responsible for creating the "future citizen community" (*Adults and Children*, 32). A more recent discussion is Cribiore, *Gymnastics of the Mind*, 1–12.

20. See Perkins, *Roman Imperial Identities*, 27.

21. Plutarch, *Life of Cicero*, 45.

22. On the "commodification of *paideia*," see Whitmarsh, *Greek Literature*, 258. For a contemporary study of the commodification of knowledge involving, in this case, the packaging of Islamic law as a "discrete body of knowledge" to be acquired by American Muslims from "authentic" experts in cities abroad, see Grewal, *Islam Is a Foreign* Country, esp. 199.

23. Greg Woolf observes, "Romans drove an ideological wedge between the inventors of civilization and the Greeks of their own day" ("Becoming Roman, Staying Greek," 120).

24. *On Salaried Posts* 25 (trans. Harmon, 453).

25. Nasrallah, *Christian Responses to Roman Art*, 64.

26. Tim Whitmarsh remarks, "Teaching is both conservative in that it replicates the social order, and subversive, in that it transforms statuses and *redistributes* social power" (*Greek Literature*, 93, italics mine). So too Whitmarsh contends that redistribution was constantly occurring along multiple axes in the Roman period, a result of the ostensible "pluralist accessibility" of *paideia*, which made "power and prestige accessible to those who [were] notionally excluded" (*Greek Literature*, 130).

27. See Whitmarsh, *Greek Literature*, 118–29.

28. On examples such as Favorinus of Gaul, see Gleason, *Making Men*, 3–20.

29. Note the salient point made by Virginia Burrus: "Who is a 'Greek'? Who is a 'Roman'? (Who, for that matter, a 'barbarian'?) Such questions, although answered with confidence by many ancient writers, raise particular challenges for the contemporary historian" ("Mimicking Virgins," 49). See too Schott, "Porphyry on Christians and Others," 277–314.

30. *The Dream* 1 (trans. Harmon, 215). On *The Dream*, see Whitmarsh, *Greek Literature*, 122–23.

31. "Thrashings" (πλήγας; *Dream* 2 [trans. Harmon, 217]).

32. Lucian, *The Dream* 2 (trans. Harmon, 217).

33. Lucian, *The Dream* 7 (trans. Harmon, 221). The personified Craft "speaks in barbarisms" (βαρβαΐζουσα; *The Dream* 8).

34. *The Dream* 11 (trans. Harmon, 225).

35. Lucian would be forced to confront criticism. He later retracted his sarcastic put-down of Greek masters in *On Salaried Posts*, acknowledging in *The Apology (for On Salaried Posts)* that he had also turned acquired *paideia* to advantage, and his performance had been rewarded with an administrative post in Roman Egypt. See Jones, *Culture and Society in Lucian* (1986).

36. *The Dream* 13 (trans. Harmon, 227).

37. *The Dream* 3 (trans. Harmon, 217).

38. *The Dream* 16 (trans. Harmon, 231).

39. *The Dream* 9 (trans. Harmon, 223, modified).

40. *The Dream* 15 (trans. Harmon, 229).

41. *The Dream* 18 (trans. Harmon, 233).

42. On the role of parents in Roman-era Greek education, see Cribiore, *Gymnastics of the Mind*, 102–24.

43. On the coherence of the three classroom episodes, see Paulissen, "Jésus à l'école l'enseignement," 153–75. While the classroom stories were likely inspired by the Lukan story of the twelve-year-old Jesus in the temple, differences in setting and characters set it off as a distinct case to which I will return in Chapter 5.

44. Davis, *Christ Child*, 100.

45. Davis, *Christ Child*, 104.

46. Readers of the Gospel of Luke know a tax collector named Zacchaeus (Luke 19:1–10).

47. *Inf. Gos. Thom.* 6.2.

48. *Inf. Gos. Thom.* 6.2b.

49. *Inf. Gos. Thom.* 6.2d.

50. See Saller, "Corporal Punishment, Authority, and Obedience," 144–65, and Shaw, "The Family in Late Antiquity," 3–51, esp. 21–24.

51. *Inf. Gos. Thom.* 6.2f.

52. *Inf. Gos. Thom.* 6.2f.

53. *Inf. Gos. Thom.* 6.3.

54. *Inf. Gos. Thom.* 6.2.

55. Cf. Aasgaard, *Childhood of Jesus*, 105.

56. David Frankfurter links this passage to "fascination with the hieroglyph" ("The Magic of Writing," 189–221, here 211). On the mystical powers of letters, see Davis, *Christ Child*, 119.

57. *Inf. Gos. Thom.* 6.4.

58. *Inf. Gos. Thom.* 13.1.

59. *Inf. Gos. Thom.* 7.1.

60. *Inf. Gos. Thom.* 7.1.

61. *Inf. Gos. Thom.* 7.2.

62. *Inf. Gos. Thom.* 7.3.

63. Talbert, "Prophecies of Future Greatness," 129–41. See too Cox, *Biography in Late Antiquity*, esp. 22–23, 34, and Carp, *"Puer senex,"* 736–39.

64. Philo, *On Moses* 1.5.21 (trans. Colson). For discussion, see Perrot, "Les récits d'enfance," 481–518, esp. 497–504 on Moses.

65. Philo, *On Moses* 1.5.22 (trans. Colson).

66. Cf. Davis, *Christ Child*, on agonistic setting. In *An Ethiopian Story*, the heroine Charicleia fights against a marriage arranged by her father, arguing that the union goes against the *paideia* he himself taught (2.33.5). For discussion, see Whitmarsh, *Greek Literature*, 93.

67. See Burridge, *What Are the Gospels?*

68. *Inf. Gos. Thom.* 7.4.

69. See Burke, *De infantia Iesu*, 287.

70. *Inf. Gos. Thom.* 10 (water), 15 (baking).

71. *Inf. Gos. Thom.* 11. On the rural motifs of the *Infancy Gospel*, see Aasgaard, *Childhood of Jesus*, 53–72.

72. *Inf. Gos. Thom.* 12.

73. *Inf. Gos. Thom.* 13.1.

74. *Inf. Gos. Thom.* 13.2.

75. *Inf. Gos. Thom.* 13.2.

76. *Inf. Gos. Thom.* 13.3.

77. *Inf. Gos. Thom.* 14.1.

78. *Inf. Gos. Thom.* 14.2.

79. See Burke, *De infantia Iesu*, 330 n. 4.

80. *Inf. Gos. Thom.* 14.2.

81. *Inf. Gos. Thom.* 14.3.

82. *Inf. Gos. Thom.* 14.3.

83. *Inf. Gos. Thom.* 14.4.

84. Foster, "The Education of Jesus," 333. Foster sees the child Jesus resisting the "inflexible intellectual gymnastics of the classroom," as described by Cribiore (*Gymnastics of the Mind*, 161–68).

85. Aasgaard, *Childhood of Jesus*, 106–7.

86. On the education of girls in antiquity, see Bloomer, "The Ancient Child in School," 448–50.

87. "Make known" (φανερώσει; *Prot. Jas.* 7.2, modified).

88. *Prot. Jas.* 7.3. Beverly Gaventa remarks, "The vivid and enchanting picture of a child dancing in the temple epitomizes Mary's sacred purity" (*Mary: Glimpses*, 113).

89. Earlier, an angel promises Anna, "Your offspring will be spoken of throughout the entire world" (*Prot. Jas.* 4.1).

90. On the temple as a source of divine knowledge and angelic visitation in early Jewish sources, see Klawans, *Purity, Sacrifice and the Temple*, 111–44.

91. For biblical background, see Smid, *Protevangelium Jacobi*, 75–80. Megan Nutzman contends that Mary represents three groups of women allowed in the temple: accused adulteresses, girl weavers of the temple curtain, and female Nazirites ("Mary in the *Protevangelium*," 551–78). On the *Proto-gospel of James*, Mary, and the temple veil in Christian tradition, see Constas, *Proclus of Constantinople*, 325–28.

92. *Prot. Jas.* 23.1.

93. Samuel's mother, Hannah, is childless for many years. She prays for a child; finally, after vowing to dedicate her offspring to the service of the Lord, she conceives and bears a son, Samuel. Once he is weaned, she leaves Samuel with the priest Eli. Samuel grows up in the house of the Lord in Shiloh. For discussion, see Smid, *Protevangelium Jacobi*, 57–58. On Christian "imitative historiography," see Fitzmyer, *Luke the Theologian*, 65.

94. *Prot. Jas.* 1.1.

95. *Prot. Jas.* 1.2–3.

96. *Prot. Jas.* 1.3. It is unclear what Joachim consults. The term "records" or "book" is not supplied in the Greek text. Smid suggests "Holy Scripture" (*Protevangelium Jacobi*, 28); Hock suggests a "genealogical register" (*Infancy Gospels*, 33, n. on *Prot. Jas.* 1.6).

97. "Until the Lord my God pays me a visit" (ἔως ἐπισκέψηταί με Κύριος ὁ θεός μου; *Prot. Jas.* 1.4, modified).

98. *Prot. Jas.* 2.1–4.

99. "Headband" (κεφαλοδέσμιον; *Prot. Jas.* 2.2).

100. Judith reproaches Anna for suspecting her of casting an evil eye: "Why would I curse you, just because you haven't listened to me?" (*Prot. Jas.* 2.3).

101. *Prot. Jas.* 4.1.

102. *Prot. Jas.* 4.2.

103. Cf. Exod 28:1–39.

104. For a discussion of the possibilities, see De Strycker (*La forme la plus ancienne*, 85). Vuong contends that Reuben is wrong: Joachim is not childless because of unrighteousness; he is instead "childless among the righteous" (*Gender and Purity*, 72).

105. *Prot. Jas.* 5.1. Cf. 1 Sam 2:1.

106. Cf. Sarah in Gen. 21:6–7.

107. δῶρον (*Prot. Jas.* 4.1). "Entire life" (πάσας τὰς ἡμέρας τῆς ζωῆς αὐτοῦ; *Prot. Jas.* 4.1).

108. Vuong, *Gender and Purity*, 80–82, 88–100, 426–29.

109. On family and sacrifice, see Townsend, "Bonds of Flesh and Blood," 214–31.

110. *Prot. Jas.* 6.1.

111. *Prot. Jas.* 7.2.

112. *Prot. Jas.* 8.1.

113. See Nutzman, "Mary in the *Protevangelium*," 563–70.

114. *Prot. Jas.* 8.2.

115. *Prot. Jas.* 8.3.

116. "Into his safekeeping" (εἰς τήρησιν ἑαυτῷ; *Prot. Jas.* 9.1).

117. *Prot. Jas.* 9.2.

118. *Prot. Jas.* 9.2.

119. *Prot. Jas.* 10.1.

120. *Prot. Jas.* 10.1.

121. *Prot. Jas.* 10.2.

122. *Prot. Jas.* 11.1–3.

123. Origen, *Against Celsus*, 1.28–32. Van Stempvoort makes the case ("The Protevangelium Jacobi," 414–15). See too Vuong, *Gender and Purity*, 35–37.

124. *Prot. Jas.* 12.1–2.

125. Matt 27:51; cf. Mark 15:38, Luke 23:44. On the significance of the temple and its destruction in the Synoptic portrayals of Jesus, see Fredriksen, *From Jesus to Christ*, 177–204.

126. Like the earlier gospels, the family gospels tell stories about a temple that no longer exists. On Christian authors blaming the destruction of the temple on the people of Israel, see Shepherdson, "Paschal Politics," 233–60, esp. 238–40. On Jewish responses, see Kirschner, "Apocalyptic and Rabbinic Response," 27–46. On place and displacement in the narrative of Luke-Acts, see Burrus, "Gospel of Luke," 133–55.

CHAPTER 4

1. *Prot. Jas.* 9.2.

2. Lily Vuong contends that the "extremely ambiguous relationship between Mary and Joseph" is designed to show that Mary "belongs exclusively to the Lord" (*Gender and Purity*, 191). See too David G. Hunter's contention that the *Proto-gospel of James* shows that "theirs was not a true marriage" (*Marriage, Celibacy, and Heresy*, 178).

3. On irony in biblical stories of bedtrick (Jacob and Leah, Judah and Tamar, Noah), see Jagendorf, "'In the Morning, Behold, It Was Leah,'" 187–92. See too Lefkowitz, "The Genesis of Gender Transgression," 408–19. My thinking is also shaped by Wendy Doniger's *The Bedtrick: Tales of Sex and Masquerade*, a massive study of cross-cultural interest in questions of sex, truth, and identity, from the Hebrew Bible to Shakespeare, from an ancient Sanskrit story about a disguised demon to Hollywood films.

4. The Gospel of Luke is vague on the point. Mary is engaged to Joseph, but no information is given about Mary's home of residence (Luke 1:26–27). Matthew, on the other hand, makes an issue of it. Andrew Lincoln argues for two perspectives on conception in Luke, one virginal and one nonvirginal (*Born of a Virgin?* 99–124).

5. See Foskett, *A Virgin Conceived*, 160–61. Cf. Vuong, *Gender and Purity*, 242.

6. Hebrew: *yadah*; Greek: γινώσκω; see Gen 4:1 in the Septuagint (Rahlfs).

7. Matt 1:25 (narrator); Luke 1:34 (Mary to angel). The usage is a "Semitism," according to Brown (*Birth of the Messiah*, 132).

8. Doniger, *Bedtrick*, 491.

9. Doniger, *Bedtrick*, 492.

10. See Doniger, *Bedtrick*, 267–69.

11. On the similarities and differences between suspense, curiosity, and surprise, see Sternberg, *Poetics of Biblical Narrative*, 264–320.

12. Smid observes that Joseph feels that "events are unavoidably coming upon him" (*Protevangelium Jacobi*, 109).

13. Did Mary menstruate, according to the *Proto-gospel of James*? Glancy says no (*Corporal Knowledge*, 111); Vuong says yes (*Gender and Purity*, 125–33).

14. *Prot. Jas.* 8.2.

15. *Prot. Jas.* 8.3.

16. *Prot. Jas.* 9.1–3. Joseph will later "fling" (ῥίπτω) himself to the ground in despair when he sees that Mary is pregnant (*Prot. Jas.* 13.3).

17. *Prot. Jas.* 9.1.

18. *Prot. Jas.* 9.1.

19. *Prot. Jas.* 9.2.

20. See Num 16:31. "Fear the Lord your God," the priest warns, "and remember everything that he did to Dathan, Abeira, and Korah, how the earth split open and they were all swallowed up because of their dispute. Now, Joseph, you should be afraid of this happening to your house as well" (*Prot. Jas.* 9.2).

21. Vuong, *Gender and Purity*, 225. Cf. Foskett, *A Virgin Conceived*, 133–34.

22. van der Horst, "Sex, Birth, Purity, and Asceticism," 62. See too Hock, *Infancy Gospels*, 24–27.

23. "Defiled" (ἐμίανεν; *Prot. Jas.* 15.2).

24. *Prot. Jas.* 9.3.

25. *Prot. Jas.* 9.3.

26. *Prot. Jas.* 11.2; cf. Luke 1:28.

27. *Prot. Jas.* 11.3. "With child by the Holy Spirit" (Matt 1:18); "overshadow" (ἐπισκιάσει; Luke 1:35).

28. *Prot. Jas.* 12.2.

29. "Forgot the mysteries" (ἐπελάθετο τῶν μυστηρίων; *Prot. Jas.* 12.2).

30. Smid, *Protevangelium Jacobi*, 97.

31. Vuong, *Gender and Purity*, 175.

32. *Prot. Jas.* 12.3. On textual variants regarding the age of Mary, see Glancy, *Corporal Knowledge*, 111–12. See too Nutzman, "Mary in the *Protevangelium*," 569–70 n. 38. I follow Glancy and Nutzman on the age of Mary as twelve.

33. *Prot. Jas.* 13.1.

34. *Prot. Jas.* 13.1.

35. *Prot. Jas.* 13.1. See Foskett's remarks: "the narrative deftly underscores Mary's difference. . . . More than the text needs Mary to redeem Eve, it needs Eve to reveal Mary as the *parthenos tou kyriou*" (*A Virgin Conceived*, 155). Glancy sees a "twist on Eve-Mary parallel . . . Mary repeats rather than reverses the sin of Eve" (*Corporal Knowledge*, 157 n. 54).

36. *Prot. Jas.* 13.2.

37. *Prot. Jas.* 13.2.

38. On Adam and Eve in the Apocryphal Acts, see Cooper, *The Virgin and the Bride*, 45.

39. Pagels, *Adam, Eve, and the Serpent*, 27.

40. Pagels, *Adam, Eve, and the Serpent*, 86. The Pastoral Epistles suggest that Eve disobeyed God but not Adam (1 Tim 2:14). On gnostic interpretations, see Pagels, *Adam, Eve, and the Serpent*, 63–68. See too Dunning, "Virgin Earth, Virgin Birth," 57–88. On Mary as the new Eve in Justin, see Shoemaker, *Ancient Traditions of the Virgin*. Cf. Cothenet, "Le Protévangile de Jacques," 4261–62.

41. Boyarin, *Carnal Israel*, 83. On Marcion, Tatian, Encratites, and the story of Adam and Eve, see Brown, *Body and Society*, 82–97. On Adam and Eve, "carnal knowing," and nakedness in the early Christian tradition, see Miles, *Carnal Knowing*, 85–116.

42. Note the parallel to Gen 3:13 in Joseph's question. In that passage, the Lord God asks Eve, "Why have you done this?"

43. "I have not known any man" (ἄνδρα οὐ γινώσκω; *Prot. Jas.* 13.3, modified).

44. NRSV, modified.

45. "I do not know" (οὐ γινώσκω; *Prot. Jas.* 13.3, modified).

46. "I have not known any man (ἄνδρα οὐ γινώσκω; Luke 1:34). For a discussion of different translations and interpretive options of the Greek in Luke, see Fitzmyer, *Gospel*

According to Luke I–IX (348–50). Fitzmyer himself favors a "vague" rendering (350). Frederick C. Grant views Luke 1:34 as a later gloss, made under the influence of debates over the virgin birth ("Where Form Criticism," 11–21, esp. 19–21). On a connection between Luke, the *Proto-gospel of James*, and the birth of Melchizedek in the difficult to date 2 Enoch 23 (71.1–8), see Schaberg, *The Illegitimacy of Jesus*, 188–90.

47. *Prot. Jas.* 14.1.

48. Joseph Marohl contends that "honor killing" is a possibility in the Synoptic accounts (*Joseph's Dilemma*, 38–61). Since "public disgrace" is a kind of social death, it could be argued that the punishments represent variations on a theme. But the threat of "public disgrace" is gynocentric, while that of a "death sentence" is not, as Joseph soon learns. See too verbatim language of humiliation in *Prot. Jas.* 13.2, 15.3.

49. *Prot. Jas.* 14.2.

50. *Prot. Jas.* 14.2.

51. Did Joseph "rest" as he reports to Annas? Cf. Vuong, *Gender and Purity*, 176 n. 87.

52. *Prot. Jas.* 15.1.

53. *Prot. Jas.* 15.1.

54. *Prot. Jas.* 15.2.

55. *Prot. Jas.* 15.3.

56. "I have not known" (οὐ γινώσκω; *Prot. Jas.* 15.3, modified).

57. *Prot. Jas.* 15.4.

58. "Kept his silence" (ἐσίγησεν; *Prot. Jas.* 15.4).

59. See Allen, "'Protevangelium of James' as an 'Historia,'" 511–12.

60. Foskett contends that Joseph's "innocence is sought less for its own sake and more as confirmation of Mary's virtue" (*A Virgin Conceived*, 156).

61. "The reader's drama is literally dramatized in and through an analogous ordeal of interpretation undergone by some character . . . with variable success but under the same constraints of human vision" (Sternberg, *Poetics of Biblical Narrative*, 49). Cf. Lily Vuong's use of Sternberg in discussing the characterization of Mary (*Gender and Purity*, 181).

62. Sternberg, *Poetics of Biblical Narrative*, 266.

63. Sternberg, *Poetics of Biblical Narrative*, 266.

64. Sternberg, *Poetics of Biblical Narrative*, 266.

65. Sternberg, *Poetics of Biblical Narrative*, 267.

66. Sternberg, *Poetics of Biblical Narrative*, 267.

67. *Prot. Jas.* 16.2–3. So too we might find evidence of a growing sympathy in Joseph's nearly verbatim repetition of Mary's vow and denial in his reply to the priest.

68. *Prot. Jas.* 16.1.

69. See Martin, "Progymnastic Topic Lists," 18–41.

70. Andrew Jacobs remarks on the Rome's "anxious ability to contain and absorb difference" (*Christ Circumcised*, 8). On the classification and management of Jews in the late antique Christian empire, see Sanzo and Boustan, "Mediterranean Jews in a Christianizing Empire," 358–75.

71. Richard Horsley sees a "direct opposition between Caesar, the savior, who had

supposedly brought peace, and the child proclaimed as savior, whose birth means peace" in the Synoptic accounts (*Liberation of Christmas*, 155). Brown likewise discerns a challenge to imperial propaganda (Brown, *Birth of the Messiah*, 45). See too Matthews, *Perfect Martyr*.

72. *Prot. Jas.* 17.1.

73. *Prot. Jas.* 17.2.

74. *Prot. Jas.* 17.3.

75. *Prot. Jas.* 19.1.

76. *Prot. Jas.* 19.1.

77. *Prot. Jas.* 23.1–3.

78. It may be a scene inspired by Jesus' condemnation of the scribes and Pharisees: "so that upon you may come all the righteous blood shed on earth, from the blood of righteous Abel to the blood of Zacharias son of Barachiah, whom you murdered between the sanctuary and the altar" (Matt 23:35). Cf. Luke 11:51, which leaves out the problematic patronym. There may be here a confusion of two Zachariases: the postexilic prophet, son of Barachiah (Zech 1:1), and Zacharias the martyr (2 Chr 24:20–22), killed by King Joash. See Jacobs, *Remains of the Jews*, 113 n. 45. My thanks to the Andrew Jacobs for this point.

79. *Prot. Jas.* 23.1.

80. In this way, the "Massacre of the Innocents" in the *Proto-gospel of James* becomes, in the words of Cleo McNelly Kearns, "the story of the preservation of the child of the collateral priestly line of the family" (*The Virgin Mary, Monotheism*, 243).

81. Perkins, *The Suffering Self*, 104–23. Cf. Matthews, *Perfect Martyr*, 99–130.

82. On Christian heroes populating Jewish holy sites in late antique Christian travel writing, see Jacobs, *Remains of the Jews*, 103–38.

83. Although they may not always be conscious of it. See James H. Cone's incisive critique of the failure of white Protestant theologians to connect the dots between crucifixion and lynching (*The Cross and the Lynching Tree*, esp. 152–66).

84. See Marcus, "Crucifixion as Parodic Exaltation," 73–87.

85. See Glancy, "Torture," 107–36, esp. 114–21. The Johannine episode of the flogging of Jesus (John 19:1–3) is an instance of Roman judicial torture. The surrounding narrative suggests that the "resistant truth of Jesus' flesh" (135) confounds the claims of empire as the baffled Roman governor Pilate is left to wonder, "What is truth?" (John 18:38).

86. Elizabeth A. Castelli observes, "Roman spectacle could at one and the same time reassuringly reinscribe and dangerously trouble the culture's prevailing values" (*Martyrdom and Memory*, 106). L. Stephanie Cobb contends that the ideal of Roman masculinity was recast in martyr accounts as "a central, Christian virtue" (*Dying to Be Men*, 91).

87. See Bauckham, "Imaginative Literature," 791–812, esp. 796.

88. *Prot. Jas.* 22.2.

89. On Augustine's view of the companionate marriage of Joseph and Mary, see Clark, *St. Augustine on Marriage*, 6–7.

90. Cooper, *Band of Angels*, 56–57.

CHAPTER 5

1. "Love of letters" (φιλογράμματον; *The Life* 2 [trans. Thackeray, 5]).

2. See Rajak, *Josephus*, 12–44.

3. Cf. Billings, " 'At the Age of Twelve,' " 70–89.

4. Today we think of childhood, from infancy through adolescence, as crucial to the formation of adults. Not so in antiquity, according to Christopher Pelling ("Childhood and Personality in Greek Biography," 213–44). Cf. Burke, "Depictions of Children," 388–400.

5. Burke, "Completing the Gospel," 113–17.

6. See Aasgaard, *Childhood of Jesus*, 46–47, 116–17.

7. On "justifiable responses," see Upson-Saia, "Holy Child or Holy Terror?" 31–39. Upson-Saia contends that the *Infancy Gospel of Thomas* answers critics of Christianity by appropriating and "domesticating" what was originally hostile source material. I think instead that the inspiration for the *Infancy Gospel* comes from a Christian source, the Gospel of Luke.

8. Luke 2:41–52, NRSV, modified.

9. Or the "Loss in the Temple," one of the "Sorrows of Mary"; see Gorman, "Sorrows of Mary," *New Catholic Encyclopedia*, 327–28.

10. "But his parents did not understand" (καί οὐκ ἔγνωσαν οἱ γονεῖς; Luke 2:43).

11. René Laurentin's theory that "after three days" foreshadows the Lukan passion and resurrection (*Jésus au Temple*, 101–2). Cf. Elliott, "Does Luke 2:41–52 Anticipate?" 87–89.

12. "Understanding" (συνέσει; Luke 2:47).

13. "In great anxiety" (ὀδθνώμενοι; Luke 2:48).

14. "Did you not know?" (οὐκ ᾔδειτε; Luke 2:49). It is tempting to hear disappointment. Brown remarks, "The tone of his question is more one of grief that his parents have known him so poorly" (*Birth of the Messiah*, 490).

15. "But they did not understand what he said to them" (καὶ αὐτοὶ οὐ συνῆκαν τὸ ῥῆμα ὃ ἐλάλησεν αὐτοῖς; Luke 2:50).

16. "Know" and "understand": γινώσκω, οἶδα, συνίημι. Negative particle: οὐ.

17. The syntax implies that the expected answer agrees with the question (Bovon, *Luke 1*, 114).

18. My translation follows that of De Jonge, "Sonship, Wisdom, and Infancy," 317–54. Cf. Dennis D. Sylva's rendering of "My father's words" ("The Cryptic Clause," 132–40).

19. "Treasured" (διετήρει; Luke 2:51). For Raymond Brown, Mary's silent pondering (Luke 2:19, 51) is the key: she may have not understood Jesus, "but she is not unresponsive to the mystery that surrounds him" (*Birth of the Messiah*, 494). Joseph Fitzmyer observes, "This is Luke's way of getting across to his readers the difficulty of understanding who Jesus is or was" (*Gospel According to Luke I–IX*, 439). See too François Bovon's salient remarks about the difference between Luke 2:19 and 2:50 (*Luke 1*, 115).

20. Nils Krückemeier contends that Luke's purpose was to proclaim the "extraordinary significance" (die außerordentliche Bedeutung) of Jesus ("Der zwölfjährige Jesus im Tempel," 307–19, at 316). If so, why depict Mary and Joseph as being unable to recognize

it? Cf. Fitzmyer, *Gospel According to Luke I–IX*, 445. François Bovon proposes that the story shows the "obsolete lawful will of earthly parents" (*Luke 1*, 115).

21. NRSV, modified.

22. On the tricky term θαυμάζω ("amaze"), see Frilingos, *Spectacles*, 50–53.

23. Brown, *Birth of the Messiah*, 480. The theological payoff, according to Brown, is to show that "the appreciation of Jesus' divine sonship was post-resurrectional" (*Birth of the Messiah*, 492). Cf. David P. Moessner's study, which adopts a Sternbergian approach to the limited knowledge of characters in Luke ("The Ironic Fulfillment," 35–50).

24. Brown, *Birth of the Messiah*, 480–81, following van Iersel, "The Finding of Jesus in the Temple," 161–73.

25. Brown, *Birth of the Messiah*, 481.

26. Joseph Fitzmyer contends, "Though Jesus recognizes his relation to his heavenly father is that of an obedient son, he is not prevented thereby from filial respect for his earthly parents" (*Gospel According to Luke I–IX*, 445). See too Brown, *Birth of the Messiah*, 493; Bovon, *Luke 1*, 115; and Horn and Martens, "*Let the Little Children Come to Me*," 79.

27. On the link between the *Infancy Gospel* and the Gospel of Luke, see De Jonge, "Sonship, Wisdom, Infancy," 347–48, and, with a theory of oral transmission, Aasgaard, *Childhood of Jesus*, 115–18. Günther Schmahl notes a difference in the smoothness of the integration of the "Finding of Jesus" into the two accounts ("Lk 2,41–52 und die Kindheitserzählung," 256). Hock conveniently provides the relevant Greek text of Luke 2:41–51 for comparison (*Infancy Gospels*, 140–42).

28. Brown, *Birth of the Messiah*, 481.

29. Elsewhere, Irenaeus describes the child Jesus as moral exemplar (*Haer.* 2.21.4); cited in Leyerle, "Children and 'The Child,'" 559–79.

30. *Inf. Gos. Thom.* 2.1.

31. *Inf. Gos. Thom.* 2.2–4 (Ga).

32. The Greek term πλάσσω ("fashion"), used here to describe how Jesus creates the clay sparrows (*Inf. Gos. Thom.* 2.2–3 [Ga]), is also used in the Septuagint translation of Genesis 2:7–8 (Rahlfs).

33. For Boyarin, the "first accent" is halakhic debate, and the "second accent" is the aggada about gigantic rabbis. "It is that incongruity that renders the text so very Menippean, that which asserts while denying but also denies while asserting the value of an intellectual practice, neither the assertion nor the denial being allowed to win the day" (Boyarin, *Socrates and the Fat Rabbis*, 235). On Menippean satire generally, see Relihan, *Ancient Menippean Satire*. See too Halliwell, "Uses of Laughter," 279–96.

34. Boyarin, *Socrates and the Fat Rabbis*, 342.

35. *Inf. Gos. Thom.* 3.2.

36. *Inf. Gos. Thom.* 4.1.

37. *Inf. Gos. Thom.* 4.2.

38. *Inf. Gos. Thom.* 5.1.

39. *Inf. Gos. Thom.* 5.2–3, modified.

40. On moral instruction in ancient Jewish households, see Yarbrough, "Parents and

Children in the Jewish Family," 39–59, esp. 43–44 on Tobit 4. See also Williams, "The Jewish Family in Judaea," 159–82, esp. 170–75.

41. Burke, *De infantia Iesu*, 305 n. 8.

42. On Zechariah and other conversions in Luke-Acts, see Balch, "ΜΕΤΑΒΟΛΗ ΠΟΛΕΤΕΙΩΝ," 139–88.

43. See Minear, "Luke's Use of the Birth Stories," 111–31, at 117.

44. *Inf. Gos. Thom.* 7.2.

45. Or, as Meir Sternberg puts it, "the gulf separating human from divine vision" (*Poetics of Biblical Narrative*, 97).

46. *Inf. Gos. Thom.* 12.2.

47. *Inf. Gos. Thom.* 16.3.

48. In addition to Burke and Aasgaard, discussed here, see Upson-Saia, "Holy Child or Holy Terror?" 31–33.

49. *Inf. Gos. Thom.* 14.3–4.

50. Burke, "Completing the Gospel," 108–9.

51. Aasgaard, *Childhood of Jesus*, 46–47, 116–17. On this point, see too Foster, "The Education of Jesus," 336.

52. *Inf. Gos. Thom.* 14.3.

53. *Inf. Gos. Thom.* 17.1.

54. *Inf. Gos. Thom.* 17.2.

55. "Great anxiety and distress" (ὀδυνώμενοι λυπούμενοι; *Inf. Gos. Thom.* 17.3). Burke suggests that the added term betrays the influence of the Western text of Luke (*De infantia Iesu*, 336 n. 4).

56. *Inf. Gos. Thom.* 17.3.

57. *Inf. Gos. Thom.* 17.4.

58. Aasgaard, *Childhood of Jesus*, 117.

59. *Inf. Gos. Thom.* 5.1. We might think of the two questions, one from Joseph and the other from Mary, as forming an *inclusio*.

60. *Inf. Gos. Thom.* 17.4.

61. *Inf. Gos. Thom.* 17.5.

62. Bovon, *Luke 1*, 113.

63. Sternberg, *Poetics of Biblical Narrative*, 36–38.

64. See Ando, *Matter of the Gods*, 149–97.

AFTERWORD

1. *Martyrdom of Perpetua* (ed. and trans. Musurillo).

2. A different approach would be to examine the way Jesus "passes" as a son in the *Infancy Gospel of Thomas* or the way that Mary and Joseph "pass" as a married couple in the *Proto-gospel of James*. For a discussion of theory and "passing" in the early Christian context, see Jacobs, *Christ Circumcised* (179–89).

3. Not until the sixth century CE is there a record of condemning, along with a host of other extracanonical writings, "the book on the infancy of the savior" and "the book of the nativity of the saviour and of Mary or the midwife." This may be found in the so-called *Decretem Gelasianum*, 519–533 CE, anonymous, traditionally and wrongly attributed to council of Gelasius 1, bishop of Rome, 492–96 (Voiçu, "Ways to Survival," 401–2). The "Decree of Gelasius" did little to stop the transmission of such stories to the medieval Christians who lived after its composition.

4. Two complementary articles describe canon and the possibilities for resistance in fourth-century Christian circles: Brakke, "Canon Formation and Social Conflict," 395–419, and Jacobs, "The Disorder of Books," 135–59.

5. Athanasius, *Festal Letter 39* (trans. Brakke), *Athanasius and Asceticism*, 326–32, at 329–30.

6. Jacobs, "The Disorder of Books," 158.

7. See Elliott, *The Apocryphal New Testament*, 68–69.

8. *Panarion* 51.20.2–3 (trans. Williams, 45). On the problem of knowing in Epiphanius, see Berzon, "Known Knowns and Known Unknowns," 75–101.

9. Voiçu, "Ways to Survival," 408.

10. *Hist. Jos. Carp.* 11.3 (trans. Ehrman and Pleše, 169).

11. *Hist. Jos. Carp.* 16.1–15.

12. *Hist. Jos. Carp.* 17.4 (trans. Ehrman and Pleše, 175).

13. *Hist. Jos. Carp.* 17.8 (trans. Ehrman and Pleše, 175).

14. *Prot. Jas.* 19–20.

15. *Hist. Jos. Carp.* 17.10–13 (trans. Ehrman and Pleše, 177).

16. *Hist. Jos. Carp.* 17.15 (trans. Ehrman and Pleše, 177).

17. *Hist. Jos. Carp.* 18.1 (trans. Ehrman and Pleše, 177).

18. *Hist. Jos. Carp.* 18.3 (trans. Ehrman and Pleše, 177).

19. Voiçu, "Ways to Survival," 408.

20. David Hunter notes, "Of all the biblical apocrypha, however, it is the *Protevangelium of James* that is by far the most significant text for its teaching of the perpetual virginity of Mary" (*Marriage, Celibacy, and Heresy*, 177).

21. Voiçu, "Ways to Survival," 413. For an overview, see Witakowski, "The Miracles of Jesus," 279–98.

22. Suras 3:49 and 5:110. For discussion, see Davis, *Christ Child*, 162–67.

23. See *Prot. Jas.* 17.3. For discussion about whether to give credit for this tradition to the *Proto-gospel of James*, see Shoemaker, *Ancient Traditions of the Virgin*, 81–98.

24. *Piacenza Pilgrim* 5 (trans. Wilkinson, 131). In addition to these late ancient sources, medieval sources reflect continuing interest in the family life of Jesus. See Dzon, "Joseph and the Amazing Christ-Child," 135–57, and Couch, "Misbehaving God," 31–41.

25. Solomon makes this point in a chapter about the Klebolds, the family whose son, Dylan Klebold, was responsible, along with his friend, Eric Harris, for the 1999 shootings at Columbine High School in Colorado (*Far from the Tree*, 588).

Bibliography

PRIMARY SOURCES

Biblical quotations are from the New Revised Standard Version (NRSV) unless otherwise stated. The Greek text of the New Testament is from *Nestle-Aland Novum Testamentum Gracae*, 27th ed., 1993.

Achilles Tatius. *Leucippe and Clitophon*. English trans. *Collected Ancient Greek Novels*. Ed. B. P. Reardon. Trans. John J. Winkler. Berkeley: University of California Press, 1989. Pp. 170–284.

Acts of Paul and Thelca. English trans. *The Apocryphal New Testament*. Trans. J. K. Elliott. Oxford: Clarendon, 1993. Pp. 350–89.

Acts of Peter. English trans. *The Apocryphal New Testament*. Trans. J. K. Elliott. Oxford: Clarendon, 1993. Pp. 390–426.

Acts of Thomas. English trans. *The Apocryphal New Testament*. Trans. J. K. Elliott. Oxford: Clarendon, 1993. Pp. 439–511.

Apuleius. *The Metamorphoses*. Text and English trans. *The Metamorphoses*. 2 vols. Ed. and trans. J. Arthur Hanson. Loeb Classical Library 44, 453. Cambridge, MA: Harvard University Press, 1989.

Athanasius. *Festal Letter 39*. English trans. David Brakke. *Athanasius and Asceticism*. Baltimore: Johns Hopkins University Press, 1995. Pp. 326–32.

Clement of Alexandria. *Stromateis*. English trans. *The Stromata, or Miscellanies*. Ed. Alexander Roberts and James Donaldson. Trans. William Wilson. Ante-Nicene Fathers 2. Edinburgh: T & T Clark, 1885. Pp. 299–567.

Epiphanius. *Panarion*. English trans. *The Panarion of Epiphanius*. Trans. Frank Williams. Nag Hammadi and Manichean Studies 36. Leiden: Brill, 2008.

Epistula Apostolorum. English trans. *The Apocryphal New Testament*. Trans. J. K. Elliott. Oxford: Clarendon, 1993. Pp. 555–88.

Heliodorus. *An Ethiopian Story*. English trans. *Collected Ancient Greek Novels*. Ed. B. P. Reardon. Trans. J. R. Morgan. Berkeley: University of California Press, 1989. Pp. 349–588.

Infancy Gospel of Thomas. Text and English trans. in Burke, *De infantia Iesu*. Pp. 301–35. Full documentation in "Secondary Sources."

Irenaeus. *Against Heresies*. Text in *Irénée de Lyon: Contre de heresies*. 5 vols. SC 100, 152–53, 210–11, 263–64. Ed. and trans. into French A. Rousseau and L. Doutreleau. Paris: Cerf, 1952–69. English trans. *St. Irenaeus of Lyons: Against the Heresies*. Trans. Dominic J. Unger. Ancient Christian Writers 55. Mahwah, NJ: Paulist, 1992.

John Chrysostom. *Homilies on John*. PG 59:23–482. English trans. *Saint John Chrysostom: Commentary on John the Apostle and Evangelist, Homilies 1–47*. Trans. Sister Thomas Aquinas Goggin. Fathers of the Church 33. New York: Fathers of the Church, 1957.

John Chrysostom. *Homilies on Matthew*. PG 57:13–472, 58:471–794. English trans. *Homilies on the Gospel of St. Matthew*. Ed. Philip Schaff. Trans. George Prevost and M. B. Riddle. Nicene and Post-Nicene Fathers 10. Edinburgh: T& T Clark, 1888.

Josephus. *The Jewish War*. Text and English trans. *Josephus, Volumes II–IV*. 3 vols. Trans. H. St. J. Thackeray. Loeb Classical Library 203, 210, 487. Cambridge, MA: Harvard University Press, 1927–28.

Josephus. *The Life*. Text and English trans. *Josephus, Volume I*. Trans. H. St. J. Thackeray. Loeb Classical Library 186. Cambridge, MA: Harvard University Press, 1926.

Justin Martyr. *First Apology*. English trans. *Early Church Fathers*. Ed. Cyril C. Richardson. Trans. Edward Rochie Hardy. New York: Collier Books, 1970. Pp. 242–89.

Lucian. *The Dream*. Text and English trans. *Lucian, Volume III*. Trans. A. M. Harmon. Loeb Classical Library 130. Cambridge, MA: Harvard University Press, 1921. Pp. 214–33.

Lucian. *On Salaried Posts*. Text and English trans. *Lucian, Volume III*. Trans. A. M. Harmon. Loeb Classical Library 130. Cambridge, MA: Harvard University Press, 1921. Pp. 412–81.

Martyrdom of Perpetua and Felicitas. Text and English trans. *The Acts of the Christian Martyrs*. Ed. and trans. Herbert Musurillo. London: Oxford University Press, 1990. Pp. 106–31.

Origen. *Against Celsus*. Text in *Contra Celse*. 5 vols. SC 132, 136, 147, 150, 227. Ed. Marcel Borret. Paris: Cerf, 1967–76. English trans. *Contra Celsum*. Ed. and trans. Henry Chadwick. Cambridge: Cambridge University Press, 1953.

Origen. *Homilies on Luke*. English trans. Fathers of the Church 94. Trans. Joseph Lienhard. Washington, DC: Catholic University of America Press, 1996.

Philo. *On Joseph*. Text and English trans. *Philo, Volume VI*. Trans. F. H. Colson. Loeb Classical Library 289. Cambridge, MA: Harvard University Press, 1935. Pp. 137–271.

Philo. *On Moses*. Text and English trans. *Philo, Volume VI*. Trans. F. H. Colson. Loeb Classical Library 289. Cambridge, MA: Harvard University Press, 1935. Pp. 273–595.

Piacenza Pilgrim. English trans. *Jerusalem Pilgrims Before the Crusades*. Warminster, England: Aris & Philips, 2002. Pp. 129–51.

Plutarch. *Advice to Bride and Groom*. Text and English trans. *Plutarch's Advice to the Bride and Groom* and *A Consolation to His Wife: English Translations, Commentary, Interpretive Essays, and Bibliography*. Ed. Sarah B. Pomeroy. Trans. Donald Russell. New York: Oxford University Press, 1999. Pp. 5–13.

Plutarch. *Life of Cicero*. Text and English trans. *Lives, Volume VII*. Trans. Bernadotte Perrin. Loeb Classical Library 99. Cambridge, MA: Harvard University Press, 1919.

Proto-gospel of James (*Protevangelium Jacobi*). Text and English trans. Ehrman and Pleše. *Apocryphal Gospels*. Pp. 40–71. Full documentation under "Secondary Sources."

Septuagint. Text in *Septuaginta*. 2 vols. Ed. Alfred Rahlfs. Stuttgart: Württembergische, 1935.

SECONDARY SOURCES

Aasgaard, Reidar. *The Childhood of Jesus: Decoding the Apocryphal Infancy Gospel of Thomas.* Eugene, OR: Cascade, 2009.

Allen, John L., Jr. "The 'Protoevangelium of James' as an 'Historia': The Insufficiency of the 'Infancy Gospel' Category." *Society of Biblical Literature Seminar Papers* 30 (1991): 508–17.

Ando, Clifford. *Imperial Ideology and Provincial Loyalty in the Roman Empire.* Berkeley: University of California Press, 2000.

Ando, Clifford. *The Matter of the Gods: Religion and the Roman Empire.* Berkeley: University of California Press, 2008.

Arnal, William. "The Collection and Synthesis of 'Tradition' and the Second-Century Invention of Christianity." *Method and Theory in the Study of Religion* 23 (2011): 193–215.

Balch, David L. "ΜΕΤΑΒΟΛΗ ΠΟΛΕΤΕΙΩΝ: Jesus as Founder of the Church in Luke-Acts: Form and Function." In *Contextualizing Acts: Lukan Narrative and Greco-Roman Discourse*, ed. Todd C. Penner and Caroline Vander Stichele, 139–88. Society of Biblical Literature Symposium Series 20. Leiden: Brill, 2004.

Barton, Carlin A. "Savage Miracles: The Redemption of Lost Honor in Roman Society and the Sacrament of the Gladiator and the Martyr." *Representations* 45 (1994): 41–71.

Barton, Carlin A. *The Sorrows of the Ancient Romans: The Gladiator and the Monster.* Princeton, NJ: Princeton University Press, 1995.

Bartsch, Shadi. *Actors in the Audience: Theatricality and Doublespeak from Nero to Hadrian.* Cambridge, MA: Harvard University Press, 1994.

Bartsch, Shadi. *Decoding the Ancient Novel: The Reader and the Role of Description in Heliodorus and Achilles Tatius.* Princeton, NJ: Princeton University Press, 1989.

Bauckham, Richard A. "Imaginative Literature." In *The Early Christian World*, ed. Philip F. Esler, 791–812. London: Routledge, 2000.

Beavis, Mary Ann. "Pluck the Rose but Shun the Thorns: The Ancient School and Christian Origins." *Studies in Religion/Sciences Religieuses* 29 (2000): 411–23.

Berlin, Adele. "Narrative Poetics in the Bible." *Prooftexts* 6 (1986): 273–84.

Berzon, Todd S. "Known Knowns and Known Unknowns: Epiphanius of Salamis and the Limits of Heresiology." *Harvard Theological Review* 109 (2016): 75–101.

Billings, Bradley S. "'At the Age of 12': The Boy Jesus in the Temple (Luke 2:41–52), the Emperor Augustus, and the Social Setting of the Third Gospel." *Journal of Theological Studies* 60 (2009): 70–89.

Bloomer, W. Martin. "The Ancient Child in School." In *Oxford Handbook of Childhood and Education*, ed. Judith Evans Grubbs and Tim Parkin, 444–61.

Bovon, François. "Beyond the Canonical and the Apocryphal Books, the Presence of a Third Category: The Books Useful for the Soul." *Harvard Theological Review* 105 (2012): 125–37.

Bovon, François. "The Child and the Beast: Fighting Violence in Ancient Christianity." *Harvard Theological Review* 92 (1999): 369–92.

Bovon, François. "Évangiles canoniques et évangiles apocryphes: La naissance et l'enfance de Jésus." *Bulletin des Facultés catholiques de Lyon* 58 (1980): 19–30.

Bovon, François. *Luke 1: A Commentary on the Gospel of Luke 1:1–9:50*. Trans. Christine M. Thomas. Hermeneia. Minneapolis, MN: Fortress, 2002.

Bovon, François. "The Reception and Use of the Gospel of Luke in the Second Century." In *New Testament and Christian Apocrypha*, ed. Glenn Snyder, 289–306. Grand Rapids, MI: Baker Academic, 2011.

Bovon, François. "The Suspension of Time in Chapter 18 of *Protevangelium Jacobi*." In *The Future of Early Christianity: Essays in Honor of Helmut Koester*, ed. Birger A. Pearson, in collaboration with A. Thomas Kraabel, George W. E. Nickelsburg, and Norman R. Petersen, 393–405. Minneapolis, MN: Fortress, 1991.

Boyarin, Daniel. *Border Lines: The Partition of Judeo-Christianity*. Divinations: Rereading Late Ancient Religion. Philadelphia: University of Pennsylvania Press, 2004.

Boyarin, Daniel. *Carnal Israel: Reading Sex in Talmudic Culture*. The New Historicism: Studies in Cultural Poetics. Berkeley: University of California Press, 1993.

Boyarin, Daniel. *Socrates and the Fat Rabbis*. Chicago: University of Chicago Press, 2009.

Bradley, Keith. "Images of Childhood: The Evidence of Plutarch." In *Plutarch's Advice to the Bride and Groom and A Consolation to His Wife: English Translations, Commentary, Interpretive Essays, and Bibliography*, ed. Sarah Pomeroy, 183–96. New York: Oxford University Press, 1999.

Brakke, David. "Canon Formation and Social Conflict in Fourth-Century Egypt: Athanasius of Alexandria's Thirty-Ninth 'Festal Letter.'" *Harvard Theological Review* 87 (1994): 395–419.

Brakke, David. "Scriptural Practices in Early Christianity: Towards a New History of the New Testament Canon." In *Invention, Rewritings, Usurpation: Discursive Fights over Religious Traditions in Antiquity*, ed. Jörg Ulrich, Anders-Christian Jacobsen, and David Brakke, 263–80. Early Christianity in the Context of Antiquity 11. Frankfurt am Main: Peter Lang, 2012.

Brown, Peter. *The Body and Society: Men, Women, and Sexual Renunciation in Early Christianity*. Lectures on the History of Religions 13. New York: Columbia University Press, 1988.

Brown, Peter. "The Notion of Virginity in the Early Church." In *Christian Spirituality: Origins to the Twelfth Century*, ed. Bernard McGinn and John Meyendorff, in collaboration with Jean Leclercq, 427–33. New York: Crossroad, 1987.

Brown, Raymond E. *The Birth of the Messiah: A Commentary on the Infancy Narratives in the Gospels of Matthew and Luke*. Updated ed. New York: Doubleday, 1993.

Burke, Tony. [Chartrand-Burke.] "Completing the Gospel: The Infancy Gospel of Thomas as a Supplement to the Gospel of Luke." In *The Reception and Interpretation of the Bible in Late Antiquity. Proceedings of the Montréal Colloquium in Honour of Charles Kannengeiser, 11–13 October 2006*, ed. Lorenzo Di Tommaso and Lucian Turcescu, 113–17. Bible in Ancient Christianity 6. Leiden: Brill, 2008.

Burke, Tony. *De infantia Iesu euangelium Thomae graece*. Corpus Christianorum Series Apocryphorum 17. Turnhout: Brepols, 2010.

Burke, Tony. "Depictions of Children in the Apocryphal Gospels." *Studies in Religion/Sciences Religieuses* 41 (2012): 388–400.

Burridge, Richard A. *What Are the Gospels? A Comparison with Greco-Roman Biography*. Society for New Testament Studies Monograph Series 70. Cambridge: Cambridge University Press, 1992.

Burrus, Virginia. "The Gospel of Luke and the Acts of the Apostles." In *A Postcolonial Commentary on the New Testament Writings*, ed. R. S. Sugirtharajah, 133–55. Bible and Postcolonialism 13. London: T & T Clark, 2009.

Burrus, Virginia. "Mimicking Virgins: Colonial Ambivalence and the Ancient Romance." *Arethusa* 38 (2005): 49–88.

Burrus, Virginia. *The Sex Lives of the Saints: An Erotics of Ancient Hagiography*. Divinations: Rereading Late Ancient Religion. Philadelphia: University of Pennsylvania Press, 2004.

Caldwell, Lauren. *Roman Girlhood and the Fashioning of Femininity*. Cambridge: Cambridge University Press, 2015.

Cameron, Averil. *Christianity and the Rhetoric of Empire: The Development of Christian Discourse*. Sather Classical Lectures 55. Berkeley: University of California Press, 1991.

Cameron, Averil. *Dialoguing in Late Antiquity*. Hellenic Studies 65. Cambridge, MA: Center for Hellenic Studies, 2014.

Carp, Teresa C. "*Puer senex* in Roman and Medieval Thought." *Latomus* 39 (1980): 736–39.

Cartlidge, David R., and J. Keith Elliott. *Art and the Christian Apocrypha*. London: Routledge, 2001.

Castelli, Elizabeth A. *Martyrdom and Memory: Early Christian Culture Making*. Gender, Theory, and Religion. New York: Columbia University Press, 2004.

Chartrand-Burke, Tony. "Authorship and Identity in *The Infancy Gospel of Thomas*." *Toronto Journal of Theology* 14 (1998): 27–43.

Chew, Kathryn. "Achilles Tatius and Parody." *Classical Journal* 96 (2000): 57–70.

Chin, Catherine M. *Grammar and Christianity in the Late Roman World*. Divinations: Rereading Late Ancient Religion. Philadelphia: University of Pennsylvania Press, 2008.

Chin, Catherine M., and Moulie Vidas, eds. *Late Ancient Knowing: Explorations in Intellectual History*. Berkeley: University of California Press, 2015.

Clark, Elizabeth A. "Antifamilial Tendencies in Ancient Christianity." *Journal of the History of Sexuality* 5 (1995): 356–80.

Clark, Elizabeth A., ed. *St. Augustine on Marriage and Sexuality*. Selections from the Fathers of the Church 1. Washington, DC: Catholic University of America Press, 1996.

Clark, Gillian. "The Fathers and the Children." In *The Church and Childhood: Papers Read at the 1993 Summer Meeting and the 1994 Winter Meeting of the Ecclesiastical History Society*, ed. Diane Wood, 1–28. Studies in Church History 31. Oxford: Blackwell, 1994.

Clivaz, Claire, Andreas Dettwiler, Luc Devillers, and Enrico Norelli, eds., with Benjamin Berth. *Infancy Gospels: Stories and Identities*. Wissenschaftliche Untersuchungen zum Neuen Testament 281. Tübingen: Mohr Siebeck, 2011.

Cobb, L. Stephanie. *Dying to Be Men: Gender and Language in Early Christian Martyr Accounts*. Gender, Theory, and Religion. New York: Columbia University Press, 2012.

Cohen, Shaye J. D., ed. *The Jewish Family in Antiquity*. Brown Judaic Studies 289. Atlanta, GA: Scholars Press, 1993.

Coleman, Kathleen. "Fatal Charades: Roman Executions Stage as Mythological Enactments." *Journal of Roman Studies* 80 (1990): 44–73.

Cone, James H. *The Cross and the Lynching Tree*. Maryknoll, NY: Orbis Books, 2011.

Constas, Nicholas. *Proclus of Constantinople and the Cult of the Virgin in Late Antiquity: Homilies 1–5, Texts and Translations*. Supplements to Vigiliae Christianae 66. Leiden: Brill, 2003.

Cooper, Kate. "Approaching the Holy Household." *Journal of Early Christian Studies* 15 (2007): 131–42.

Cooper, Kate. *Band of Angels: The Forgotten World of Early Christian Women*. New York: Overlook, 2013.

Cooper, Kate. *The Virgin and the Bride: Idealized Womanhood in Late Antiquity*. Cambridge, MA: Harvard University Press, 1996.

Cooper, Kate, and James Corke-Webster. "Conversion, Conflict, and the Drama of Social Reproduction: Narratives of Filial Resistance in Early Christianity and Modern Britain." In *Conversion and Initiation in Antiquity: Shifting Identities, Creating Change*, ed. Birgitte Secher Bøgh, 169–83. Early Christianity in the Context of Antiquity 16. Frankfurt am Main: Peter Lang, 2015.

Cothenet, Edouard. "Le Protévangile de Jacques: Origine, genre, et signification d'un premier midrash chrétien sur la Nativité de Marie." In *Aufstieg und Niedergang der römischen Welt: Geschichte und Kultur Roms im Spiegel der neueren Forschung*, ed. Hildegard Temporini and Wolfgang Haase, 2.25.6: 4252–69. New York: de Gruyter, 1988.

Couch, Julie Nelson. "Misbehaving God: The Case of the Christ Child in MS Laud Misc. 108 'Infancy of Jesus Christ.'" In *Mindful Spirit in Medieval Literature: Essays in Honor of Elizabeth D. Kirk*, ed. Bonnie Wheeler, 31–43. New York: Palgrave Macmillan, 2006.

Cox, Patricia L. *Biography in Late Antiquity: A Quest for the Holy Man*. Transformation of the Classical Heritage 5. Berkeley: University of California Press, 1983.

Cribiore, Raffaela. *Gymnastics of the Mind: Greek Education in Hellenistic and Roman Egypt*. Princeton, NJ: Princeton University Press, 2001.

Davis, Natalie Zemon. "The Rites of Violence: Religious Riot in Sixteenth-Century

France." In *Society and Culture in Early Modern France: Eight Essays*, 152–87. Stanford, CA: Stanford University Press, 1975.

Davis, Stephen J. *Christ Child: Cultural Memories of a Young Jesus*. Synkrisis. New Haven, CT: Yale University Press, 2013.

De Jonge, Henk J. "Sonship, Wisdom, and Infancy: Luke 2:41–51a." *New Testament Studies* 24 (1978): 317–54.

De Strycker, Émile. *La forme la plus ancienne du Protévangile de Jacques*. Subsidia Hagiographica 33. Brussels: Société des Bollandistes, 1961.

Dixon, Suzanne. "The Sentimental Ideal of the Roman Family." In *Marriage, Divorce, and Children in Ancient Rome*, ed. Beryl Rawson, 99–113. Oxford: Clarendon, 1991.

Doniger, Wendy. *The Bedtrick: Tales of Sex and Masquerade*. Worlds of Desire: The Chicago Series on Sexuality, Gender, and Culture. Chicago: University of Chicago Press, 2000.

Dungan, David L. *Constantine's Bible: Politics and the Making of the New Testament*. Minneapolis, MN: Fortress, 2007.

Dunning, Benjamin H. "Virgin Earth, Virgin Birth: Creation, Sexual Difference, and Recapitulation in Irenaeus of Lyons." *Journal of Religion* 89 (2009): 57–88.

Dzon, Mary. "Joseph and the Amazing Christ-Child of Late-Medieval Legend." In *Childhood in the Middle Ages and the Renaissance*, ed. Albrecht Classen, 135–57. Berlin: Walter de Gruyter, 2005.

Ehrman, Bart D. *Lost Christianities: The Battles for Scriptures and the Faiths We Never Knew*. New York: Oxford University Press, 2003.

Ehrman, Bart D., and Zlatko Pleše. *The Apocryphal Gospels: Texts and Translations*. New York: Oxford University Press, 2011.

Elliott, J. K. *The Apocryphal New Testament: A Collection of Apocryphal Christian Literature in an English Translation*. Oxford: Clarendon, 1993.

Elliott, J. K. "Does Luke 2:41–52 Anticipate the Resurrection?" *Expository Times* 58 (1971–72): 87–89.

Elliott, John H. "The Jesus Movement Was Not Egalitarian but Family Oriented." *Biblical Interpretation* 11 (2003): 173–210.

Enslin, Morton. "Along Highways and Byways." *Harvard Theological Review* 44 (1951): 81–92.

Fewell, Danna Nolan, and David Gunn. "Tipping the Balance: Sternberg's Reader and the Rape of Dinah." *Journal of Biblical Literature* 110 (1991): 193–211.

Fitzmyer, Joseph A. *The Gospel According to Luke I–IX*. Anchor Bible 28. Garden City, NY: Doubleday, 1981.

Fitzmyer, Joseph A. *Luke the Theologian: Aspects of His Teaching*. Mahwah, NJ: Paulist, 1989.

Foskett, Mary F. *A Virgin Conceived: Mary and Classical Representations of Virginity*. Bloomington: Indiana University Press, 2002.

Foster, Paul. "The Education of Jesus in the Infancy Gospel of Thomas." In *Texts and Traditions: Essays in Honour of J. Keith Elliott*, ed. Peter Doble and Jeffrey Kloha, 327–47. New Testament Tools, Studies and Documents 47. Leiden: Brill, 2014.

Foster, Paul. "The Reception of the Canonical Gospels in the Non-Canonical Gospels." *Early Christianity* 4 (2013): 281–309.

Francis, James A. *Subversive Virtue: Asceticism and Authority in the Second-Century Pagan World*. University Park: Pennsylvania University Press, 1995.

Frankfurter, David. *Evil Incarnate: Rumors of Demonic Conspiracy and Ritual Abuse in History*. Princeton: Princeton University Press, 2006.

Frankfurter, David. "The Magic of Writing and the Writing of Magic: The Power of the Word in Egyptian and Greek Traditions." *Helios* 21 (1994): 189–221.

Frede, Michael. "Origen's Treatise *Against Celsus*." In *Apologetics in the Roman Empire: Pagans, Jews, and Christians*, ed. Mark Edwards, Martin Goodman, and Simon Price, 131–55. Oxford: Oxford University Press, 1999.

Fredriksen, Paula. *From Jesus to Christ: The Origins of the New Testament Images of Jesus*. 2nd ed. New Haven, CT: Yale University Press, 2000.

Frilingos, Christopher A. "For My Child, Onesimus: Paul and Domestic Power in Philemon." *Journal of Biblical Literature* 119 (2000): 91–104.

Frilingos, Christopher A. " 'It Moves Me to Wonder': Narrating Violence and Religion Under the Roman Empire." *Journal of the American Academy of Religion* 77 (2009): 825–52.

Frilingos, Christopher A. "No Child Left Behind: Knowledge and Violence in *The Infancy Gospel of Thomas*." *Journal of Early Christian Studies* 17 (2009): 27–54.

Frilingos, Christopher A. "Parents Just Don't Understand: Ambiguity in Stories About the Childhood of Jesus." *Harvard Theological Review* 109 (2016): 33–55.

Frilingos, Christopher A. *Spectacles of Empire: Monsters, Martyrs, and the Book of Revelation*. Divinations: Rereading Late Ancient Religion. Philadelphia: University of Pennsylvania Press, 2004.

Gager, John G., and Mika Ahuvia. "Some Notes on Jesus and His Parents: From the New Testament Gospels to the *Toledot Yeshu*." In *Envisioning Judaism: Studies in Honor of Peter Schäfer on the Occasion of His Seventieth Birthday*, vol. 2, ed. Ra'anan Boustan, Klaus Herrmann, Reimund Leicht, Annette Yoshiko Reed, and Guiseppe Veltri, with the assistance of Alex Ramos, 997–1019. Tübingen: Mohr Siebeck, 2013.

Gager, John G., ed., with contributions by Catherine F. Cooper, David Frankfurter, Derek Krueger, and Richard Lim. *Curse Tablets and Binding Spells from the Ancient World*. New York: Oxford University Press, 1992.

Gamble, Harry Y. "The New Testament Canon: Recent Research and the Status Quaestionis." In *The Canon Debate*, ed. Lee M. MacDonald and James A. Sanders, 272–94. Peabody, MA: Hendriskson, 2002.

Garnsey, Peter. *Social Status and Legal Privilege in the Roman Empire*. Oxford: Clarendon, 1970.

Garnsey, Peter, and Richard Saller. *The Roman Empire: Economy, Society and Culture*. Berkeley: University of California Press, 1987.

Gaventa, Beverly Roberts. *Mary: Glimpses of the Mother of Jesus*. Columbia: University of South Carolina Press, 1995.

Gibson, Jack J. "Ephesians 5:21–33 and the Lack of Marital Unity in the Roman Empire." *Bibliotheca Sacra* 168 (2011): 162–77.

Glancy, Jennifer A. *Corporal Knowledge: Early Christian Bodies*. Oxford: Oxford University Press, 2010.

Glancy, Jennifer A. "Torture: Flesh, Truth, and the Fourth Gospel." *Biblical Interpretation* 13 (2005): 107–36.

Gleason, Maud W. *Making Men: Sophists and Self-Presentation in Ancient Rome*. Princeton, NJ: Princeton University Press, 1995.

Gleason, Maud W. "Mutilated Messengers: Body Language in Josephus." In *Being Greek Under Rome*, ed. Simon Goldhill, 50–85. Cambridge: Cambridge University Press, 2001.

Gleason, Maud W. "Truth Contests and Talking Corpses." In *Constructions of the Classical Body*, ed. James I. Porter, 287–313.

Golden, Mark. "Did the Ancients Care When Their Children Died?" *Greece & Rome* 35 (1988): 152–63.

Goldhill, Simon, ed. *Being Greek Under Rome: Cultural Identity, the Second Sophistic, and the Development of Empire*. Cambridge: Cambridge University Press, 2001.

Goldhill, Simon. "Introduction. Setting an Agenda: 'Everything is Greece to the Wise.'" In *Being Greek Under Rome*, ed. Simon Goldhill, 1–25. Cambridge: Cambridge University Press, 2001.

Gorman, J. C. "Sorrows of Mary." In the *New Catholic Encyclopedia*, ed. J. C. Gorman, vol. 13, 327–28. 2nd ed. Detroit, MI: Gale, 2003.

Grant, Frederick C. "Where Form Criticism and Textual Criticism Overlap." *Journal of Biblical Literature* 59 (1940): 11–21.

Grewal, Zareena. *Islam Is a Foreign Country: American Muslims and the Global Crisis of Authority*. Nation of Newcomers: Immigrant History as American History. New York: New York University Press, 2014.

Grubbs, Judith Evans, and Tim Parkin, eds., with the assistance of Roslynne Bell. *Oxford Handbook of Childhood and Education in the Classical World*. Oxford: Oxford University Press, 2013.

Halliwell, Stephen. "The Uses of Laughter in Greek Culture." *Classical Quarterly* 41 (1991): 279–96.

Himmelfarb, Martha J. *Tours of Hell: An Apocalyptic Form in Jewish and Christian Literature*. Philadelphia: University of Pennsylvania Press, 1983.

Hock, Ronald F. *The Infancy Gospels of James and Thomas*. The Scholars Bible. Santa Rosa, CA: Polebridge, 1995.

Hodge, Caroline Johnson. *If Sons, Then Heirs: A Study of Kinship and Ethnicity in the Letters of Paul*. Oxford: Oxford University Press, 2007.

Hopkins, Keith. *Death and Renewal*. Sociological Studies in Roman History 2. Cambridge: Cambridge University Press, 1983.

Horn, Cornelia B., and John W. Martens. *Let the Little Children Come to Me: Childhood and Children in Early Christianity*. Washington, DC: Catholic University of America Press, 2009.

Horner, Timothy J. "Jewish Aspects of the *Protevangelium of James*." *Journal of Early Christian Studies* 12 (2004): 313–35.

Horsley, Richard A. *The Liberation of Christmas: The Infancy Narratives in Social Context.* Eugene, OR: Wipf and Stock, 2006.

Hunter, David G. *Marriage, Celibacy, and Heresy in Ancient Christianity: The Jovinianist Controversy.* Oxford Early Christian Studies. Oxford: Oxford University Press, 2007.

Jacobs, Andrew S. *Christ Circumcised: A Study in Early Christian History and Difference.* Divinations: Rereading Late Ancient Religion. Philadelphia: University of Pennsylvania Press, 2012.

Jacobs, Andrew S. "A Family Affair: Marriage, Class, and Ethics in the Apocryphal Acts of the Apostles." *Journal of Early Christian Studies* 7 (1999): 105–38.

Jacobs, Andrew S. "The Disorder of Books: Priscillian's Canonical Defense of Apocrypha." *Harvard Theological Review* 93 (2000): 135–59.

Jacobs, Andrew S. *Remains of the Jews: The Holy Land and Christian Empire in Late Antiquity.* Divinations: Rereading Late Ancient Religion. Stanford, CA: Stanford University Press, 2003.

Jaeger, Werner. *Early Christianity and Greek Paideia.* Rev. ed. New York: Belknap, 1961.

Jagendorf, Zvi. "'In the Morning, Behold, It was Leah': Genesis and the Reversal of Sexual Knowledge." *Prooftexts* 4 (1984): 187–92.

Johnston, Sarah I. "Charming Children: The Use of the Child in Ancient Divination." *Arethusa* 34 (2001): 97–117.

Jones, Christopher P. *Culture and Society in Lucian.* Cambridge, MA: Harvard University Press, 1986.

Kaster, Robert A. *Guardians of Language: The Grammarian and Society in Late Antiquity.* Transformation of the Classical Heritage 11. Berkeley: University of California Press, 1988.

Kazen, Thomas. "Sectarian Gospels for Some Christians? Intention and Mirror Reading in the Light of Extra-Canonical Texts." *New Testament Studies* 51 (2005): 561–78.

Kearns, McNelly Cleo. *The Virgin Mary, Monotheism, and Sacrifice.* Cambridge: Cambridge University Press, 2008.

Kellhoffer, James A. "'How Soon a Book' Revisited: EUAGGELION as a Reference to 'Gospel' Materials in the First Half of the Second Century." *Zeitschrift für die neutestamentliche Wissenschaft und die Kunde der älteren Kirche* 95 (2004): 1–34.

Kermode, Frank. *The Genesis of Secrecy: On the Interpretation of Narrative.* Cambridge, MA: Harvard University Press, 1997.

Kirschner, Robert. "Apocalyptic and Rabbinic Response to the Destruction of 70." *Harvard Theological Review* 78 (1985): 27–46.

Klawans, Jonathan. *Purity, Sacrifice and the Temple: Symbolism and Supersessionism in the Study of Ancient Judaism.* New York: Oxford University Press, 2006.

Klutz, Todd. "The Value of Being Virginal: Mary and Anna in the Lukan Infancy Prologue." In *The Birth of Jesus: Biblical and Theological Reflections*, ed. George J. Brooke, 71–87. Edinburgh: T & T Clark, 2000.

Koester, Helmut. *Ancient Christianity Gospels: Their History and Development*. London: SCM Press, 1990.

Konstan, David. *Sexual Symmetry: Love in the Ancient Novel and Related Genres*. Princeton, NJ: Princeton University Press, 1994.

Kraemer, Ross S. "Jewish Mothers and Daughters in the Graeco-Roman World." In *Jewish Family in Antiquity*, ed. Shaye J. D. Cohen, 89–112.

Krückemeier, Nils. "Der zwölfjährige Jesus im Tempel [Lk 2.40–52] und die biografische Literatur der hellenistischen Antike." *New Testament Studies* 50 (2004): 307–19.

Lacey, W. K. "Patria Potestas." In *The Family in Ancient Rome: New Perspectives*, ed. Beryl Rawson, 121–44. London: Croon Helm, 1986.

Lassen, Eva Marie. "The Roman Family: Ideal and Metaphor." In *Constructing Early Christian Families: Family as Social Reality and Metaphor*, ed. Halvor Moxnes, 103–20. London: Routledge, 1997.

Laurentin, René. *Jésus au Temple: Mystère de Paques et Foi de Marie en Luc 2, 48–50*. Paris: Librairie Lecoffre, 1966.

Lefkowitz, Lori Hope. "The Genesis of Gender Transgression." *Jewish Quarterly Review* 101 (2011): 408–19.

Leyerle, Blake. "Appealing to Children." *Journal of Early Christian Studies* 5 (1997): 243–70.

Leyerle, Blake. "Children and 'The Child' in Early Christianity." In *Oxford Handbook of Childhood and Education*, ed. Judith Evans Grubbs and Tim Parkin, 559–79.

Lieu, Judith M. *Christian Identity in the Jewish and Graeco-Roman World*. Oxford: Oxford University Press, 2004.

Lieu, Judith M. *Image and Reality: The Jews in the World of the Christians in the Second Century*. London: T & T Clark, 1996.

Lillis, Julia Kelto. "Paradox *in Partu*: Verifying Virginity in the *Protevangelium of James*." *Journal of Early Christian Studies* 24 (2016): 1–28.

Lincoln, Andrew T. *Born of a Virgin? Reconceiving Jesus in the Bible, Tradition, and Theology*. Grand Rapids, MI: Eerdmans, 2013.

Lyman, Rebecca. "The Politics of Passing: Justin Martyr's Conversion as a Problem of 'Hellenization.'" In *Conversion in Late Antiquity and the Early Middle Ages: Seeing and Believing*, ed. Kenneth Mills and Anthony Grafton, 36–60. Rochester, NY: University of Rochester Press, 2003.

MacAlister, Suzanne. *Dreams and Suicides: The Greek Novel from Antiquity to the Byzantine Empire*. New York: Routledge, 1996.

MacDonald, Dennis R. *The Legend and the Apostle: The Battle for Paul in Story and Canon*. Philadelphia: Westminster, 1983.

MacDonald, Margaret Y. "Beyond Identification of the Topos of Household Management: Reading the Household Codes in Light of Recent Methodologies and Theoretical Perspectives in the Study of the New Testament." *New Testament Studies* 57 (2007): 65–90.

MacMullen, Ramsay. "Judicial Savagery in the Roman Empire." In *Changes in the Roman*

Empire: Essays in the Ordinary, by Ramsay MacMullen, 201–17. Princeton, NJ: Princeton University Press, 1990.

MacMullen, Ramsay. *Roman Social Relations: 50 B.C. to A.D. 284*. New Haven, CT: Yale University Press, 1974.

Maier, Harry O. *Picturing Paul in Empire*. London: Bloomsbury, 2013.

Maier, Harry O. "Sly Civility: Colossians and Empire." *Journal for the Study of the New Testament* 27 (2005): 323–49.

Marcus, Joel. "Crucifixion as Parodic Exaltation." *Journal of Biblical Literature* 125 (2006): 73–87.

Marohl, Matthew J. *Joseph's Dilemma: "Honor Killing" in the Birth Narrative of Matthew*. Eugene, OR: Cascade, 2008.

Marrou, Henri I. *A History of Education in Antiquity*. Trans. George Lamb. London: Sheed and Ward, 1956.

Martin, Dale B. *Inventing Superstition: From the Hippocratics to the Christians*. Cambridge, MA: Harvard University Press, 2007.

Martin, Michael W. "Progymnastic Topic Lists: A Compositional Template for Luke and Other *Bioi?*" *New Testament Studies* 54 (2008): 18–41.

Matthews, Shelly. *Perfect Martyr: The Stoning of Stephen and the Construction of Christian Identity*. New York: Oxford University Press, 2010.

Meeks, Wayne A. *First Urban Christians: The Social World of the Apostle Paul*. 2nd ed. New Haven, CT: Yale University Press, 2003.

Meeks, Wayne A. "The Man from Heaven in Johannine Sectarianism." *Journal of Biblical Literature* 91 (1972): 44–72.

Miles, Margaret. *Carnal Knowing: Female Nakedness and Religious Meaning in the Christian West*. New York: Vintage, 1989.

Minear, Paul S. "Luke's Use of the Birth Stories." In *Studies in Luke-Acts*, ed. Leander E. Keck and J. Louis Martyr, 111–31. Nashville, TN: Abingdon, 1966.

Mitchell, Margaret M. "Patristic Counter-Evidence to the Claim That 'The Gospels Were Written for All Christians.'" *New Testament Studies* 51 (2005): 36–79.

Moessner, David P. "The Ironic Fulfillment of Israel's Glory." In *Luke-Acts and the Jewish People: Eight Critical Perspectives*, ed. Joseph B. Tyson, 35–50. Minneapolis, MN: Augusburg, 1998.

Morales, Helen A. *Vision and Narrative in Achilles Tatius' Leucippe and Clitophon*. Cambridge Classical Studies. Cambridge: Cambridge University Press, 2004.

Morgan, J. R. "History, Romance, and Realism in the *Aithiopika* of Heliodorus." *Classical Antiquity* 1 (1982): 221–64.

Moxnes, Halvor. *Putting Jesus in His Place: A Radical Vision of Household and Kingdom*. Louisville, KY: Westminster John Knox, 2003.

Muehlberger, Ellen. *Angels in Late Ancient Christianity*. Oxford: Oxford University Press, 2013.

Mussies, Gerard. "Reflections on the Apocryphal Gospels as Supplements." In *Empsyhcoi Logoi, Religious Innovations in Antiquity: Studies in Honour of Pieter Willem van der*

Horst, ed. Alberdina Houtman, Albert De Jong, and Magda Misset-Van De Weg, 597–611. Ancient Judaism and Early Christianity 73. Leiden: Brill, 2008.

Nasrallah, Laura S. *Christian Responses to Roman Art and Architecture: The Second-Century Church and the Spaces of Empire*. Cambridge, MA: Harvard University Press, 2010.

Nasrallah, Laura S. "Grief in Corinth: The Roman City and Paul's Corinthian Correspondence." In *Contested Spaces: House and Temples in Roman Antiquity and the New Testament*, ed. David L. Balch and Annette Weissenrieder, 109–40. Wissenschaftliche Untersuchungen zum Neuen Testament 285. Tübingen: Mohr Siebeck, 2012.

Nutzman, Megan. "Mary in the *Protevangelium* of James: A Jewish Woman in the Temple." *Greek, Roman, and Byzantine* Studies 53 (2013): 551–78.

Osiek, Carolyn. "The Family in Early Christianity: 'Family Values' Revisited." *Catholic Biblical Quarterly* 58 (1996): 1–24.

Osiek, Carolyn, and Margaret Y. MacDonald, with Janet H. Tulloch. *A Woman's Place: House Churches in Earliest Christianity*. Minneapolis, MN: Fortress, 2006.

Pagels, Elaine. *Adam, Eve, and the Serpent*. New York: Random House, 1988.

Paulissen, Lucie. "Jésus à l'école l'enseignement dans l'évangile de l'enfance selon Thomas." *Apocrypha* 14 (2003): 153–75.

Pelling, Christopher. "Childhood and Personality in Greek Biography." In *Characterization and Individuality in Greek Literature*, ed. Christopher Pelling, 213–44. Oxford: Clarendon, 1990.

Penn, Michael Philip. *Kissing Christians: Ritual and Community in the Late Ancient Church*. Divinations: Rereading Late Ancient Religion. Philadelphia: University of Pennsylvania Press, 2005.

Peppard, Michael. *Son of God in the Roman World: Divine Sonship in Its Social and Political Context*. Oxford: Oxford University Press, 2011.

Perkins, Judith. "Fictive *Scheintod* and Christian Resurrection." *Religion and Theology* 13 (2006): 396–418.

Perkins, Judith. *Roman Imperial Identities in the Early Christian Era*. New York: Routledge, 2009.

Perkins, Judith. *The Suffering Self: Pain and Narrative Representation in the Early Christian Era*. London: Routledge, 1995.

Perrot, Charles. "Les récits d'enfance dans la haggada antérieure au IIe siècle de notre erè." *Recherches de science religieuse* 55 (1967): 481–518.

Petersen, William L. "OUDE EGŌ SE [KATA] KRINŌ: John 8:11, the Protoevangelium Jacobi, and the History of the *Pericope adulterae*." In *Sayings of Jesus: Canonical and Non-Canonical: Essays in Honour of Tjitze Baarda*, ed. William L. Petersen, Joan S. Vos, and Henk J. de Jonge, 191–221. Supplements to Novum Testamentum 89. Leiden: Brill, 1997.

Piper, Ronald A. "The One, the Four, and the Many." In *The Written Gospel*, ed. Markus Bockmuehl and Donald A. Hagner, 254–73. Cambridge: Cambridge University Press, 2005.

Porter, James I., ed. *Constructions of the Classical Body*. Body, in Theory: Histories of Cultural Materialism. Ann Arbor: University of Michigan Press, 1999.

Potter, David S. "Performance, Power, and Justice in the High Empire." In *Roman Theater and Society: E. Togo Salmon Papers I*, ed. William J. Slater, 129–59. Ann Arbor: University of Michigan Press, 1996.

Rajak, Tessa. *Josephus: The Historian and His Society*. 2nd ed. London: Duckworth, 2002.

Rebell, Walter. *Neuetestamentliche Apokryphen und Apostolische Vater*. Munich: Kaiser, 1992.

Reed, Annette Yoshiko. "The Afterlives of New Testament Apocrypha." *Journal of Biblical Literature* 134 (2015): 401–25.

Reed, Annette Yoshiko. "Εὐαγγέλιον: Orality, Textuality, and the Christian Truth in Irenaeus' *Adversus Haereses*." *Vigiliae Christianae* 56 (2002): 11–46.

Relihan, Joel C. *Ancient Menippean Satire*. Baltimore: Johns Hopkins University Press, 1993.

Rescher, Nicholas. *Forbidden Knowledge and Other Essays*. Boston: Reidel, 1987.

Saller, Richard. "Corporal Punishment, Authority, and Obedience in the Roman Household." In *Marriage, Divorce, and Children in Ancient Rome*, ed. Beryl Rawson, 144–65. Oxford: Clarendon, 1991.

Sanzo, Joseph E., and Ra'anan Boustan. "Mediterranean Jews in a Christianizing Empire." In *The Cambridge Companion to the Age of Attila*, ed. Michael Maas, 358–75. Cambridge: Cambridge University Press, 2014.

Schaberg, Jane. *The Illegitimacy of Jesus: A Feminist Theological Interpretation of the Infancy Narratives*. The Biblical Seminar 28. Sheffield: Sheffield Academic Press, 1995.

Schellenberg, Ryan S. "Suspense, Simultaneity, and Divine Providence in the Book of Tobit." *Journal of Biblical Literature* 130 (2011): 313–27.

Schmahl, Günther. "Lk 2,41–52 und die Kindheitserzählung des Thomas 19,1–5: Ein Vergleich." *Bibel und Leben* 15 (1974): 249–58.

Schott, Jeremy. "Language." In *Late Ancient Knowing*, ed. Catherine M. Chin and Moulie Vidas, 58–78.

Schott, Jeremy. "Porphyry on Christians and Others: 'Barbarian Wisdom,' Identity Politics, and Anti-Christian Polemics on the Eve of the Great Persecution." *Journal of Early Christian Studies* 13 (2005): 277–314.

Schroeder, Caroline T. "Embracing the Erotic in the Passion of Andrew: The Apocryphal Acts of Andrew, the Greek Novel, and Platonic Philosophy." In *The Apocryphal Acts of Andrew*, ed. Jan N. Bremmer, 110–26. Leuven: Peeters, 2000.

Shaw, Brent D. "The Family in Late Antiquity: the Experience of Augustine." *Past and Present* 1987 (115): 3–51.

Shepherdson, Christine. "Paschal Politics: Deploying the Temple's Destruction Against Fourth-Century Judaizers." *Vigiliae Christianae* 62 (2008): 233–60.

Shoemaker, Stephen J. *Ancient Traditions of the Virgin Mary's Dormition and Assumption*. Oxford Early Christian Studies. Oxford: Oxford University Press, 2002.

Shoemaker, Stephen J. "Early Christian Apocryphal Literature." In *The Oxford Handbook of Early Christian Studies*, ed. Susan Ashbrook Harvey and David G. Hunter, 521–48. New York: Oxford University Press, 2008.

Sim, Davd C. "Matthew's Use of Mark: Did Matthew Intend to Supplement or to Replace His Primary Source?" *New Testament Studies* 57 (2011): 176–192.

Sylva, Dennis D. "The Cryptic Clause '*en tois tou patros mou dei einai me*' in Luke 2:49b." *Zeitschrift für die neutestamentliche Wissenschaft und die Kunde der älteren Kirche* 78 (1987): 132–40.

Smid, Harm Reinder. *Protevangelium Jacobi: A Commentary*. Trans. G. E. van Baaren-Pape. Apocrypha Novi Testamenti 1. Assen: Van Gorcum, 1965.

Smit, Peter Ben. "Something About Mary? Remarks About the Five Women in the Matthean Geneaology." *New Testament Studies* 56 (2010): 191–207.

Solomon, Andrew. *Far from the Tree: Parents, Children, and the Search for Identity*. New York: Scribner, 2012.

Sternberg, Meir. "Biblical Poetics and Sexual Politics: From Reading to Counterreading." *Journal of Biblical Literature* 111 (1992): 463–88.

Sternberg, Meir. *The Poetics of Biblical Narrative: Ideological Literature and the Drama of Reading*. Bloomington: Indiana University Press, 1985.

Sundberg, A. C., Jr. "Toward a Revised History of the New Testament Canon." *Studia Evangelica* 4 (1968): 452–61.

Talbert, Charles A. "Prophecies of Future Greatness: The Contribution of Greco-Roman Biographies to an Understanding of Luke 1:5–4:15." In *The Divine Helmsman: Studies on God's Control of Human Events, Presented to Lou H. Silberman*, ed. James L. Crenshaw and Samuel Sandmel, 129–41. New York: Ktav, 1980.

Townsend, Phillipa. "Bonds of Flesh and Blood: Porphyry, Animal Sacrifice and Empire." In *Ancient Mediterranean Sacrifice*, ed. Jennifer Wright Knust and Zsuzsanna Várhelyi, 214–31. New York: Oxford University Press, 2011.

Treggiari, Susan. *Roman Marriage: Iusti Coniuges From the Time of Cicero to the Time of Ulpian*. Oxford: Clarendon, 2002.

Upson-Saia, Kristi. "Holy Child or Holy Terror? Understanding Jesus' Anger in the *Infancy Gospel of Thomas*." *Church History* 82 (2013): 31–39.

van der Horst, Pieter W. "Sex, Birth, Purity, and Asceticism in the *Protevangelium Jacobi*." In *The Feminist Companion to Mariology*, ed. Amy-Jill Levine with Maria Mayo Robbins, 56–66. Feminist Companion to the New Testament and Early Christian Writings 10. London: T & T Clark, 2005.

van Iersel, Bastiaan Martinus Franciscus. "The Finding of Jesus in the Temple: Some Observations on the Original Form of Luke 2, 41–51a." *Novum Testamentum* 4 (1960): 161–73.

Van Stempvoort, Pieter A. "The Protevangelium Jacobi: The Sources of Its Theme and Style and Their Bearing on Its Date." In *Studia Evangelica* III, part 2, ed. Frank L. Cross, 413–23. Berlin: Akademie–Verlag, 1959.

Voiçu, Sever J. "Ways to Survival for the Infancy Apocrypha." In *Infancy Gospels: Stories and Identities*, ed. Claire Clivaz et al., 401–17.

Vuong, Lily C. *Gender and Purity in the* Protevangelium of James. Wissenschaftliche Untersuchungen zum Neuen Testament 2: 358. Tübingen: Mohr Siebeck, 2013.

Vuong, Lily. " 'Let Us Bring Her Up to the Temple of the LORD': Exploring the Boundaries of Jewish and Christian Relations Through the Presentation of Mary in the *Protoevangelium of James*." In *Infancy Gospels: Stories and Identities*, ed. Claire Clivaz et al., 418–32.

Watts, Edward J. *City and School in Late Antique Athens and Alexandria*. Transformation of the Classical Heritage 41. Berkeley: University of California Press, 2006.

Watts, Edward J. "The Student Self." In *Religion and the Self in Antiquity*, ed. David Brakke, Michael L. Satlow, and Steven Weitzman, 234–51. Bloomington: Indiana University Press, 2005.

Weitzman, Steven. "Before and After *The Art of Biblical Narrative*." *Prooftexts* 27 (2007): 191–210.

Weitzman, Steven. *Surviving Sacrilege: Cultural Persistence in Jewish Antiquity*. Cambridge, MA: Harvard University Press, 2005.

Whitmarsh, Tim. *Beyond the Second Sophistic: Adventures in Greek Postclassicism*. Berkeley: University of California Press, 2013.

Whitmarsh, Tim. *Greek Literature and the Roman Empire*. Oxford: Oxford University Press, 2001.

Whitmarsh, Tim, ed. *Local Knowledge and Microidentities in the Imperial Greek World: Greek Culture in the Roman World*. Cambridge: Cambridge University Press, 2010.

Wiedemann, Thomas J. *Adults and Children in the Roman Empire*. London: Routledge, 1989.

Williams, Margaret. "The Jewish Family in Judaea from Pompey to Hadrian—the Limits of Romanization." In *The Roman Family in the Empire: Rome, Italy, and Beyond*, ed. Michele George, 159–82. New York: Oxford University Press, 2005.

Witakowski, Witold. "The Miracles of Jesus: An Ethiopian Apocryphal Gospel." *Apocrypha* 6 (1995): 279–98.

Woolf, Greg. "Becoming Roman, Staying Greek: Culture, Identity and the Civilizing Process in the Roman East." *Proceedings of the Cambridge Philological Society* 40 (1994): 116–43.

Yarbrough, O. Larry. "Parents and Children in the Jewish Family of Antiquity." In *Jewish Family in Antiquity*, ed. Shaye J. D. Cohen, 39–59.

Young, Frances M. *Biblical Exegesis and the Formation of Christian Culture*. Cambridge: Cambridge University Press, 1997.

Index

Acknowledgments

My name is on this book, but that is only part of the story. The rest of the story belongs to others, and it is a pleasure to recognize them here.

My first encounter with the *Infancy Gospel of Thomas* was in a course taught by Dr. W. Barnes Tatum of Greensboro College in Greensboro, North Carolina. He passed away in 2016. He was a respected biblical scholar, a generous teacher, and a kind and dedicated mentor. I explored in more detail the *Infancy Gospel* and the *Proto-gospel of James* as a graduate student at the University of North Carolina at Chapel Hill. My advisor, Dr. Bart D. Ehrman, now James A. Gray Distinguished Professor, encouraged my interest in these unusual gospels in a seminar on early Christian apocrypha. His support at that time gave me the confidence to return to these sources years later.

The writing of this book was aided by research funding from the Wabash Center for Teaching and Learning in Religion and Theology. Research funding was also awarded by the College of Arts and Letters at Michigan State University. I thank Arthur Versluis, chair of the Department of Religious Studies, my home department, for standing behind my applications for research funding. Undergraduate students in my courses at Michigan State University listened to my ideas about the family gospels, and their questions helped me to spot things in the family gospels that I would not have otherwise. One of our best students, Julia Johnson, now a graduate student at Yale University, served as my research assistant, finding and annotating scholarship about family and early Christianity. Colleagues in the Department of Religious Studies, especially Amy DeRogatis, Benjamin Pollock, and Mohammad Khalil, read portions of the manuscript and offered important suggestions.

I presented earlier versions of chapters to thoughtful audiences at meetings of the North American Patristics Society, the Society of Biblical Literature, and the American Academy of Religion. One paper was read at the 2013

International Meeting of the Society of Biblical Literature at St. Andrews University, Scotland, the school where I had earned a graduate degree two decades before. Time flies. Audiences at Michigan State University, the University of Minnesota, and Central Michigan University listened to presentations of my work and asked perceptive questions. In January 2011, I participated in an international workshop on religion and violence, organized and hosted by Kate Cooper of Manchester University, which helped to shape my view of violence in the family gospels.

I have published technical studies of the family gospels in academic journals. Material from these articles is used here by permission. Portions of Chapter 2: " 'It Moves Me to Wonder': Narrating Violence and Religion Under the Roman Empire," *Journal of the American Academy of Religion* 77, no. 4 (2009): 825–52. Portions of Chapter 3: "No Child Left Behind: Knowledge and Violence in the *Infancy Gospel of Thomas*." Copyright © 2009 The Johns Hopkins University Press and the North American Patristics Society. This article first appeared in the *Journal of Early Christian Studies* 17, no. 1 (2009): 27–54. A different version of Chapter 5 appeared first as "Parents Just Don't Understand: Ambiguity in Stories About the Childhood of Jesus," *Harvard Theological Review* 109, no. 1 (2016): 33–55.

I want to thank my editor at the University of Pennsylvania Press, Jerome Singerman, for shepherding the manuscript through the review process. So too I wish to thank his assistant, Hannah Blake, for answering all of my questions. For her patience and expertise during the copyediting stage, I thank Erica Ginsburg. And I am grateful for the support of this project by the Series Editors of Divinations: Daniel Boyarin, Virginia Burrus, and Derek Krueger. Anonymous readers for the press pushed me to sharpen my arguments, and I thank them for the nudge.

It took me a while to write this book. During that time, I incurred many debts to friends and colleagues at other schools. Some read parts of the manuscript; others read earlier versions or followed up with me about papers. The list includes Reidar Aasgaard, Ra'anan Boustan, David Brakke, Virginia Burrus, Bart D. Ehrman, Jennifer Glancy, Andrew S. Jacobs, Melanie Johnson-DeBaufre, Charles Mathewes, Shelly Matthews, Ellen Muehlberger, Laura Nasrallah, Michael Penn, Judith Perkins, Taylor Petrey, Nathan Rein, Jeremy Schott, Caroline T. Schroeder, Stephen Shoemaker, Gregory Smith, Kristi

Upson-Saia, and Steven Weitzman. They did their best to steer me in the right direction. I alone am responsible for veering off course.

Of these colleagues, I want to single out Andrew Jacobs, a friend since graduate school days whose generosity knows no bounds. It was Andrew who first suggested to me the phrase "family gospels." Suddenly, it all made sense—to me, at least.

I have a set of friends who meet together at least once but no more than twice a year. I don't know what I would do without them. Thank you, Andrew, Becky, Laura, and Carrie.

My wonderful parents, Tony and Judi Frilingos, are also wonderful grandparents to my children. They host us when we visit, and when they visit, they bring warmth and joy. My brothers, Daniel and Timothy, have both made the mistake of asking, "How's the book going?" I'm happy to answer that question now.

It is hard to find words to express how I feel about my spouse, Amy, and my children, Emma and Joe. Every day they teach me what family means. I thank them for their patience. I still have a lot to learn.